Taking the Pulse
of
Basingstoke

*Memories from before the National Health Service
and up to the present day*

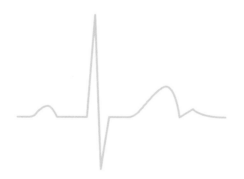

Compiled and edited by Barbara Applin

BASINGSTOKE
TALKING HISTORY

BASINGSTOKE ARCHAEOLOGICAL
& HISTORICAL
SOCIETY

ISBN: 0-9508095-2-7

Acknowledgements

The editor and Basingstoke Talking History wish to thank the following for their kind permission to reproduce the items listed on the pages given below:

Photos
Barbara Applin *5L, 8 top & bottom), 12, 16, 18L, 19, 31, 35, 50R, 52L, 54, 57, 62, 74, 88, 103, 109, 113*
Bob Applin *10, 13R, 14, 26,, 48L*
(Basingstoke) Gazette *28, 29R, 47, 48R, 50L, 77R, 78, 79, 82, 90,103*
A Bearne *48, 75L, 90 bottom*
Robert Brown *24, 27, 29L, 37R, 67 top, 77L, 85*
Burberrys *25*
Fitness League *23*
Guy's Hospital *13L*
Hampshire Clinic *109*
Hampshire Museums & Archives Service *1L, 2R, 5R, 22, 44, 45, 93*
Hampshire Record Office *36, 38R (47M94), 89 (279M87/84/3)*
Nina Koch *75R*
Eli Lilly *18R, 63,64*
North Hants Hospital Trust *98, 107R*
Sid Penney *49*
Rooksdown Club Magazine *40*
St Michael's Hospice *110, 111 bottom*
Nicola Stanley *104, 105, 107L, 108L*
Willis Museum *37L, 42; Attwood Collection 1R, 34, 58*

Drawings
Monica Graves *39*
Dr Hugh Hamber *53*

Cartoons
John Dinan (Danni) *6L, 6R, 9, 23, 27, 35, 36, 38, 47, 68, 70, 84, 87*
Alan Turton *12, 13, 20, 51, 56, 59, 62, 83*
Nicola Turton *73*

Maps
Peter Heath, John Feuillade & Howard Rogers

Text
Dr Peter Arblaster *Extract from* The Making of a Hospital, *94*
Basingstoke Gazette (Hants & Berks Gazette) *Advertisements 10, 11, 12, 14, 15; report of court proceedings, Feb 10th 1906, 30-31; report 6th January1900,34; letter to the editor, 81*
Dilys Eaton *Extracts from unpublished* History of Basingstoke Hospital, *24; extract from unpublished* History of Infectious Diseases Hospital, *30*
Hampshire Record Office *Basingstoke Cottage Hospital report 1899-1900 (8 M 62/7 printed) 25; extracts from Minute Book of Lord Mayor Treloar Hospital, 43; Extracts from Minute Book, Park Prewett Hospital Management Committee, 35, 86 & 87*
Eli Lilly *Extracts from unpublished history 17, 18, 19, 63*
The Rooksdown Club *Extracts from Magazine 40-41, 91*
Willis Museum *Health Week Booklet 26, 32; poster 31*

COVER
Photos
Robert Brown *Cottage Hospital, Basing Road Hospital*
Eli Lilly *Eli Lilly building*
Basingstoke Gazette *Jeanette Patterson and fellow nurses*
Sid Penney *New St surgery*
Hampshire Museums & Archives Service *Stomach pump and stethoscope*

Cartoon
John Dinan (Danni)

If any source is not acknowledged, we would be glad to have details.

Contents

Our Backers

We are most grateful to the various organisations and individuals who have supported this publication and would like to give them the opportunity to say something about themselves.

Assisted by *Basingstoke and Deane*

Basingstoke & Deane Borough Council was established in 1974 and exists to provide statutory services to the residents, businesses and visitors of the borough. The borough covers an area of 245 square miles. Basingstoke is the main town and Deane is the smallest parish. Wordfest is the Borough Council's literature development programme, which aims to support literature in all its forms through participatory workshops, author events, theatre and poetry.

Hampshire County Council

Since the Hampshire County Council was constituted in 1889, and re-formed in 1974, it has served the community in education, recreation, protecting the natural and historic environment, caring for people and protecting the public.

The Four Lanes Trust

The Four Lanes Trust has been active in Basingstoke and the surrounding area for over 30 years. It seeks to help groups and organisations with projects that benefit local people, especially in the fields of education, the arts and community. To apply contact Bob Carr at 5 Ferguson Close, Basingstoke, RG21 4AP or telephone 01256 477990 or e-mail bobcarr@fourlt.fsnet.co.uk

Macmillan Publishers

Macmillan takes an interest in local matters. Money raised by staff for various causes has often been matched and proceeds from its staff Book Sales are divided among a number of charities.

Friends of the Willis Museum

The Friends of the Willis Museum aim to further the development of the museum collections and facilities, to encourage public awareness of the museum and its services and to support and encourage an interest in the history and development of the local area. They organise lectures and outings and publish regular Newsletters. They have supported the Basingstoke Talking History project by providing some essential equipment, as well as supporting this publication.

The Hampshire Field Club & Archaeological Society was founded in 1885 and for over one hundred years has been Hampshire's most active association for the study of the country's past and natural history. It has a regularly issued journal, *Hampshire Studies* (formerly *The Proceedings of the Hampshire Field Club* and still named as such for the purposes of academic references, that publishes articles on natural history, geology, landscape, archaeology, history, historic buildings and industrial monuments.

The aim of the Friends of Basing House, by their activities, is the education of the public by promotion, support, assistance, improvement and preservation of the Ruins of Basing House.

Answers That Matter.

Eli Lilly and Company opened its first overseas manufacturing facility in Basingstoke in 1939 and the town has been a critical part of the company's strategy ever since. From the very earliest days in Basingstoke, Eli Lilly and Co have played an active rôle in the community, with a reference in the archives to a donation in 1940 of 'a goodwill gift to the local hospital of a cooker and X-ray equipment'. Lilly is delighted to support the publication of this book, which has had contributions from a number of ex-Lilly employees.

UnumProvident

'Keeping dreams and ambitions alive even when accident or illness strikes'

UnumProvident is the UK's leading provider of group income protection insurance, with over 30 years of experience. Its critical illness and life insurance products offer a comprehensive protection package. while income protection customers benefit from expertise in the specialist areas of disability, rehabilitation and return-to-work.

At the end of 2004, UnumProvident protected over 2.1 million lives through more than 19,800 schemes. Its staff are encouraged (and paid) to give part of their working week for voluntary work on community projects. One has worked as an assistant physiotherapist, others help wrap Christmas presents in aid of Shopmobility. Others have helped Kempshott Junior School to built a new access path and clear away 'green' waste from a big gardening/pruning exercise, and there are many jobs to be done at Crabtree Plantation and Black Dam Ponds. For more information visit www.unumprovident.co.uk

the string group
Health & Wellness Management

The String Group has been established for approximately six years., with its head office in the 100-year-old Lutyens designed building in Bilton Road. It was founded by a group of professionals committed to the delivery of health and wellness services to individuals, associations, groups and companies. This involves: how we look after ourselves on a physical and emotional basis, who we interact with and socialise with, what we enjoy for ourselves and our lives in general and, when we are unhappy, learning what to do about it. Departments cover Lifestyles, Social Events, My World (psychotherapy, hypnotherapy, NLP, stress management and relaxation techniques and training) and Corporate (workshops and presentations for stress, healthy living, injury prevention, hereditary illnesses and work: life balance). 'The name can suggest a 'string' of services or a further 'string' to our bow: For more information contact Katie Stroud, 01256 300460 www.stringonline.co.uk http://www.stringonline.co.uk

THE MANYDOWN COMPANY

The Manydown Charitable Trust was formed about nine years ago and concentrates its charitable giving to local organisations and concerns. The Trustees are pleased to be able to support The Basingstoke Archaeological & Historical Society in the launch of their book.

BASINGSTOKE ARCHAEOLOGICAL & HISTORICAL SOCIETY

Members of the Basingstoke Archaeological & Historical Society
Scott Childs, Paulline Williams and Bob Applin.

Foreword

Basingstoke and Deane

By The Worshipful The Mayor of Basingstoke and Deane, Councillor Mrs Paula Baker

I was delighted to be invited to write a Foreword to this splendid book. *Taking the Pulse of Basingstoke* tells the story of health care in the local area from just before the National Health Service, its beginnings, and up to the present day.

This is a local history, told by local people, and gives a wonderful insight into medical care before the Heath Service when few people could really afford it, up to the present time when health care is available to us all.

The generosity of our residents, which still prevails today, is shown in the way that the Cottage Hospital and the Hospice, to name but two, have been provided. Care and concern for others has always been in abundance locally and means that our health care is second to none.

It is fascinating to read individual stories from people who have received health care and from those who provide it, like our doctors, nurses and ancillary workers. To all of them, I say a big thank you for sharing your memories with us and for providing a living history of the Pulse of Basingstoke.

Mayor of Basingstoke and Deane
Councillor Mrs Paula Baker

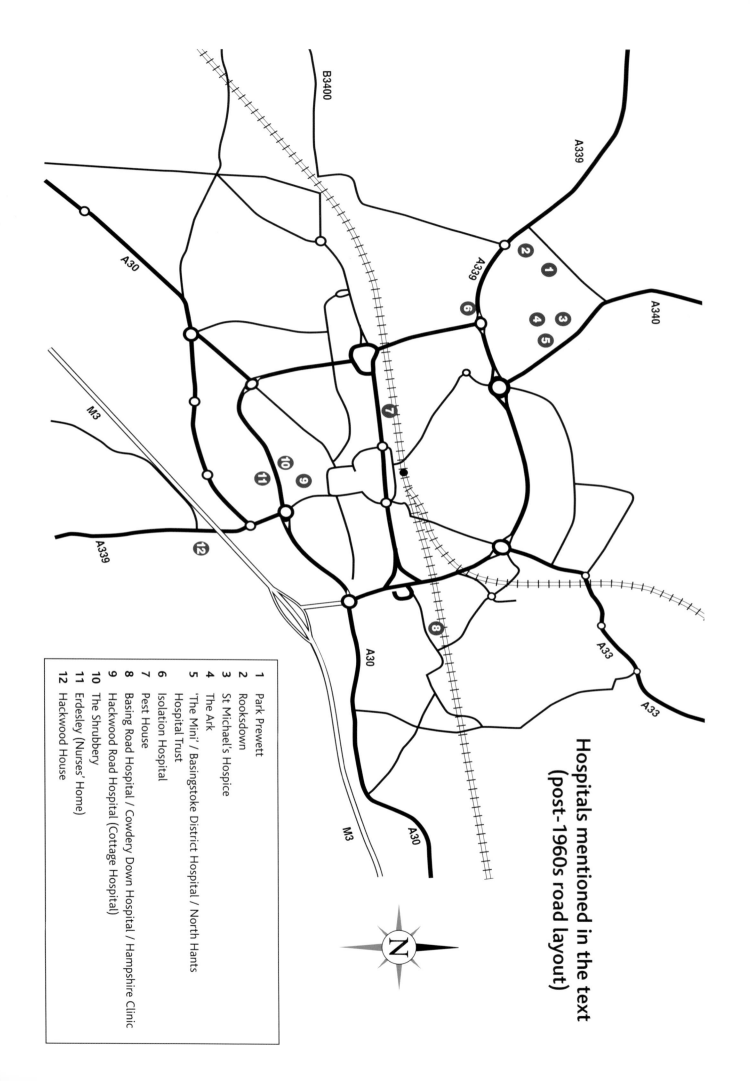

Hospitals mentioned in the text (post-1960s road layout)

1 Park Prewett
2 Rooksdown
3 St Michael's Hospice
4 The Ark
5 'The Mini' / Basingstoke District Hospital / North Hants Hospital Trust
6 Isolation Hospital
7 Pest House
8 Basing Road Hospital / Cowdery Down Hospital / Hampshire Clinic
9 Hackwood Road Hospital (Cottage Hospital)
10 The Shrubbery
11 Erdesley (Nurses' Home)
12 Hackwood House

Some Basingstoke doctors, dentists, chemists and opticians from the 18th century to the present day (pre-1960s road layout)

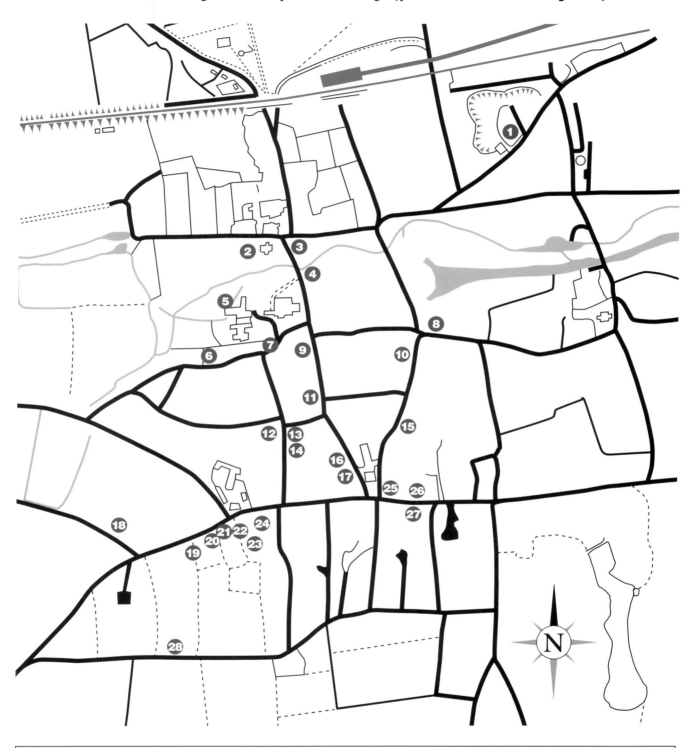

1	Steam Dell	12	Kenneth Reed (chemist)
2	Chute House	13	No 1 New Street / Cross Street surgery
3	Gittoes (chemist)	14	No 3 New Street surgery
4	Hospital of St John	15	Jukes (chemist)
5	Church Cottage	16	Solomon (chemist)
6	Church Square surgery	17	Gelstone (homoeopathic chemist)
7	Dr Potter, Dr Housden	18	Bramblys Grange / Church Grange health centres
8	Jeff Dodd (dentist)	19	Dr Bowen-Jones
9	Dudman (dentist)	20	No 14 Winchester Street surgery
10	Jeff Dodd (dentist)	21	Winton House
11	Gyles Lyford	22	Clement Clarke (optician)
		23	Bobby Pearce (dentist)
		24	Bateman (optician)
		25	Timothy Whites (chemist)
		26	Boots (chemist)
		27	Turner (chemist)
		28	Peters / Jeff Dodd (dentists)

Equivalent Money Values

Based on a leaflet produced by the Bank of England: *Equivalent Contemporary Values of the Pound: A Historical Series 1270 to 2004)* giving the amount of money required at June 2005 to purchase the goods bought by £1 at the dates shown.

Expressed in decimal coinage:

1600	1700	1800	1900
£101.53	£78.79	£32.46	£57.57

1910	1920	1930	1940	1950	1960	1970	1980	1990	2000	2005
£57.57	£21.40	£33.72	£28.98	£22.98	£15.43	£10.37	£2.88	£1.52	£1.13	£1.00

Introduction

Taking the Pulse of Basingstoke is an attempt to investigate one particular aspect of this Hampshire town - how its recent medical history has affected people who lived and worked here. Editorial comments are given in italics, while to give some historical perspective, short items are inserted about even earlier medical matters in the town. Mainly, however, the book consists of first-hand accounts taken from interviews recorded on tape for Basingstoke Talking History, a project run by the Basingstoke Archaeological & Historical Society in conjunction with the Willis Museum.

It was the 50th anniversary of the National Health Service in 1998 that inspired us to begin to gather this material together so that we can compare the days **Before the National Health Service** with those **On the National Health**.

Sometimes Basingstoke had an important part to play. In the First World War, Park Prewett Hospital was diverted from its original purpose as a mental health hospital to house Number 4 Canadian General Hospital. In the Second World War, it was Hackwood House that was taken over by the Canadians while Park Prewett was home to the Emergency Medical Service, with the famous Burns Unit and Plastic Surgery Unit at Rooksdown. We hear from the secretary who

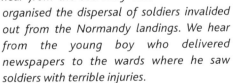

organised the dispersal of soldiers invalided out from the Normandy landings. We hear from the young boy who delivered newspapers to the wards where he saw soldiers with terrible injuries.

Sometimes Basingstoke experiences are typical and more everyday. We hear, for instance, from a district nurse, a midwife, a doctors' dispenser and from patients who went into the Isolation Hospital with infectious diseases or had a broken leg set at home on the dining room table. There are serious moments – the harshness of a system

that made a woman run to her brothers' workplace to raise the few shillings needed for the ambulance taking her dying mother to hospital. And there are comic moments – the door of the district nurse's little car flying open to deposit a clutch of commodes under the wheels of a bus coming down the Kingsclere Road.

'And did the National Health Service make a difference?' we asked. 'Oh yes,' was one reply. 'At last if we were ill we hadn't the terrible worry of doctors' bills.' 'Oh yes,' said the district nurse. 'We had a lot more forms to fill in.' 'Oh yes,' said the dentist. 'Lots of people suddenly wanted full sets of dentures.'

Doctors, nurses, dentists, pharmacists, health workers of all kinds and a variety of patients show us what effect the National Health Service watershed had on our town, and later how Basingstoke's sudden and massive expansion in the 1960s revolutionised hospitals and health care. More recently Basingstoke has seen the birth of important new developments. A state of the art Diagnosis and Treatment Centre has been opened, while consultants Bill Heald and Myrddyn Rees have put the town well on the medical map with their pioneer work in the treatment of bowel and liver cancer, and The ARK provides 'a centre of excellence for the sharing of medical knowledge'. The Hampshire Clinic offers private hospital treatment, while Primary Care Trusts and HantsDoc are giving new backing for General Practitioners (GPs), reinforced by their new contracts introduced in 2003.

St Michael's Hospice provides care for the terminally ill from all of North Hampshire. In the words of professional staff, volunteer carers and patients, we hear of one of Basingstoke's greatest medical and social success stories. Long may it continue!

The various topics covered in this book are closely inter-related, but in general each is considered more or less chronologically. So, for instance, after taking Doctors up to the 1940s we return to the 19th century for the Medical Officer of Health and the Dentists.

These extracts are taken from interviews recorded from 1992 to 2005. One speaker may have something to say under several headings, and when we can we say when the speaker was born and when they were interviewed.

We can't claim that all these memories are completely accurate, of course – no-one's memory is infallible, but the fact that people now are giving these accounts of their experiences has its own validity.

The master tapes (M1-98 and BAHS 1-133 etc) are held at the Wessex Film and Sound Archive, with copies in the Resources Room of Basingstoke's Willis Museum. Many thanks to the speakers for giving us permission to publish their words, to the interviewers and the transcribers. If we were unable to contact any speakers we would be glad to hear from them or their family.

Thanks to the members of the Basingstoke Archaeological & Historical Society for their moral and financial support for this project. Thanks also to Peter Heath, John Feuillade for the maps and for Howard Rogers for making them work. Thanks to Bob Applin and Paulline Williams for their meticulous work on proofs and index. Above all, thanks to Gary Fielder for his patience, generosity and creative flair in designing this book.

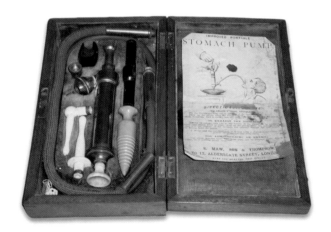

Before the National Health Service

First, a quick look at Basingstoke itself. Over the centuries Basingstoke has developed as a market town, playing its part in the woollen industry and serving farms and villages around. Our map, based on the Archer Davis map of 1851, shows a pattern of main streets and the roads, radiating out to London, Reading and the West Country. This had changed little from medieval times, apart from the addition of the canal and the railway.

In the eighteenth and nineteenth centuries the Basingstoke Canal and the railway brought expansion and by 1860 new housing had spread out around the town. An area called 'Newtown' was specifically built for railway employees, although the Railway Works originally proposed for Basingstoke went to Bishopstoke (Eastleigh). Major employers were the engineering works of Thornycrofts and Wallis & Steevens.

The 1920 Kelly's Directory notes, 'Basingstoke is situated in the centre of an extensive agricultural district and has a considerable trade in corn, malt, coal, timber and other merchandise. Here are large iron foundries for the manufacture of agricultural and other implements and motor engines, clothing and leather factories, carriage works and breweries, and in the district are brick works.' It was also the home of one of Hampshire's two psychiatric hospitals. Between the two World Wars, the town gradually expanded, with 'homesteads' for ex-servicemen, poultry farms and smallholdings, and with Council housing available for many who had been living in sub-standard housing. During the second half of the 1930s, several new industries such as Kelvin, Bottomley & Baird (later part of Smiths Industries) and the pharmaceutical company Eli Lilly, became substantial additional employers, bringing more people to the town.

After the Second World War, further companies like Lansing Bagnall were attracted here, so that by 1948 the town had a wide range of industries, with a bias towards engineering and science.

Such changes called for increased health provision, and we can hear in their own words how this affected the people of Basingstoke, even before the great 'watershed' of the introduction of the National Health Service.

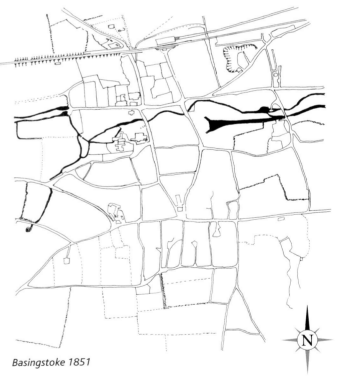

Basingstoke 1851

Why the NHS was needed

Jo Kelly had considerable experience of hospital orthopaedic treatment under the National Health (see pages 92-94) but here she is telling two family stories which vividly illustrate conditions in the 1930s, well before she was born. The stories show what bureaucratic regulations were imposed. The 'great and the good' mentioned in the first story might have been local landowners or solicitors, bank managers and owners of important businesses in the town. The second story illustrates the strength of local politics: if ambulances crossed county borders they had to be paid for. We see too what little consideration was given to the feelings of the people concerned. In today's terms. Jo's mother would have had to run down Sarum Hill, past BCOT (the Basingstoke College of Technology) and right along Worting Road to the roundabout for the Thornycrofts Industrial Estate/Morrisons supermarket.

Jo Kelly

born 1947   *Interviewed 1999*

As I grew up in Basingstoke, my parents, especially my mother, were always saying how important it was to have the National Health Service. She told me two stories about her family to make her point.

The first was of the occasion when my grandmother needed a surgical corset. My grandfather was disabled and from his late thirties he'd been unable to work, so they had managed but they had never got much money to spare. And at that time, if you needed the Borough of Basingstoke to pay for something like a surgical corset, you had to get the signatures of six worthies of the town, including the mayor. My mother can remember at the age of 15 going round with her mother to collect these signatures. She found the whole enterprise embarrassing, having to go and wait while the maid went away to see if the man would see you, and then sitting in the room being interviewed. She never could understand where this list came from. You were given a list of about 12 names and you had to get signatures from six of them. You had to explain why you couldn't afford to pay for the corset yourself, to each of these worthies.

Mum said that she felt some people enjoyed it more than others. Other people just signed the piece of paper and said, 'Oh, leave it with us,' but there were a couple of gentlemen of the town who obviously delighted in the idea of having the power over whether you got the surgical corset or not. And of course you'd still have to go to a panel of two doctors before you actually were given the piece of paper that said that you needed the corset.

The other thing was when my grandmother died in 1938, just before the Second World War. She had been ill and the doctor had come to see her and had said that she had stomach cramps. When she was obviously very ill, the doctor came back and said that it was an emergency and she would have to go into hospital.

At that time, if you paid into the Panel for the local doctors, that meant that you could have an ambulance for sixpence that would take you to the County Hospital at Winchester, because they were going to have to operate because she had got a stoppage. But when the ambulance turned up it wasn't the Hampshire ambulance, it was an ambulance that was going to take her to the Royal Berkshire Hospital at Reading. And that meant that the money that you 'paid in for Hampshire' wouldn't do because you were going across the border.

So they needed more money. My mother was at home with her mother and didn't have enough money - which I think was the grand sum of three shillings and sixpence - to pay to the Berkshire people, so she had to run down the road to the gatehouse of Thornycrofts and call out one of her brothers, who both worked there, and he came out and had a rake round and gave her the money. And then she ran up the hill, gave it to the ambulance drivers and off they went to the Royal Berkshire Hospital.

If it had been local - if it had been 'in-county' - it would have just gone through with the ordinary paperwork. It was no further to Reading than it would be to Winchester but it was 'across county' so they needed the money up-front.

So these were the sort of things that our family felt very strongly about, that finished when the NHS came in. I was told all the time that you'd got to guard the NHS.

Paying for treatment

As was the case all over the country, the Panel system and National Insurance gave some help but It was still a struggle for families to pay for doctors' visits and medicine, particularly when sickness also meant loss of earnings. Clubs and Friendly Societies were a godsend to many and some doctors lowered their fees for poor families.

Dr Sandy Smeaton

born 1916   *interviewed 1998 and 1999*

Before the Health Service, the working man with an income of under about £400 or £450 a year was covered by the Panel system which had been brought in with amendments over the years since about Lloyd George's time. But it was only the working man who was covered, not his family.

Doug Warsop

born 1917   *interviewed 2001 and 2002*

I can go back 80 years, because I'm now pretty well 85, and I can remember as a boy the doctor coming to the house and charging four shillings and sixpence, and then there'd be a bottle of medicine perhaps, for which you'd be paying half a crown (two shillings and sixpence). In those days that was quite a lot of money. The cost of the medicine might depend on the doctor, who might put his own charge.

Hilda Applin

born 1907   *interviewed 1999*

Before the National Health, there was medical aid for children – not very popular with doctors, probably it didn't pay them very well. It was a contributory scheme, you paid into a club like Oddfellows and got medical aid free, till you were 14. You paid seven shillings a visit, not including medicine.

National Insurance then just covered sick pay, not medicines or doctors' visits. Going on sick pay was called 'going on the club' (probably because Friendly Societies helped to run it). You got twopence or threepence per sick child.

Phyllis Ferguson

born 1930   *interviewed 2004*

My mother paid into the Saturday Hospital Fund, sixpence a week , and then you could get treatment for nothing.

Ken Toop

born 1930   *interviewed 1993*

The patients in the Isolation Hospital didn't have to pay for the care. They wouldn't have gone if they had, they'd have stayed at home and died, wouldn't they! There was no money changed hands. Of course, before the National Health Service there were Friendly Societies which were approved by the Ministry and you paid a contribution every week, like the Hearts of Oak Benefit Society. But they were not by any means or stretch of the imagination a total health care service, they were just purely and simply to help you out in time of need, that's all. There was no money changed hands at all. Because there wasn't any money.

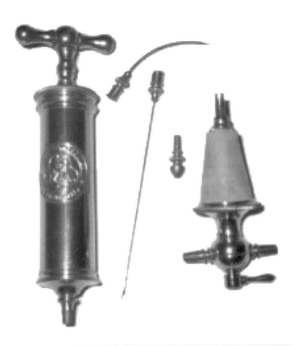

Treat the doctor with the honour that is his due,
in consideration of his services...
The doctor's learning keeps his head high,
and the great regard him with awe.

Ecclesiasticus, 38.1, 3 (Jerusalem Bible)

Doctors

'It is not his title and his eloquence, nor his knowledge of languages, not the number of books he has read, which are the requirements of a doctor, but the most profound knowledge of the nature of things and the secrets of nature, which simply and solely offset everything else . . . The task of the doctor is to diagnose the various types of illness, to discover the causes and symptoms, to prescribe remedies astutely and assiduously, and to do his utmost to further the process of healing according to the circumstances and peculiarities. . . '

Paracelsus, Theophrastus Works II, ed Peuckert, W.E.

The first mention of a physician in Basingstoke records is in 1627 when Mary Venables left 'to my physician, Andrew Twychin, gentleman, £5 in plate.' There are references in the Overseers' Accounts of 1684, 1695 and 1698 to Mr Ives, the bonesetter and to Dr Crompton, who is also mentioned in records of payments for cures between 1701 and 1708.

Rupert Willoughby, in his book **Sherborne St John and the Vyne in the Time of Jane Austen***, mentions several doctors in and around Basingstoke, including the Rev. Alexander Lytton 'who was Vicar of Sherborne St John till 1747, Master of Basingstoke's Grammar School and a practitioner of physic'. Rupert Willoughby quotes Gilbert White as saying it was quite common then for clergymen to assume a medical character.*

*The place of the doctor in Hampshire society is illustrated by the fact that Gyles Lyford, surgeon, leased a house in Church Street from Lord Bolton in 1753, while John Lyford (another surgeon, possibly his son) was, like Jane Austen's clergyman brother, a regular visitor at the Vyne. Rupert Willoughby quotes Edward Austen-Leigh's description of him as 'a fine, tall, old man, with such a flaxen wig as is not to be seen or conceived by this generation' and says that 'as an act, supposedly of charity, Lyford used to donate his used wigs every second year to an old man in the parish.' His son and successor was Charles Lyford of Basingstoke, the doctor who attended Jane Austen's mother at Steventon in 1798 (when he would have been just 20). He diagnosed incipient jaundice and prescribed 12 drops of laudanum in a soothing dandelion tea, before bed. Jane Austen said, 'He wants my mother to look yellow and to throw out a rash, but she will do neither.' (***Letters***, no 50) He also prescribed a balm of cotton moistened with oil of sweet almonds for Jane Austen's sister-in-law who suffered from deafness. She called him 'the melancholy Mr Lyford', though*

Austen-Leigh said that he 'really knew something about hunting' and 'enjoyed it exceedingly.' Charles Lyford was a Commissioner for Basingstoke's Pavement Act in 1815, subscribed £5.5.0 for the new Town Hall in 1832-4, was Mayor in 1837-8 and died at Bath in 1859, aged 81. He is buried in the Liten, Basingstoke. Jane Austen knew his son, another John, and his daughter, Sukey.

His uncle was Mr Giles King Lyford, who attended Jane Austen in her last illness at Winchester Both Giles King Lyford and his father, another Charles Lyford, were Surgeons at the Royal Hampshire County Hospital there and became Freemen and Mayors of Winchester. Giles King Lyford's son, Henry Giles Lyford, succeeded him at the County Hospital.

Other families of doctors can be found in Basingstoke records: Charles and Edward Covey, Maurice and Thomas Workman were all listed in directories as surgeons. Charles Covey and Maurice Workman were Commissioners for the Pavement Act, while Thomas Workman was a member of the Old (pre-1835) Basingstoke Council and Edward Covey was an Alderman on the new Council and a magistrate. Rupert Willoughby gives more information about Dr Thomas Workman, a widower who married Caroline Wiggett from the Vyne; she describes him in her memoir as 'the respected surgeon of the neighbourhood', not her equal socially but 'the perfect gentleman in his address, and excellent husband and father, a good friend and taught me the way to Heaven'; the couple built Old Bramblys which was later owned by Tom Thornycroft and became Bramblys Grange (see page 53 and elsewhere).

Patients' memories of different doctors from about 1918 into the 1930s and 1940s can no doubt be matched all over the country. By the 1940s the growth of practices called for the appointment of trained dispensers and secretaries and we can follow changes in working practice.

Mary Felgate

born 1912   interviewed 1992

When I was very small I was often poorly and Mother was always having to send for the doctor. I'm sure he was a lovely doctor but he certainly was no good for children. He was a great big man with a square face and a straight mouth and black eyes that looked all through you. His hair stood straight up and was cut short and it sort of went straight across his square forehead. To me it looked rather like the photographs of Germans in Mother's *Windsor* magazine. I was terrified of him.

Mother hated sending for him when I was poorly. She didn't if she could help it because she said to me one day, 'I do hate sending for the doctor for you, because as soon as I mention his name you go quite white with fear.' As soon as he came in he always offended my sense of decency, because he always said, 'Have the bowels been opened?' And the next

thing was, 'Open your mouth.' Mother had to give him one of our dessert spoons and he stuck the handle of the dessert spoon right down my throat till I nearly choked, to see what my throat was like. There was always a clean soap and towel ready and the kettle on the hob when the doctor came. He washed his hands in the kitchen.

But when I had a mastoid abscess, he was really very good to me. He came every single day. He used to put something in my ear that used to bubble bubble bubble. I had the most dreadful earache but he really did put it right, the mastoid, without having to have an operation.

When I was six, I broke my leg. I used to jump over a rope which was tied loosely to the apple tree, and where the washing was hung. One day my brother tied it too tightly, he only used to do one tie, and it didn't undo as I jumped through, and I caught my foot in it and I fell and I broke my leg. Oh, it was awful! And that was when they sent for the doctor.

I had to be laid on the table and given chloroform to put me under while the doctor, whom I hated, put my leg straight. They had to bring down a low folding camp bed from Father's spare room upstairs and the dining-room had to be turned into a sort of bedroom for me. And the bed had on it an iron frame which was heavy steel round both sides, and it came over my head in a sort of square so that I could put my hands on it and lift myself up and down to get a bit of exercise. But my right leg was bandaged tightly against the right side of this great steel bar. Goodness knows how many weeks I was in that.

That's when Aunt Annie had to come and live with us and look after me while the rest of the household carried on as best they could as usual with the front room instead of the dining-room. And Aunt Annie had another camp bed so that she slept beside me all night. Her bed wasn't absolutely close to mine, and I remember one night I must have been so restless and moving about, and she was sleeping, and she didn't know, and I fell right out of my bed onto the floor sideways, still strapped into this great iron frame. She had to wake Father up to come down and lift the whole thing up, with me in, back on the bed. It was a very unhappy time.

I can't remember how long I was in bed. Eventually I was allowed outdoors to sit in a chair and eventually to take a few hesitating steps, helped by members of the family, and so to recovery.

Blanche Bunkle (Woodley)
born 1908   *interviewed 1998*

I attended Fairfields School for nine months and had to leave at 13 to have my tonsils removed by Dr Bethel, sitting in a chair, as the Cottage Hospital was closed. I saw these tonsils come out into a bowl of water. It was pink. I was very, very weak for three months and only gradually got stronger, so that was the end of my schooldays.

I've been very healthy, actually, since then. It must have done some good, although I can't sing. I just have to mime if I go to church.

Susan Richmond
born 1924   *interviewed 1992*

In the old days we had Dr Bethel, who was considered a very good diagnostician, because he could diagnose very well and very quickly. I remember my mother and father liked him very much and had great respect for him. If we got any of the odd children's complaints - measles, whooping cough, chicken-pox - he used to say, 'Throw them all in together. Let's get it all over with,' and it sort of ran through the family, the four of us, and that was it, over and finished.

Joyce Clark
born 1912   *interviewed 1992*

Nobody else had a car near here when I was a child, only the doctor. I was a puny child, so I used to see the doctor quite a lot, but I'm nearly 80 now so I didn't do so badly. If my parents sent for the doctor, they had to pay five shillings, which in those days was quite a bit, so you didn't go to the doctor more than you had to. But if you sent for the doctor he would come.

Ivy Kneller
born 1918   *interviewed 2001*

You didn't send for the doctor until you were really, really, ill. I remember one occasion, my grandfather had to have the doctor and I was not feeling very well myself. We had a gate-legged table and when the doctor came I was snuffling away under there, out of sight. The doctor lifted the leaf up and he looked at me and said, 'It looks if you want the doctor more than your grandad.' But, of course, children got different things and you didn't have the doctor for normal infectious diseases, they came and went. Because it was so expensive. And the money in those days just about paid for the food and the rent and that was it.

I did have tummy problems when I was a child. I had to get a special certificate because the school attendance officer was very strict in those days. They came very regularly. I had to have a certificate to say that I was permitted to stay away from school at certain times, because of this tummy trouble. Fortunately I grew out of it, so it's all right.

Margot Woodcock
born 1903   *interviewed 1992*

There was a Dr Macpherson. He lived somewhere in Winton Square – a big house which stands back, which belongs now to Telecom. It was a very big building and we used to think he must be a very wealthy doctor to live there.

Phyllis Ferguson
born 1930   *interviewed 2004*

The first day of the school holidays the year before I started at the High School in 1937, I gashed my leg very badly on a rusty nail, cut a great lump out of it. I've still got that scar, because it cut right down to the bone. There were army medicals billeted next door who gave me first aid.

I went up to the Cottage Hospital and they put me in a little room and eventually my own doctor, Dr Rowe, came to stitch it up. I think it was the Matron who held me down and they stitched it without any anaesthetic at all and of course by then the shock had worn off because I'd been there for two or three hours. Anyway they stitched it up and I came home and my mother had to push me about in a pushchair for a while and then it all went septic and nasty and my eldest brother's wife, who had trained as a nurse, dressed it twice a day with a hot poultice that hurt me.

'…put her in the garden.'

I had half a term off school because it was still septic. Eventually Dr Rowe healed it up, he put elastoplast from knee to ankle and said, 'I'm going to leave that on for a week. If she smells too much, put her out in the garden.' So he came back after a week and cut the elastoplast and I was waiting to yell when he pulled it off, but he just got hold of it and pulled it off before it hurt. 'Oh,' he said, 'that'll be all right,' and did it again and he did it two or three times and it healed up.

A doctor's secretary

Mrs Zena Labanowska (née Beagley)

born 1921   *interviewed 2003*

My first job on leaving school was as a secretary at Airpak, in Overton. Dr Rowe, my mother's doctor, used to come to the house to see her, and I didn't realise my mother was dying. He came downstairs after going to see her one day and he said, 'What work do you do?' I said, 'I'm a secretary.' 'Oh,' he said, 'I need a secretary. Would you like to be my secretary?' I said, 'Oh, I can't do that, they're keeping my job open for me at Overton for when my mother is better.' 'Oh,' he said, 'well, think about it.' Well, when my mother died, I didn't want to leave Dad all day and every day and I went to Dr Rowe and said, 'Does your offer still stand?' He said, 'When can you start?'

Winton House

And so, in 1940 I started working for Dr Rowe in Winton House. I just took dictation and did all the letters and accounts. It was a beautiful big house facing towards Sarum Hill. And going into it, from the left-hand side as you're facing it, one came straight into the patients' waiting room, and the dispensary was that side as well. So I had my typewriter in the dispensary and I used to take dictation in Dr Rowe's consulting room, which was the big room facing Sarum Hill. Before I got to the surgery, often Dr Rowe would have been there and he would have laid out on his consulting couch all

the letters that we were going to be dealing with at that particular session and anything he might want me to do before. So his children always called the consulting couch 'Miss Beagley's bed'. And if by any chance I didn't have time to get the typing finished by the time surgery started, if Dr Rowe had been held up and we were both late, I would hump this huge typewriter, which was an old-fashioned one and very, very heavy, into the dining room and continue the typing in the dining room.

We had a surgery in the morning, 9 to 10 if I remember rightly, and then he did his visits and had another surgery in the evening, probably 6 to 7. There was no dispenser, no nurse in Winton House, just Dr Rowe. The only treatments carried out at the surgery were the ones he could do there and then on the spot. He made up the medicines himself. He had the big Winchester bottles with all the different medicines and he'd go in and make up a bottle of medicine, it would be wrapped up in white paper and sealed with sealing wax. He taught me how to do that. Things were done so differently in those days. You weren't handed the bottle of medicine, it was wrapped in white paper and sealed with sealing wax.

The patients had to pay for the medication, there was no National Health Service in those days. But most of the parents had their children belonging to what was called 'Medical Aid', which was a help. Private patients' records were all kept in a separate filing cabinet.

In Winton House days there weren't many telephone calls. Mostly people used to come and ask for a doctor, because not a lot of people knew how to use a telephone, they didn't have one and they were a bit scared of using a public telephone.

I was bringing up a family at the same time. When I was still working at Dr Rowe's house I took my little baby with me and had her in the garden. But then when my son was born not quite two years later, I took one child with me and my father took the other one. So my family were never left at all, they were always cared for, and that was very important. And the doctors knew that that had to be. I wouldn't have stayed otherwise

I joined the Fire Service just before the war started as a part-timer, a telephonist, and had to report on every siren. So I would turn up at Dr Rowe's surgery with my gas mask on my back and my tin hat. But the surgery continued as normal during the war.

The doctors' dispensary

Doctors used to have their own dispensary attached to their surgery. Hilda Applin gives a patient's view, while Eleanor Goddard tells of the training and the work involved.

Hilda Applin

born 1907   *interviewed 1999*

Just after the War, going to the doctors' dispensary for pills, you used to have to provide your own container. Grandad used to send tobacco tins to put them in. Then they started giving you cardboard pill pots.

Eleanor Goddard

born   *interviewed 1998*

1930 was the year when I came to Basingstoke to live and start working. Since qualifying as an Associate of the Apothecaries' Hall, I had had no paid employment, although I had done voluntary work at two Public Dispensaries in south west London. This qualification is better known as a Pharmacy Technician or Dispenser today. Because of the general slump, jobs were difficult to obtain, but the voluntary work gave me experience. Dr Potter and Dr Housden, who lived in Church Square, and had a medical practice there, had engaged me as their dispenser, book-keeper, and assistant nurse when necessary.

The south side of Church Square was particularly attractive, with a 16th century house on the corner of the square and Church Street, occupied by a dentist and his practice. Next door was Dr Potter's grey Georgian-type house, and at the far end, adjoining Mortimer Lane, Dr Housden's red-brick Victorian house. Between the last two were outhouses and, I think, old stables but they had been converted into waiting-rooms, and Dr Housden's consulting-room and the dispensary. All three houses had beautiful walled gardens. Dr Potter's consulting-room was the large room to the right of his front door.

There was a morning surgery daily, and an evening one from six o'clock until it finished, except on Thursdays. One doctor was on call after the morning surgery, then I was free from lunch-time. It was possible to get a train to London after 4 pm for half a crown (2s 6d) and return on the midnight one which arrived at five minutes to one.

I used to go to the theatre with my family or friends, and have a snack at Waterloo. It was a cheap journey.

When the morning surgery finished, I spent the time until lunch keeping the book-keeping entries up to date. An hour for lunch-time and then the doctors came in with the medications needed for patients they had visited at the latter part of the morning.

On Wednesdays, two carriers came into town and came to the surgery with messages from patients in other villages. One came from Dummer and the other from North Waltham. They arrived about eleven o'clock and called back for answers and medicines during the afternoon. They also shopped for their customers and their vans were fitted as crude buses.

There was a special surgery for country patients from two to three. Dr Housden held a special Baby Clinic and surgery on Tuesday afternoons. He was particularly interested in babies and wrote three books about them and young children. Saturday evening surgery was usually long. I often went home to London for the weekend (such as it was) and rarely caught the 7.30 pm train. Sometimes Dr Potter drove me up to the station to be in time for the 9 pm. He then returned to finish his remaining panel patients.

There was a small passage-type of room where I could test urine specimens when needed, as this was part of my training. Also the sterilisation of used instruments was carried out there.

The accounts were sent out quarterly and I used to take the money either by post or from the patients. Then I had the accounts to balance and I took the money to the bank. I also had to pay regular visits to the firm's accountants, and order the drugs under the doctors' supervision. The charge for a visit, plus medicine or tablets, ranged from three shillings and sixpence to five shillings, and a surgery consultation about two shillings and sixpence. There were also the PMS patients (I think that was the 'People's Medical Service'). Each family belonging paid a penny a week to some agency and the doctors supplied consultation and medicine free of charge. Bottles were brought when the patients arrived - some very odd ones.

It was a varied and fascinating job and I was very interested in the different types of people, especially the country folk. An old shepherd used to give me, before Christmas, a bunch of primroses and violets and very early leaves from a very special place he knew.

The actual type of medicine prescribed was very different from today, more liquid forms of medicine. Each dispensary had a row of stock bottles, that held 80 liquid ounces and were called 'Winchester Quarts', usually for the common ailments like coughs and indigestion and there were smaller bottles of linctus. There were shelves of tablet bottles, arranged according to their use. Medicines were dispensed in special glass bottles, in several sizes, labelled with instructions for the patient and wrapped in a special way in white demy paper, with name and address, looking very neat. Similarly, tablets were boxed, labelled and wrapped.

In New Street, opposite the old General Post Office, was a house with large bow windows on each side of the front door. This was another practice of three doctors: Dr Bethel, Dr Keith Williams and another who moved away about 1932. As Dr Housden and Dr Keith Williams had trained at Guy's Hospital together, the two firms joined together. So we had five doctors, Dr Charles Cobb becoming the fifth. He specialised in ophthalmic work mostly. I continued to dispense and answer the phone about visits, etc, and Dr Bethel's dispenser/book-keeper, a much older man, took over all the accounts. The Panel patients had a very long waiting-room, approached down the back garden. Upstairs was the eye surgery room and a small flat where the caretaker lived. She also gave the Panel patients their cards in an envelope. She was on call day and night.

I was called up on the day war was declared in 1939, because I had become a 'Mobile V.A.D.' with the Red Cross.

This was due to Dr Bethel's advice two years before. I was attached to the army and dispensed in military hospitals, based to begin with at The Royal Victoria Hospital, Netley, near Southampton. There was a large separate dispensary there, with one V.A.D. pharmacist and four dispensers. During the war I was moved to various hospitals and Camp Reception Stations (usually 40-bedded hospitals) in Wiltshire, Hampshire, Dorset and Berkshire. In 1942 I married a Basingstoke man. I was demobbed in September 1945 and my husband six months later. Dr Potter asked me if I would return as their book-keeper as both Dr Bethel and his book-keeper had retired. This I did for four years.

Dr Michael Williams comments that a five-handed partnership was unusually large in those days. Dr Housden left the practice in the late 1940s to join the Ministry of Health as an adviser in Parentcraft and Dr Stewart Weston arrived in 1943.

V.A.D. – Voluntary Aid Detachment

Medical Officer of Health

Advertisement in the Hants & Berks Gazette:

BASINGSTOKE UNION

MEDICAL OFFICER WANTED

The guardians of this Union will, at their meeting to be held at the UNION WORKHOUSE, Basing, near Basingstoke, on FRIDAY the 17th day of JANUARY 1879, proceed to the election of a duly qualified medical practitioner to act as MEDICAL OFFICER for the No. 4 District comprising the parishes of Basing, Bramley, Eastrop, Nately Scures, Newnham, Sherborne St John and Sherfield, and containing an area of about 14029 acres, and a population according to the census of 1871, of 3598.

The salary is £85. Per annum, exclusive of the authorised fees for surgical and midwifery cases, and for visiting lunatic paupers.

The gentleman elected will also in probability be appointed PUBLIC VACCINATOR and MEDICAL OFFICER OF HEALTH respectively for the District. The vaccination fees for the year ended on Ladyday last, amounted to £13. 18s. 6d. The appointment of Medical Officer of Health is an annual one, salary £25. Per annum. The appointments will be subject to the approval of the Local Government Board, and also subject to any alteration in the extent of the district which may hereafter be made.

Applications for the appointments, accompanied by testimonials of recent date, and evidence of qualification under the Medical Act of 1858, to be sent to me on or before THURSDAY, the 16th day of JANUARY next.

No candidate need attend on the day of election unless requested.

By order of the Board
GEORGE LEAR, Clerk
Basingstoke, 20th December, 1878

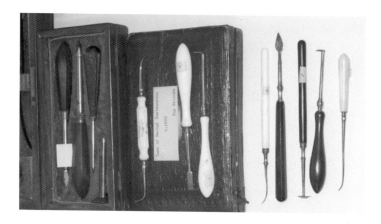

Dentists

The Dentists Act of 1879 led to the foundation of the British Dental Association in 1880. But it was not until the 1920s that dentists had to be qualified and registered and that advertising was banned, as in the medical profession. Why, then, are dentists permitted to advertise today?

Dental instruments c 1800

1870

Mr J D Frampton Surgical & Mechanical Dentistry

Respectfully informs the Nobility, Clergy, Gentry & Inhabitants of Basingstoke & Vicinity, that at his residence in New St he will give prompt attention to every requirement in all branches of the Dental Profession, and trusts that the great experience he has had in England & France, combined with moderate charges for Extracting, Stopping, Scaleing & Regulating the Teeth, as also for the supply of Complete or Partial Sets in Gold or other Material of his own sound work, upon the most recent & Improved Principles will ensure him the constant support of all who may please to honour him with their patronage. Hours 9 to 4, except Saturdays, when he attends at 43 Jewry St, Winchester.

1879

Painless Dentistry

MR WEBB, SURGEON DENTIST OF 27, New Bond Street, London, may be consulted at Mr Adams', Winchester-street, BASINGSTOKE EVERY WEDNESDAY

(an arrangement which has been carried on for many years).

ARTIFICIAL TEETH fixed by atmospheric pressure, and with all the latest improvements, fitted Without Pain and Without Removing any Teeth or Roots of Teeth. They are made without springs or other unsightly fastenings and support instead of injuring any teeth that remain in the mouth, and, as they are made with imperishable soft-gums that can be altered as the mouth changes, they can be worn by the most nervous patients over roots of teeth on tender gums, and last for years.

PERFECTLY PAINLESS EXTRACTIONS with Laughing Gas and Ether Spray. Decayed teeth painlessly filled with Pure Gold and White Enamel, which is the same colour as teeth and never becomes discoloured, and lasts for years, while it prevents the decay proceeding.

Irregular teeth rectified and every dental operation performed painlessly.

TERMS MOST MODERATE.

Half fees to servants and others the first and last hours of attendance.

ALL CONSULTATIONS FREE.

1886

Mr J E Carter, Zinjan House, Reading, Surgical & Mechanical Dentist

Still continues to visit Basingstoke, and finds it necessary to do so every Wednesday for the convenience of his Patients, and those who may wish to consult him on all cases of Dentistry, at Mr Hilliers, Jeweller, London St. Hours ten till four.

Father Charles Cooksey S.J., writing to Mrs Elizabeth Moody, remembered his boyhood in Basingstoke before 1885.

When I had been nearly suffocated by a brute of a dentist who put a rubber sheet over mouth and nose, you comforted my mother and I with a lovely tea.

Hants & Berks Gazette, 31st March 1900

Many ladies and gentlemen have by them old or disused false teeth, which might as well be turned into money. Messrs R.D. & J.D. Frazer, of Prince's Street, Ipswich (established since 1833) buy old false teeth. If you send your teeth to them they will remit to you by return of post the utmost value or, if preferred, they will make you the best offer and hold the teeth over for your reply. If reference necessary, apply to Messrs Bacon & Co, Bankers, Ipswich.

Ian Carey

born 1936

interviewed 2000

Mr Dudman, the dentist, had a nice big residential property in Church Street. Mr Dudman was one of the last people to be pulling teeth without qualifications. When they introduced whatever health act it was before the war, they allowed people who had already been in practice to continue. So if you wanted a tooth out, you went to see Mr Dudman and he would do it. That was it. There was no fillings or anything, he would just extract a tooth.

Jill Pickering

born 1933

interviewed 2000

Grandfather Charlie Munford apparently had to have some new false teeth, and they must have been sort of china, very fragile. And the dentist said to him, 'Don't sneeze, don't cough, because they will come out.' They probably weren't fitted in like they are today. Apparently he got to the door, opened the door, the sun shone in his eyes, and he sneezed, and out came the teeth and broke. And he hadn't even got outside!

Mary Felgate

born 1912   *interviewed 1992*

When we were very young there was no such thing as nice-tasting toothpaste and we had a very large metal box of carbolic toothpaste, which was gritty and tasted absolutely revolting. And we were told we had to scrub our teeth with it, but of course we didn't scrub very well because we had this mouthful of dreadful gritty pink carbolic powder. And because of it being so gritty, Father always told us we had to rinse our mouths out at least five times to get rid of the powder. It really was horrid.

So no wonder both we and other children had awful teeth because really we didn't clean our teeth properly!

If we had toothache Father used to go to Gelstone's, the chemist, in Church Street, and get a little bottle of essence of cloves. And he put some on this cotton wool and you had to put it on the tooth that was aching.

A pre-1948 dentist took a little girl's tooth out, charging 10s 6d at a time when her father's weekly wage was £3.10s at the most. Because she was so good during the operation, he kindly gave her back 6d.

Bobby Pearce

born 1924   *interviewed 2002*

I started in January 1946 as a Dental Student at Guy's Hospital. The course leading to a qualification was for five years. The first year of clinical dentistry was in the prosthetic department, where you were taking impressions and making dentures. You used your hands to fabricate all the dentures, - metal dentures, gold dentures, cast dentures, whatever - and you were actually handling human beings. You would do that for a year before you went on to the conservation room, where you dealt with conserving teeth.

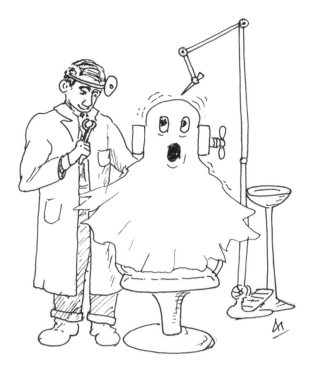

 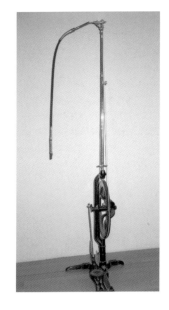

Treadle

You spent a month in the phantom head room. The phantom heads were made of highly polished wood in vices, about 3 or 4 feet apart on a long bench. The jaws that we had on the phantom head were lined with a material like sealing wax, which when heated was malleable but when cold was solid. When anyone had a tooth out at Guy's Hospital, the extracted tooth was put into a bin of formalin. We were each given a great bowl of teeth to fit our heads up with the correct teeth in all the right places. It was upon these phantom heads that we were taught to drill and shape the cavities for fillings. We only had foot treadle machines to drill the teeth, and we stood up, of course, behind the phantom heads. There were only a few electric drills for the seniors.

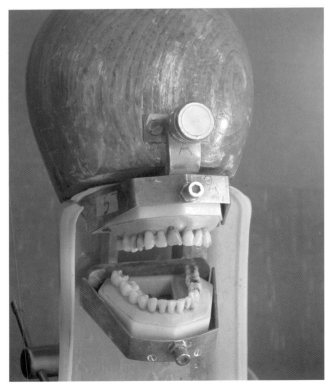

Phantom head, Guy's Hospital

Equipment saved from an old dentist's surgery included a cauterising machine that plugged into a light bulb and dangled down under the patient's eye!

Jeffrey Dodd

born about 1915   *interviewed 1998*

When I came to Basingstoke in December 1946, on coming out of the army, I'd taken over a dental practice in Wote Street. I should think it must be one of the oldest qualified dental practices in the country, because I know it was a dental practice in 1904 and there were not many qualified dentists in 1904.

Basingstoke wasn't a big town then, it was a small market town and people from the surrounding area also came in. Wednesday was market day, and there was always a market in Basingstoke, and my premises were in Wote Street, which was two-way traffic. Lansleys, who were butchers in Wote Street, had a slaughter-house behind the shop, and every Wednesday they drove a flock of sheep to it, on market day, so it was very different. It's no longer a farming community, Basingstoke!

But I was busy every day, not just on market day. One of the troubles about dentistry is that if you're not there, then there's no work done, and you still have to pay the people you employ. That's one of the reasons why the army is a much better bet, and I think that the standard of dentistry in the army is probably on balance higher than a lot of National Health Service dentistry.

I think there's a big change in attitude from the days prior to the start of the Health Service, and what goes on now. I used to get young people with basically decent mouths, who refused to have any fillings, and the excuse you used to hear was, 'Well, my mum doesn't hold with it.' It was all a question of they didn't want to pay, and I haven't heard that excuse for years. It was difficult to get round, because they were the people who really needed it. If they'd agreed to have it done, their teeth would probably last them the rest of their lives. But I don't think anybody really values their teeth until they get to middle age. Then they say, 'I wish I'd taken a bit more notice a bit earlier.'

Many people had worn dentures for 20 years, who should have only had them for ten years. They were mostly full upper and lower dentures, because we were a nation of denture-wearers. A lot of working-class people had all their teeth out, whether they needed it or not, and they'd have dentures,

because they thought that that was the end of the thing and it wouldn't cost them any more money. They weren't insured. There was a form of insurance, but the insurers wouldn't pay out until they were 21, so all the damage in children was done between 14 and 21. And if they hadn't had any dentistry in that time, in a lot of cases it was too late.

So you got quite a lot of young adults then having full sets, people under, say, 30. This was mostly before the war.

I always had an X-ray machine, right from the start.

Chemists

In 1532 the mercer, Thomas Lane, sold drugs, oils and salves, some of which may have been for animals rather than humans, and in 1636 we have the will of William White, apothecary, whose inventory lists many medical items in his shop.

HOMOEOPATHY

—— *(Gazette 1878)* ——

The great increase in the number of families practising Homoeopathy in the minor ailments of everyday life proves its value in the treatment of common complaints, as well as in the more serious disorders calling for professional Homoeopathic advice. With a few bottles of the most used remedies and a small book of directions, heads of families may treat coughs, colds, rheumatism, indigestion, constipation, piles, head-ache, and all common disorders with the utmost safety and certainty of success, and so prevent much suffering and often prevent slight ailments developing into serious illness.

W. E. BOND, having proved the value of homoeopathy, has for some years been agent for the sale of the medicines prepared by ASHTON AND PARSONS, Homoeopathic Chemists, London, and supplies them in phials for internal or external use, at 6d. and 1s. each, as well as in complete family chests from 6s. upwards.

W. E. BOND will be happy to give the benefit of his knowledge and experience to any one wishing to obtain an insight into Homoeopathy.

8 WESTERN TERRACE, BASINGSTOKE.

A small book, 64 pages, containing "Plain directions for the treatment of common complaints" free on application.

Mary Felgate
born 1912
interviewed 1992

Gelstone's the homoeopathic chemist in Church Street, had a big curved window on the right hand side with just a few bottles of various things on the lower shelf, and on the top shelf there were two enormous glass bottles with huge glass stoppers. I think one was bright green and one was bright red. Father used to go there to get all sorts of homoeopathic medicines for us when we were children. One of the favourite ones he used to get was Mr Gelstone's own mixture for when we had a cold. I can remember Aunt Annie telling me it was good because it had pure alcohol in it! I wonder how many people used to walk in and out of the shop without ever noticing the words in mosaic under their feet: 'HOMOEOPATHY: LIKE CURES LIKE'. The mosaic was moved to the Willis Museum when the shop was demolished.

Mr Haines

born 1920   *interviewed 1992*

Mr Haines worked for Mrs Solomon (chemist in Church Street, now the florist's, Nicola Too) from about 1934-1935.

I used to go up to the Basingstoke Hospital at Hackwood Road. You had to leave the stuff there in a special place and bring the empties back. Or the customers used to leave their prescription and have it delivered.

I got paid 12s 6d – an extra 2s 6d because you worked in the evenings with the surgery. They had to get the prescriptions done up and if it couldn't wait they got it sent round. So I worked 6 am to 8pm.

There may have been two, three or four or five deliveries to do, you never could tell. Sometimes nobody came to the surgery that night. It varied. If there were no deliveries, I used to have to go downstairs and tidy up bottles. All the new medicine bottles used to come in and you had to stack them away, 4 oz bottles, 6 oz bottles, all in racks. Mr Solomon used to go down and bring up the bottles from the cellar. He and his wife were a very nice couple, very well liked in the town. He was a family chemist.

Most of the chemists had big houses up Cliddesden Road. All business people seemed to live up Cliddesden Road. Great big houses, five- or six-bedroom places.

Doug Warsop

born 1917   *interviewed 2001 and 2002*

Doug was a pharmacist with Eli Lilly in Basingstoke for many years (see pages 19-22, 64-65), but he had begun his career with college training and a four-year apprenticeship with Boots in Birmingham. He has made a special study of the various chemists' shops in Basingstoke. When he arrived in 1942 Doug found seven chemists' shops, making up prescriptions from the Pharmaceutical Codex.

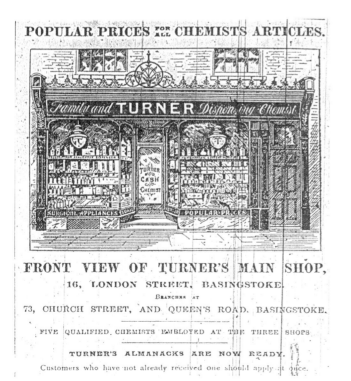

We had Boots in London Street, and across the road was Turner. On the corner of London Street and Wote Street we had Timothy Whites. Part way down Wote Street there was Jukes, and then in Church Street we had Solomon, and at the bottom of Church Street, near Brook Street, we had Gittoes. And then Ken Reed was in New Street.

Despite the reference to National Health, this was 1936!

Source: Attwood collection, Willis Museum

Some doctors had their own dispensers too. Otherwise, in those days you could only get medicines from a chemist's shop. Some of the medicines were very simple. There used to be an idea, I think left over from the Victorian times, that on Friday nights you should have some sort of laxative to cleanse the body for the weekend: remedies like Epsom Salts, which was very simple to use and very cheap. You got a whole range of things like Bile Beans and Beecham's Pills, and people who wanted to have something a little better than Epsom Salts would probably have Syrup of Figs. And then you'd get other things like cough medicines and bandages.

People used to go to the chemist's in those days for advice - if they had a bit of a cough or a cold, perhaps, or indigestion, they'd go along to get something from the shop. And some chemists would provide a little first aid if someone had a bee or a wasp sting or even cut their finger. When Basingstoke was a small town with just a few shops, you got to know the pharmacist and the pharmacist got to know you, and of course he was aware of your background and perhaps what you'd been suffering from and what drugs you'd been taking

The other thing you got in the chemist's shop was cosmetics. The names come to me of Ponds and Yardleys - they used to supply face powder, lipstick, and that sort of thing. When you went to a chemist's shop there was an odour in there, a mixture of antiseptic and the sweet smell of cosmetics.

Prescriptions were done quite differently in those days.

The doctor would probably use prescriptions from the National Formulary. And then you'd go to the chemist's shop and he'd follow the instructions, make up a bottle of medicine or whatever was asked for - because in those days they also made up all sorts of things like pills and suppositories and creams and lotions. It was quite a lengthy business and it meant people might have to wait half an hour or more, or maybe they'd go off and do shopping and then come back again. It was quite labour-intensive in those days, not as it is today.

There was a bit of a friendship between pharmacists and if one hadn't got the necessary ingredients, sometimes he'd slip out through the back door, or at least send someone, to the next chemist, to borrow or buy it. Most of the things were from local wholesalers. I think there was one in Reading and one in Southampton. And you could send off an order each evening and then get a delivery next morning, which was quite useful. In those days it meant you were buying in small quantities and you probably had to contribute towards the cost of the transport and things like that. It wasn't so economical as it is perhaps today.

If you went into a chemist's shop, you were probably aware of these lovely coloured jars with Latin names on the front. And of course there were also bottles for syrups and liquids and so on, again with Latin names. Most of the powders were in colourless jars and a lot of the syrups were in a blue-coloured bottle, which I suppose was thought to protect it to a certain extent against the ultra-violet rays or whatever. I remember from my days as an apprentice, going back before the War, it was my job to go round and top the bottles up. So it would mean there'd be something in the bottle that had been there perhaps for several weeks and then you'd add some more to top it up, and it makes you wonder just what the quality was like in storage.

The pharmacist spent most of his time in those days in the dispensary. He would use the British Pharmaceutical Codex, which was a tremendously thick book, with 1,800 pages. It started off by listing all the drugs that were available and it gave information for the pharmacist about how you arrived at the drug, and instructions to the manufacturer as to the quality standards that they should attain when they were preparing this drug. The last part of the book gave you the formulae for all the various medicines and suppositories and tablets and capsules and so on. That's the thing that the pharmacist would have to follow. And there were a few little tips about how to dispense.

ung.sulph

ext.opium

lin.alba   digitalis

Doug describes his training.

Before the Second World War, to be a pharmacist you did four years' apprenticeship, starting at about 16, and then you went to college. As an apprentice, I started with ten shillings a week, finished up at twenty-five shillings after about four years. I always remember that when I put my hand out for my first ten shillings, I only got about eight-and-something, and I looked a bit puzzled, and of course there was National Insurance and things deducted, which rather surprised me. Before the War, you were expected to provide your own white coat, which you had to wear in the shop. We had to keep them washed and cleaned ourselves. So you had to have two: one in the wash and one to put on. You'd best have a spare in case there was an accident and you perhaps spilled something down the front of the coat, because you had to present the right image.

My training was with Boots, and I have a feeling that they probably did a better job training people than perhaps the small pharmacist on his own. You had to fill up all the jars with the different powders and liquids and memorise the names and so on. And then eventually perhaps take a hand in the dispensary and do a few little jobs under supervision by the pharmacist. And that's where I began to pick up skills. A lot of the things were straightforward, just tipping powders and liquids into a bottle after weighing or measuring and adding the water. But there were some tricky things if you were making an emulsion or a cream or something of that sort. You had to get the right consistency and mix it properly and so on, mix it in the right order. There was no sort of quality control, really. It was just entirely the responsibility of the pharmacist to make sure that the medicine handed out was right. It makes you think, doesn't it!

To start with, most of the products available were from natural sources: plants and such like. If you had a very bad sickness - say, perhaps like tonsillitis - you'd probably go and get a prescription that would reduce the temperature and ease the pain but it wouldn't cure the tonsillitis. With  pneumonia, people used to go through a crisis and they either died or they came out of it. Then, before the War, pharmaceutical companies started looking at chemicals that would kill the bacteria responsible for the illness, like pneumococcus that caused pneumonia. And I think the story goes that, after 693 different products had been produced, May and Baker (M & B) came up with sulphapyridine that actually cured pneumonia by killing the pneumacocci that were responsible for it. That was a great step forward, and then after the War more and more chemicals were being produced. At the same time there was the work of Professor Fleming and Professor Florey with penicillin.

You could possibly see different prices for medicines in different pharmacies. I spent my early days with Boots - not in Basingstoke - and if there was a private prescription (for which you paid, of course) they put a code number on so that, whichever branch of Boots you went to, you paid the same price.

Before the War, they charged about twopence for a bottle and then, of course, people were encouraged to take the bottles back, so that they didn't have to keep paying their twopences, but on the other hand it left the pharmacist with the problem sometimes of cleaning out rather dirty bottles. They would have to be washed thoroughly, because sometimes you get powders sticking to the walls of the bottle and very difficult to remove.

When I went to work at Boots first, I went in my best suit and went on to start this career to be a pharmacist - because my father thought it was a job for life; he lived through a lot of unemployment in Birmingham. At least, if people were sick, even if they were poor and out of work, they still needed medicine, didn't they? And very soon after I started, the errand-boy went sick and the manager asked me if I would go out delivering some medicines. Well, I was not going to go out with a bicycle with a big basket on the front with a Boots label stuck on the side. So I went on my own bicycle. And I was a bit annoyed about it. When I came back, I spent some time in the back there, washing my bike down and cleaning it. This was all a sort of mild protest at having to be an errand-boy when I went to be a pharmacist!

The chemists themselves played an important part in the social life of the town and became very popular figures.

Kenneth Reed had a little photographic club where we used to meet, perhaps once a month, in that pub outside the station, the Station Hotel. Mr Gittoes - affectionately known as Pop Gittoes - always used to organise the Carnival once a year.

I look back on the pharmacy with a certain amount of interest and I have noticed many changes. When I was at college, the head of the department was a Communist, and he'd publish any research he did in a scientific paper, because he didn't want it to fall into the hands of a company that would make a profit out of what he'd done. And I was rather influenced by him. I can always remember when I was leaving Boots to join Eli Lilly, the General Manager came to me and said, 'Why are you leaving Boots?' and I said 'Well, I can't see any future for Boots, because I think in the future everything will be done in some national sort of centre where there'll be the doctors and the dispensers and so on and there'll be no need for people like Boots.' And he assured me, 'Young man, Boots is here to stay for a long, long time'- and, as you know, they have certainly grown.

Brian Spicer

born 1928   *interviewed 1982*

The chemist's shop was just one room with counters on either side and at the end, I suppose it was about 14 feet, 15 feet square, and dozens and dozens of little drawers with little knobs on where all the pills and potions were stored. And then there were all the bottles around the top, with coloured liquid in., and that sort of thing. It looked quite attractive.

Eli Lilly

Eli Lilly and Company was founded by Colonel Eli Lilly in 1876 in Indianapolis, USA.

In 1939 the company set up its first manufacturing facility outside the USA in Basingstoke

It isn't recorded why Lilly chose Basingstoke but the reasons are not hard to guess. High on the list of priorities must have been the sophisticated railway link-ups which put Basingstoke in touch with the whole country. The transport of coal, for example, from the coalfields of South Wales and the North, was a relatively easy matter; Basingstoke coal merchants even had their own railway wagons. This, for an industry depending on power, and on coal for its power production, must have been a prime consideration.

So must the accessibility of London, and of a main port - Southampton - through which supplies from Indianapolis could be shipped. Not the least attractive feature must have been the availability of building land and its relative cheapness.

Lilly bought quite a lot of land - 23 acres on the outskirts of town - providing for further expansion even as it was expanding. It was a patch of grazing, surrounded by cultivated land, bordering the Kingsclere Road - unspoilt country rich with dog roses, blackberries and violets in the spring. There were also poppies. Older employees can remember them springing up in season all over the factory site, thousands of poppies forming an expansive red carpet.

From an unpublished history p 53

Eric Godden

born 1925   *interviewed 2001*

When he left St John's School at 14, Eric went for an interview at Eli Lilly and Company.

Eli Lilly advertised at the Employment Exchange, who came to the headmaster and he suggested that if I was interested I should go for an interview. So I went, saw the receptionist, who escorted me to the lift. The liftman took me up and escorted me to the Company Secretary's office, knocked on the door and showed me in, and I thought, 'This is rather good treatment for a 14-year-old.' I was taken on straight away. I left school on the Friday and started work on the Monday.

It was an open-plan office. Going in, all one could see was quite a number of girls sitting there, looking at you. They were mostly girls in the office and the factory, quite an age range. Most of the supervisors in the factory were older than the girls working on the packaging line. But it was a mixture even then. The bosses on the factory floor were chemists.

My first impression of the office was a sense of space. There wasn't a lot of partitioning then. I think there were only three major offices initially that were solid walls. Very clean and pretty empty as well. The office was on the third floor, the packaging floor was the one below, and the production floor was the one below that - the ground floor, with warehousing in the basement for a while.

The person I worked with first was Stanley Watcham. I reported to him for a number of things, and then another chap who looked after accounts gave me some training in accountancy. It was very much an office-boy-cum-messenger job. One of the early things was to go the bank and the post office. In fact, later on I used to collect the wages at the bank, on my bike, of course. I had to provide my own bicycle. I bought it from Charlie Everett's shop in Potter's Lane and paid for it at the rate of half-a-crown a week. It was a Hercules, with a three-speed, so that made it cost a guinea more.

Initially we started at eight o'clock and finished at five o'clock. That was everyone: factory, office, directors as well, everyone. On Saturdays there wasn't normal working, but some people from each department would go in, certainly the warehouse, and the office as well, because if urgent orders came in on a Saturday then they were dispatched on the Saturday. I probably took them to the post office on some occasions, unless they were big packets for wholesalers that would be delivered by van. It was fairly normal to work one Saturday in three. You were paid three times a month: the 10th, 20th and last day of the month. I don't know why. I think it was an American idea. Our two board directors were both Scottish and we hadn't really a lot of direct American influence initially. Over the years it changed quite a lot. Americans came to work in the factory and we had a number of American managing directors.

The firm didn't really develop on a very great scale for some time because that was in 1939, and when the war started there were quite a number of limitations. Shortly afterwards what had started as a bright white building was camouflaged all over, including the windows. And then the windows were scraped and we had clear glass during the day, but in the evening we had to put shutters up to complete the camouflage.

The building drew attention to itself. Floodlit by night, it shone out for miles around - as far as the Isle of Wight, employees liked to say. Atop the building was a neon sign, LILLY OF BASINGSTOKE in red and green. Neon was then something of a rarity outside Piccadilly Circus, and the sign gave a colourful touch of all-American pizazz.

It would never be illuminated, however. The building's prominence was all very well in peacetime; in war it was a positive drawback. The neon had scarcely been erected before it was taken down, leaving only the skeletal gantry against the sky. The floodlighting stopped - leaving searchlights to monopolise the night. And the sugarwhite "House on the Hill" was camouflaged, maroon and brown. Even the windows were painted, even the approach roads - employees, it was said, sometimes missed the entrance.

A fairy tale in reverse: the building, born a white swan, turned ugly duckling

Unpublished history p 53

Eric Godden

born 1925   *interviewed 2001*

In the factory, things developed slowly. Most of the products were imported initially and despatched. Early in the war, Kelvin, Bottomley & Baird came and took over the basement and part of the ground floor. They called the Lilly portion of their firm 'Kelvinettes'. They were doing war work and were more security conscious. I think that was the time when the gatehouse and fencing around the grounds were built. You had to have an identity card and show it when you went in.

In the early days, the research was done in America. At Basingstoke the laboratory staff carried out development work: checking new products and trying them out - how to pack them and how to punch them on the tablet punch or mix them, and the best way to pack them. Later, a research laboratory was set up at Windlesham.

During the war, the range of products was rather limited. Tablets were made or compressed in the tablet room and capsules were filled in the capsule-filling room, and eventually capsules were made in a separate capsule plant. We weren't making capsules early on, but importing them, but eventually we started making things like anti-burn jelly. Some of that was made specifically for the Services.

In 1941 Mr Armstrong reported that 'the demands from the Services for Gentian Violet Jelly are phenomenal. We have a batch ready for tubing every day of the week and still we cannot keep up with the demand' - this despite the fact that Basingstoke was turning out, daily, some 8,000 five ounce tubes of the stuff (requiring over a ton of material). Mr Armstrong continued, 'Every airman who leaves the ground now carries a tube in his pocket, in addition to the standard equipment of large size tubes in first-aid kits on aeroplanes.' It was also carried on battleships.

Unpublished history p 53

Eric Godden

born 1925   *interviewed 2001*

We also made a foot powder for the Services. It made the floors rather slippery in the factory area, because it was mainly talc, which somehow got onto the floors. We also made ointments, jellies, cream.

One Lilly employee, Miss Margaret Coombs, recalled that 'It was not infrequent to travel up in the lift first thing in the morning with an enormous container of uncooked livers. It was enough to make the hastily consumed and partially digested cornflakes and scrambled egg turn turtle.'

Unpublished history p 53

Eric Godden

born 1925   *interviewed 2001*

When we started making tablets and filling capsules for penicillin, there were people who were allergic to penicillin. And when we started making the contraceptive pill, they had to wear special clothing, in a special room.

There was the sterile area where liquids and powders were filled into ampoules, for injection. As things developed, there were areas where you had to change clothing completely and shower, but in the early days workers seemed all right with much less protection.

Doug Warsop

born 1917 *interviewed 2001, 2002*

When I came to Eli Lilly in 1942, I wanted to get onto the manufacturing side. I spent the first six months in the laboratory, and then there was a vacancy in the department making sterilised injections, and that's where I started. During that time I was making morphine hydrochloride tablets for the armed forces.

When I first came in the laboratory there would be about a dozen there, probably two or three qualified chemists or pharmacists, then young people who had come from the local school, perhaps with some qualification in chemistry. In the laboratory it was all open work on benches and old-fashioned methods. You made precipitates, and weighed the result, and worked out from that the strength of the drug you were examining. In other cases you would make up solutions and use burettes, do titrations, get an end point, and again use that information to work out the strength of the drug. You used logarithms and slide rules. A sample would be taken to the laboratory, and it would go through the complete test to check that production was working properly and standards were right. You had to be very careful to take a sample from the whole of the batch, not just the end. You had to take it from the beginning, from the middle and from the end, perhaps as a tablet machine was running.

We had written procedures for everything. It was a thing that impressed me first when I went there. The manufacturing ticket must have been, oh, I suppose, ten feet long, and gave all the instructions step by step. The operators had to read it and carry out an operation and then sign with the date. This record was kept after the batch was finished, filed away so we could always check to see who did it, what ingredients were used, and things of that sort.

We used reputable drugs which we also tested in the laboratory before they were issued to the manufacturing area. So the quality of the drug was okay at the start, and the operators were very closely supervised. In each department you probably had a qualified pharmacist. Then under him you'd have trained operators, and they would go through a period when they would be working along with a senior operator, who would watch them very carefully to make sure they got the right procedures. And of course there wasn't any question of rushing the work. There was no piece work, there was no pay for output. So people weren't harassed at all. They could take their time, do the job properly. The strength of Eli Lilly, right from the start, was on quality control, which is a very good thing.

Protective clothing was somewhat limited. In the laboratory you just had a white coat, that was all. You could have glasses if you thought there was a possibility of some flare-up. In manufacturing, the fellows just had white overalls. In some cases rubber gloves were available, more to protect the worker than the product, perhaps. There were cloth masks available, that fitted round the back of the ears, which was some protection from dust. Though, I must admit, in those days there was a certain amount of dust in the atmosphere, which was unavoidable with the way we worked.

Bottles used to come in crates packed in straw, and they would go down and be washed with strong detergent. Sometimes, if the girls were not wearing their rubber gloves, you would find that their skin was starting to peel in that detergent. And of course all the bottles had to be washed, then rinsed in clear water, and then stacked in racks and put into cupboards where they were dried, before we could use them.

When Doug started, it was war-time, so there was a limited range of Lilly products.

We made all sorts of things like water-sterilising tablets, then tablets to follow up to remove the taste. Later on in the war we were making tablets for dysentery, which we shipped abroad for the soldiers.

We used to get cans of orange juice sent over from America. The cans were emptied, put into big vats with syrup, preservative and water to make up to the right volume, then bottled off. It was available for expectant mothers and children. Old ladies who used to work at Eli Lilly on the packaging line like to talk about this. You can imagine that when we opened these cans of juice, it did attract wasps in the summer-time, so we had to have wasp remedies always freely available for any of the operators who got stung. Then, of course, we had to be very careful to put everything through a strainer, in case a wasp had actually got into the

mixer and went down with the orange juice. So we had to be very careful with the packaging. We used to squash the empty cans, so you could get more cans to the lorry load, and I think they went off to some steel-manufacturing company up in the Midlands somewhere, to be made into razor blades. From time to time a steam roller would come up from the local firm who made steam rollers, Wallis & Steevens, and flatten all the cans. Of course, the poor old operator on the steam roller would have swarms of wasps all around him. He had to take that risk. When he had flattened all the cans, we would hose down his rollers with a hosepipe. He was cleaned up to go back down, I think this was part of his road test.

We did government contracts. We used to make a preventative ointment which was used for troops, to prevent venereal disease. It was all packed away in a special room by elderly ladies who wouldn't say what they were doing. Of course the young women would say, 'What are they doing in that special room?' 'Oh, it's some secret war work.' Of course in those days you wouldn't want to talk about this preventative ointment. I think a leaflet was dished out with each tube of ointment.

The factory had been opened at just about the time when war was declared. So there was a limited amount of equipment there and the basement and half of the ground floor was taken over by a firm which later became Smiths Aviation. In those days it was Kelvins, and they made instruments like barometers and altimeters for the aircraft industry. Because of that, the whole factory was surrounded by barbed wire. Very carefully controlled. I think we had an anti-aircraft gun in the centre of the field there. I was never very sure if it was used or not. Then we had volunteers for the Home Guard. We did have practice evacuations. Bells would sound and everybody would go outside and stand in lines. The supervisors would check that all members of their team were present and correct. I don't think there was an air-raid shelter.

If there was a fire alarm or perhaps enemy aircraft, we would just go out into the field. But luckily, all the time we were there we didn't have a raid on the factory or anywhere near. They very quickly camouflaged the building because it was bright white and people claimed that it could be seen from Southampton quite clearly, and was a good target for planes advancing from the continent.

There would be about five or six hundred employed by Eli Lilly, I should think, in those days because a lot of the work was being done by hand. Packaging: rows of girls sitting there counting out tablets with special paddles with certain numbers of holes. They would inspect the quality, then pour the tablets into a bottle. The next girl would be stuffing in cotton wool. The girl after that would be putting on a cap. A girl further down the line would have a paste board, a pot of paste, a brush and she would paste the labels and stick them on by hand. Another girl would inspect and polish the bottle. The bottle would be put into an individual carton, and then the cartons would be put into dozens. 'Music while you work' would be playing. I think the women used to sit there and sing; they were all quite happy.

Doug only stayed six months in the laboratory as he was very determined to get into production.

Then I moved to a department making sterilised injections. We had glass ampoules which were filled by machine. The girls would sit there with a sort of blow torch and a pair of tweezers and would rotate the ampoule in the flame and seal the glass ampoule by hand. And the vials were sealed under sterile conditions. This was done with a rubber cap. A machine would put a seal round it afterwards and hold the rubber cap in position. That was in the early days before we started mechanising. All this was done in a sterile area. The girls used to put on special hats, coats and overshoes and suchlike, and sit in this area, where the air coming in was filtered through special filters. Everything was done with strict sterilisation; all the equipment was sterilised in a big steam steriliser and such like.

> The war brought out the spirit of 'making do' which so warms the cockles of the British heart. Children combed the fertile hedges of Hampshire for rose hip berries, which they then brought to the official area collecting point, our Basingstoke site. Lilly then sent the berries on elsewhere to be made into Rose Hip Syrup. Self-help was the order of the day.
>
> *Then and Now: A Pictorial Account of Lilly, Basingstoke: 50 years 1939-1989*

As a pharmacist, I could make certain decisions on my own with my expertise which I had learnt at college. For instance, I was making some antibiotic tablets and they were falling apart in the coating department, so obviously I was going to do something about it. So I added about 0.5% of gelatine to the formulation when we were making the granule, before we compressed the granules to make the tablets. It held the tablets together and it didn't interfere with the test afterwards to make sure that the tablet would disintegrate or dissolve properly. So that's where I used my knowledge, but today that wouldn't be allowed. It would have to go through quite different tests. In those days, I had the freedom to make changes as I thought fit with my training.

The processes were quite elaborate.

In the Granulation Department the powders were mixed in big mixers, operated by electricity. They were about five feet long and probably three feet in each direction: a trough and blades rotating. There would be a trap door at the bottom for the material to fall through. The granules would be put on trays and dried on a rack. And then we had a large mixing table with a sort of parapet all the way round. People would run their fingers backwards and forwards to mix all the powders together by hand.

Then it was all put into bins and transferred to the Tablet Compression Department where you would have a chargehand looking after the machines. He was making sure that the operators were working properly and perhaps training a newcomer.

It was the same with the tablet machines, Once you got everything set up, the compression machine would start, so the granules would be fed into the die that had a hole in the middle, while the lower punch was down. You could decide how far down the lower punch would go, and the further down it went, the more granules you got in the hole in the die. So that was a way of measuring the amount of material you were putting into the machine. Then the lower punch would start to come up as the upper punch would come down. Between the two, you would compress the tablets. Then the lower punch would continue to rise until the tablet was ejected from the turntable, it would be knocked out of the way and fed into a drum. The machines were rather noisy: I have a feeling that over the course of years, one or two people's hearing was not as good as it should be.

After compression, in some cases, tablets would be coated and that would be a separate department where again we had big revolving drums. The tablets would be trundling round inside, and people with jugs would be pouring on syrups and things, containing perhaps dyes to give a coloured effect. After you had wet the tablets, they would all be taken out and put onto trays and put in the oven to be dried. They would be brought back and again another coat applied, and this would go on perhaps for a week or so, building up coats on the tablets. So it was all very time-consuming.

There were different tablets being made at different times. Where possible, you would perhaps make two or three lots of the same granules, one after the other, to save some of the cleaning. Otherwise all the equipment would have to be thoroughly cleaned and inspected before you put a different product on. Samples would be taken of all stages and submitted to the laboratory. When they were okayed, they went to the Packaging Department, where there would be one product being packed on one line. Then samples would be taken again to the laboratory to do a final check to see all was well, the right labels on the right tablets. From there everything would go to Dispatch. That was a separate department. It was then sent out to medical centres, wholesalers, hospitals and, of course, some for export.

Sometimes the machines had to be adjusted.

Mechanics would always be available at short notice to do any repairs or adjustments that were necessary. Then, while the tablets were being made, the fellow would be taking tablets every few minutes and weighing them in tens on scales to make sure he had got the right weight. And if there was any variation, you would make an adjustment to the machine, because we were allowed a slight variation up or down in the weight of a tablet, plus or minus perhaps 0.5% or something like that.

Security was necessary.

There was a strict rule that people could be searched on the way out. If they were caught with drugs, then they would be dismissed straightaway. We did have one case where we found that some barbiturates were being sold in a pub in the town and it was traced back to a fellow who was there. And, of course, he was dismissed. In some cases you would get the police involved. But there was a very strict rule that people could be searched at any time. Their lockers could be searched. There was one unfortunate case where a machine setter had got some tablets which he had been using to set up the machine, and he put them into his locker. When the security guard was going around doing a routine check, he found these barbiturates in this man's locker. And although the man said that he had only used them for setting the machine, it was an offence to take the tablets from the department, and I am afraid that he was sacked.

In those days it could be an eight-hour day and five and a half days a week. We didn't have unions at all. There were one or two, like the electricians, who were in a union, but nothing to do with production. We like to think, you see, that Eli Lilly was a very caring family firm, who looked after the people, and I think that our rates of pay and hours of work and all that were very competitive. We were quite independent in those days, doing our own thing.

Blanche Bunkle (née Woodley)

born 1908   *interviewed 1998*

During the War, I went to work at Lilly's on an old bike, three shillings an hour, in all weathers. Oh and it was such a struggle to get up Chapel Street! And if you were punctual they gave you a three shilling bonus. We were bottling orange juice, a sticky old job that was, and then I was put on bottling tablets.

Opticians

Doris Galop

born 1911   *interviewed 1992*

I went into glasses at 10 years old. I had my eyes tested at the surgery at the doctor's and went to Ackrell, the optician at the top of Church Street.

Muriel Wilson

born 1912   *interviewed 1998*

My husband was a dispensing optician. The doctor tested the eyes and the patients came to him with the prescription and he took the measurements of their face and what have you and saw the specs made up. There was a fair choice of spectacles. But of course when he started there was no National Health so anything you had you paid for. Prices were low, but if you think of the average wage, I think you could have got a pair of specs then for £2 or £3. I don't know what the lenses would have cost, but not any more - but I suppose if your specs cost you £6 it was quite a big amount. If you had real tortoise-shell frames, you paid for it. But the average person couldn't think of that. And then of course they reduced the prices when some sort of composition came in - plastic didn't really come in until round the war time.

He had had very rigorous training. When he left Technical College he had three years' apprenticeship and then, by the time he was about 20, he went as a very very junior to a firm, in the Royal Exchange building in London. But he wasn't there too long and he got a position with Clement Clarke's in Wigmore Street. He was made a roving manager for two or three years, to replace managers for holiday time, and then he was himself offered the managership of Maidstone, and on the strength of that we got married. Then Clement Clarke rang up my husband on a Friday and said, 'Can you go to Basingstoke on Monday and take over Basingstoke branch?' He was here over 16 years. He had the full responsibility of doing it all, and his salary was £6 a week, plus 1% commission - well, you've got to go some at the prices they were then to make anything at 1% commission.

During the Second World War he was in a reserved occupation but he had to do fire service - every time the siren went he went down to the fire station. He was sent to Southampton, Portsmouth, Plymouth in their blitzes. And not only that, as soon as he was home he was doing his other work as well. He couldn't recuperate like the permanent men could, have their time off and sleep. He also had to put the glasses or specs in goggles in 200 pairs of airmen's helmets every week.

First-Aid and Clinics

Mrs Margot Woodcock

born 193[?]   *interviewed 1992*

I must have been ever so small but I've never forgotten it. The kettle was on the fire and I was sitting in front of it with nothing on my feet. Suddenly the kettle boiled and all the boiling water came out on to my toes, and I remember quite well my mother rushing out into the kitchen. She said, 'Oh, I must go and peel a potato, because potato peelings are good for burns.' An extraordinary remedy!

Pat Wright

born 1930   *interviewed 2003*

My Mother was a VAD (in the Voluntary Aid Detachment) I think, and she started in the Red Cross in early 1930 or just before, and she used go to the hospital for training . Then during World War 2 she was at the First-Aid post, which was underneath where the Haymarket is in Basingstoke. Mum helped when the bombs dropped in Church Square and also one day a despatch rider happened to come off his motorbike around Basingstoke and he had gravel wounds on his arms and I believe she put Friar's Balsam on them, which must have been very, very uncomfortable.

An inaugural meeting of the National Birth Control Association was held in Basingstoke in 1934 and the Basingstoke and District Mothers' Clinic set up in rooms in Castons Road.

St John Ambulance Brigade

An account of the history of the St John Ambulance Brigade tells us that their first meeting in Basingstoke was held in the Library, New Street, in 1929, and almost immediately they began to patrol danger spots on main roads. Over the years they met at the Southern Railway station, in the Station Hill workshops of Wallis & Steevens, the London Street Congregational Schoolroom, the old Friends' Meeting House in Wote Street, the Methodist Schoolroom and Church Cottage.

When Mr Solomon, the Church Street chemist, became vice-president of the St John Ambulance Brigade in the town in 1930, he offered its members a 10% discount off all purchases of medical supplies.

In the summer of 1935 the superintendent of the Basingstoke division of the St John Ambulance Brigade, Dr H Radford Potter, was on holiday in the Lake District when he rescued a lady from drowning. He gave her artificial respiration and she made a complete recovery.

During the Second World War, members not serving in the Forces were involved in ARP duties and the social committee arranged to take entertainment to the war wounded at Park Prewett Hospital every Sunday evening. The Brigade was responsible for providing an ambulance service for the town and they gave excellent first-aid training. One of the founder members of the group in Basingstoke worked nights at Thornycrofts and then during the day was driving an ambulance around Basingstoke.

Nancy Powell

born 1906   *interviewed 1992*

When I joined, in 1941, the Ladies' Division had been running one year. I became a member in 1942 and remained a member until 1970, by which time I had become Divisional Superintendent.

I have been to fairs on duty, dealing with casualties like people getting knocked over, banging their heads, or going round in one of those whirly things and then coming off and feeling horribly sick. We used to have duties at gymkhanas and fêtes, not only in Basingstoke but in the surrounds, and point-to-points and open gardens.

The St John Ambulance Brigade doesn't get any help from the Government whatsoever. You have to raise the funds yourself from bazaars or rummage sales - people seem to be more generous these days, curiously enough.

Women's League of Health & Beauty

Mrs Muriel Wilson

born 1912   *interviewed 1992*

The Women's League of Health and Beauty started up here and this friend and myself decided we'd like it better than the pictures. At that particular time Prunella Stack started these exercises - instead of being jerks, they were all stretch and relax movements and they were really super. And we had exhibitions in the Park. We had little black satin trunks, cut quite high for those days - they weren't shorts, just with elastic in the legs, cut on the cross. They were very cleverly designed so that they fitted tightly to your body and gave with you, all the movements that you did. And then you had a white sleeveless top with just a collar, and your badge, and the badge was of a girl leaping, with her legs almost doing the splits in mid-air. And that was in black on this white satin badge edged with black on the white blouse. They were very attractive.

We did the exercises to music. I went once down to the Portsmouth offices training ground and it was fantastic. There were over a thousand women, all doing these same things, with Prunella Stack in the middle. I suppose she was in her twenties, leading us. We'd all rehearsed separately. We came from all over the county and it was really quite something.

I used to go to the classes on Friday night - tired, at the end of the week. And by the time I'd got to the class, done my exercises, I felt quite rejuvenated and I could walk home - in fact, I could hurry home. Sometimes it was an effort to make myself go to the class but I was always glad because it really did something to your muscles and you did really get benefit from it. But unfortunately, as the War started, then the class stopped.

We had a huge class. We had a little children's class too; my eldest one was two and a half when she joined. She's 57 now.

Hospitals

The first Hospital recorded in Basingstoke was the Hospital of St John the Baptist, set up around 1240 by Walter de Merton (who was the son of a Basingstoke woman, the founder of Merton College, Oxford and later Bishop of Rochester). However, it was rather different from modern hospitals and certainly not open to all. At first it was intended for poor and sick travellers, shortly afterwards also for ailing priests, and later for aged and infirm fellows of Merton College. Henry III took an interest in the hospital and granted it perpetual freedom from taxation and payment of subsidies, re-affirmed by Edward I and later kings. However, it became derelict by the 16th century and Merton Farmhouse was built on the site in 1778, to be replaced in 1901 by St John's School, and in the 1960s by part of the new shopping centre.

Basingstoke's Cottage Hospital in Hackwood Road was small but patients appreciated its friendly atmosphere, 'a real little country hospital', and townspeople went to considerable trouble to support it. The Shrubbery Maternity Home, too, raises many fond memories. Basing Road Hospital, on the other hand, suffered from its association in people's minds with the dreaded Workhouse, while patients at the Isolation Hospital, having been almost snatched from home in the famous yellow ambulance, had to have their belongings fumigated and were kept in strict isolation. Park Prewett had a particularly interesting history, diverted from its rôle in mental health to a new wartime use, particularly with the associated Burns Unit at Rooksdown.

On the Saturday after Armistice Day, 1918, there was a grand procession from Thornycrofts works around the town, with floats showing a realistic operating theatre made by the staff of the Canadian Hospital at Park Prewett, and 'Old Bill in Bed' made by nurses from West Ham House, which was being used as a convalescent home. Collections were taken for the Cottage Hospital and the St Dunstan's Homes.

Hackwood Road Hospital

In 1867 a public meeting was called of Inhabitants of the Parish of Basingstoke concerning the proposed sale of the Pest House and establishing a Village Hospital (sometimes called the Cottage Hospital). Local 'bigwigs' like Mr Wyndham S Portal of Malshanger, Mr Bates of Manydown and the Misses Simmons of Highfield gave donations, but the hospital was not opened until 1879, with eight beds and one nurse.

The Cottage Hospital, Basingstoke.

In March 1880 the first surgical operation was performed in the hospital. Mr Walker, a veterinary surgeon, had his right eye removed by two of the honorary medical staff. How a one-eyed vet may get on is open to question but at least the operation itself seems to have been a success. By June 45 patients had been admitted, 20 had recovered, 8 had 'benefitted', 12 had been 'relieved', there were currently four patients and presumably there had been one death.

In 1887, the year of Queen Victoria's Golden Jubilee, Basingstoke got a new town clock and the Cottage Hospital got the Victoria Ward. Ten years later, celebrating the Diamond Jubilee, Colonel John May presented the Hospital with the May Wing, costing £700. This consisted of two four-bedded wards on the ground floor and one on the first floor, each with bathrooms and lavatories. They were warmed by modern stoves, lighted by incandescent burners and ventilated by Tobin tubes with outlets in the chimney flues. On the ground floor was a linen store with an arrangement for drying and airing linen.

From History of Basingstoke Hospital by Dilys Eaton

Basingstoke Cottage Hospital Reports, 1st June 1899 to 31st May 1900

1899-1900

Gifts:

7/6	from Anonymous, Tunworth
£1.1.0	[?Borough] Constitutional Club collected by Dog 'Jack'
£1.0.0	Basingstoke Cycle Club
15/6	result of Billiard Handicap, Mechanics' Institute
£15.5.8	proceeds of Concert given by the Banjo & Mandoline Orchestra per Miss Tyrrell
£34.6.9	Proceeds of Entertainment given by Mrs E Adams

Gifts:	Bagatelle board, crutches, goose, hens, old linen, rabbits, turkeys, etc

A Mortuary was created 'through the munificence of W S Portal of Laverstoke', and a gardener's cottage was given by Mrs Arthur Wallis of Coombehurst.

1903-4

The Committee would like to draw attention to the fact that owing to the great success of the Hospital Pound Day and to the generous gifts of game during the season the cost of provisions has been materially less than last year although more patients have been treated.

Report of Ladies' Committee:

On the first Wednesday in July last year the Ladies' Committee organised a Pound Day which was most successful; nearly 200 children from the different schools came in troops with their offerings, in charge of their teachers, to whom for their kindly help and trouble taken the Ladies' Committee owe their best thanks.

1904-5

Many domestic servants also showed their appreciation of the good work done among their class by several generous offerings. The girls in Mr Burberry's workroom brought a contribution of £2.10s which was expended in the purchase of two lounge chairs, to which tablets have been attached bearing the following inscription 'Given by the workers in Messrs Burberry Factory, July 1904' . Employees of J Mares and Wallis & Steevens also contributed £6.17.5 and £7.16.2.

Burberry girls

1905-6

Pound Day was again celebrated by '...over 1000 children from the Council Schools, St John's School and Miss Dunn's and Mrs Coates' Private Schools. The money was spent on two wicker easy chairs for the wards, two canvas reclining chairs, one invalid self-propelling chair and two dozen yards of flannelette for children's nightgowns.

1906-7 Report of Committee:

The Hospital Pound Day, organised and carried out by the Ladies' Committee, proved, as usual, successful in adding largely to the stores of provisions.

Hampshire Record Office, 8 M 62/7 (Printed)

Basingstoke Hospital

(in 1924 the Cottage Hospital at Hackwood Road was renamed Basingstoke Hospital)

By P. DOWSLAND JONES, Esq.
Chairman of the Basingstoke Hospital Committee

In spite of the stress and strain of the War period it was found possible during the years 1915 and 1916 to modernise and enlarge the Operating Theatre, to install the heating apparatus and the electric light.

In 1918-19 the May Wards were enlarged and accommodation for the Night Nurses and store rooms increased. 1921 saw the addition of the Board Room, Private Wards and the X-Ray Room and plant. In 1922 the electric lift and the sterilising room were added. The Children's Ward was erected and other extensions carried out in 1923. In 1926-27 further improvements were made in the heating arrangements and domestic quarters. A development in 1929 was the installation of a Permain Water Softening Plant and an up-to-date sterilising plant.

During 1930, to meet modern requirements, an up-to-date X-Ray Plant was installed and the X-Ray Room enlarged and in the same year a generous friend provided a complete Refrigerating Plant. During the present year (1932) a sum of over £400 is being expended on long-needed additions and on renovations to the building. To-day, all kinds of cases can be dealt with in the Hospital in the manner most approved by the best medical and surgical authorities. A special feature is the provision of a number of private Wards where patients able and willing to pay for their treatment can be accommodated.

Surgeons' knives

The Hospital is held in trust for public service by five Trustees and is governed by a Committee of nine. There is also a Committee of Lady Visitors and the Hospital is served by a devoted staff of Surgeons and Physicians, Dentists, Radiologists and others. The Matron and Nurses, that loyal band of tireless workers, must not be forgotten.

Last year, 489 In Patients and 807 Out Patients were admitted to the Hospital. In addition there were 413 X-Ray and 106 Ophthalmic cases. Altogether the number of patients receiving treatment was 1815 and 640 operations were performed. The private wards were used by 39 patients during the year.

From the Borough of Basingstoke's 1932 Health Week booklet

The patients were treated by GPs with the support and help of the London consultants, described by Dr Michael Williams as the 'visiting honoraries', figures of considerable awe, who used to come down and hold their clinics and then go back to the 'big smoke.'

In 1934 an appeal was launched for £40,000 to fund a new building scheme. Pound Day continued until 1946 and from 1937 Annual Carnivals were held to raise this amount, but it became clear that the target of £40,000 would not be enough and the land acquired in the 1930s became Beaconsfield Road.

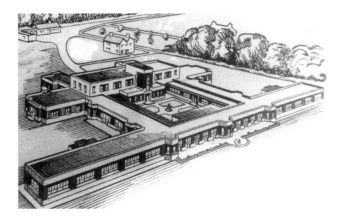

The Nurses' Home was at Tangier House in Wootton St Lawrence in the Second World War, until it was moved to Erdesley, in Cliddesden Road..

Barbara Green
born 1921   *interviewed 2001*

Before Hackwood Road Hospital was nationalised, it was run by a Trust. And we had a lovely time. Christmas was lovely. We all had a present, all the patients had a present, from the people on the Hospital Board.

Irene Hill
born 1911   *interviewed 1992*

When I was at Brook Street School we used to have a Pound Day and we would all march up to Hackwood Road Hospital with a pound of something, a pound of sugar, a pound of flour, a pound of soda, anything our parents could spare. And that was the school's contribution to the Hackwood Road Cottage Hospital once a year, and we used to love that because it got us away from school for half a day.

Pound Day

It was a real little country hospital and we were shown round the hospital after they had collected all of their goods. I suppose that it took the fear of going into hospital away from us all because they were so friendly and nice. The hospital was small but homely. Oh, I loved it. We all looked forward to Pound Day, going up to the hospital. That's one of my happiest memories.

I suppose there were about 25 to 30 in each class and there were about seven classes at Brook Street School. And we'd all go up at the same time to the hospital. Each school went on a different day. Our school all went together, and then Fairfields School would go, St John's School would go. To see all of us kiddies marching up with our pounds of stuff! It was great fun.

Pat Wright
born 1930   *interviewed 2003*

When I was at Brook Street School, one day a year we would be walked from the school, very proudly carrying a pound of something, whether it was a pound of rice, or a pound of sugar, or flour, or something from Dad's allotment, to the Cottage Hospital. And when we got there Matron was standing at the door and there was the Sister there with her and Matron would take the things from us and pass them to Sister, and Sister would put them on the table inside the hospital. We didn't go in, we just sort of filed past the door and she said, 'Thank you very much,' for whatever we had bought and then we would be taken back to school again. I remember going two or three times. I think I must have been probably aged between five and seven.

I can also remember the Hospital Carnivals which were used to raise money for the hospital. My Grandparents, Stockwell, had a tobacconists' shop in London Street. They lived over the shop and so when there was a Carnival we would go up into their sitting room and they would put a cushion on the window ledge and I would sit on the cushion and watch the Carnival procession go by. One Carnival that I particularly remember, there was a clown who came rolling along the street on a great, big ball and he was almost level with me as he went past the window so I shall never forget that. We used to have Carnivals quite regularly, every year, I think, and one of my uncles who worked in Thornycrofts used to play the tuba in the Thornycroft band and they used to walk past and it was great fun to see them all lined up and going past.

Margot Woodcock
born 1903   *interviewed 1992*

I was ill when I was 5. I had poisoning. I don't know what caused it, but I used to lick the paint, most peculiar, lick the paint on the cupboards and scrape the paint with my teeth. And I don't remember it, but I must have been taken to hospital with this stomach poisoning.

Ivy Kneller
born 1918   *interviewed 2001*

I went to the Hackwood Road hospital to have my tonsils out when I was 13. I had to stay for two or three days, and I can remember coming down the stairs and fainting at the bottom of the stairs.

You did not have your own transport in those days. When you came out of the hospital, if you could put one foot in front of the other, you came home on the bus.

Doris Galop

born 1911   *interviewed 1992*

I was desperately ill when I was 17. I had tonsillitis very badly. I kept having it and at last the doctor said, 'You'll have to go into hospital and have your tonsils out.' 'What, at my age?' I was in the Cottage Hospital and I lost a terrific lot of blood. Mother and father were called and they were up with me all night but I got over it. It was a very clean and tidy hospital. The nurses and matron were very kind.

Barbara Green

born 1921   *interviewed 2001*

When I was seven years old, I had my tonsils removed. It was either Dr Williams or Dr Potter who removed my tonsils. You had chloroform and you had a nozzle over your nose, and you had to breathe it in gradually, till you went to sleep. It was quite frightening, it wasn't nice at all. I just stayed in there for the day. There was a parrot in the children's ward and we used to talk to the parrot, and he used to answer us.

There was a lovely brass plaque on the wall in the hospital with the names of people and how much money they'd given - £100 was a lot of money then. John May, the brewers, had done a lot. But the building has been pulled down and nobody knows where that beautiful plaque's gone.

Susan Richmond

born 1924   *interviewed 1992*

I was knocked off my bicycle by a car and I was taken to the Cottage Hospital and the doctor had to be called because I'd hit my head. He stitched me up and I was taken home by my father. The little hospital was very antiquated. The casualty department was very small. I remember my youngest brother going in and having his tonsils out, and visiting him there. There wouldn't have been more than about six to eight beds in the children's ward in those days.

In the garden at Hackwood Road Hospital c 1937

Eleanor Goddard

                             interviewed 1998

The doctors also had to visit their patients in the Hackwood Road Cottage Hospital, now pulled down. It had two large wards, one for men, the other for women, one three-bedded ward called 'Malshanger' and three or four private wards. There was a theatre and the necessary kitchen with cook and domestic staff, as well as Sister and nurses. Each doctor in the town used it for his patients. There was an anaesthetist on call

and surgeons came up from Winchester Hospital or Southampton. Orthopaedic cases were usually sent to the Lord Mayor Treloar Hospital at Alton. Matron ruled supreme over all her staff. She saw all patients every day and did nearly all the secretarial work herself..

In 1919 the role of State-Registered-Nurse was created by the Nurses Registration Act.

Miss Nightingale had believed that the work of nurses depended on the standard set by the Matron, and no good ever came of anyone interfering between the head of a nursing establishment and her nurses. Nurses were not to be passive, devoted and obedient.

From Miss Nightingale's Notes on Nursing: what it is and what it is not (quoted in Barbara Carpenter Turner's History of the Royal Hampshire County Hospital

Based on an article from the Basingstoke Review, (date and author unknown)

A small home-made X-ray machine, operated at a house in Chequers Road, Basingstoke, in 1906, produced the first plate made for medical reasons in the town. This machine, 'a mass of wires and gadgets', was operated by a Mr Albert Thumwood and Mr 'Bunny' Lunn, a woodwork master at a local school. The patient was Mr Lunn's father, who had sustained a severe fracture of the wrist.

An interested spectator on that occasion was Mr Edmund Knight, of Worting Road, Basingstoke, who later spent much of his World War 1 service as a radiographer and became radiographer at the Hackwood Road Hospital. Interviewed for the *Basingstoke Review*, he said that modern techniques have resulted in it being almost a push-button job and that people entering the profession now have little idea of the conditions that pioneer operators had to work under, or of the 'amateur state' of the apparatus.

Albert Thumwood

born 1903   *interviewed 1992*

My uncle built the first X-ray machine in Basingstoke. He made it in my grandfather's workshop in Church Street and took it down to Chequers Road, where my grandfather used to live, and set it up in the front hall. He practised on it down there until he got it more or less perfect. Then he took it up the Cottage Hospital and he used it there until the First World War broke out. Then he gave it to another chap to take it over and run it and he went on to a London hospital and worked on the big X-rays in London.

> At the end of World War 1, when the American Military Hospital at Hursley Park was closed, they gave their X-ray plant to the Royal Hampshire County Hospital at Winchester, which in turn passed on its old X-ray plant to the Basingstoke General Hospital
>
> *From A History of the Royal Hampshire County Hospital by Barbara Carpenter Turner, quoting Peach DI: Merdone: The History of Hursley Park, 1976, pub by IBM UK Laboratories*

Basing Road Hospital

Basing Road Hospital suffered from its association in people's minds with the dreaded Workhouse, especially since it specialised in geriatric care.

Dr Sandy Smeaton

born 1916   *interviewed 1998, 1999*

The Workhouse was a common feature of Victorian England. They provided food and accommodation, usually on a temporary basis, for 'down-and-outs' in return for some form of manual labour from the men and 'in-house' contribution from the women. Basingstoke's workhouse had been built on the road to Old Basing in 1836. Part of it was demolished in

the late 1940s and what remained became a geriatric unit, also housing physiotherapy: the Basing Road Hospital. It was never popular with the elderly townsfolk, who still looked upon it as the workhouse.

The name was then changed to the Cowdery Down Hospital, to emphasise that it was not connected with the Workhouse, but many local people refused to be convinced. The site now houses the private Hampshire Clinic.

Barbara Broadbridge

born 1918   *interviewed 1992*

My mother died in the Basing Road Hospital, and two of my aunts were down there as well. Everybody, poor old souls, didn't want to finish their days down there because they all remembered it as the Workhouse, but it was a wonderful hospital and it did look after them till the end. Two of my aunts were down there as well. So there have been good things in the town.

The Shrubbery Maternity Home

A midwife, Mrs Mary Annie Hardwick, was listed at 7 Penwith [Penrith] Rd in 1920 and at 23 Essex Rd in 1923.

Many Basingstoke people have fond memories of the Shrubbery Maternity Home, opened in 1946. They tell of excellent standards of care, although in emergencies mothers might have to be sent on to Winchester.

Dr Sandy Smeaton

born 1916   *interviewed 1998, 1999*

The Shrubbery had been a private house belonging to the Burberry family. I think it was called the Shrubbery because they imported lorry loads of soil to grow flowers. It was a very nice house. The billiard room was turned into a 6-bedded ward and so on. There was an upstairs room which was the labour ward, a nursery for the babies, and other bedrooms became one- and two-bedded wards. There was no lift, so patients had to be taken up in a sort of chair, I suppose, by the ambulance men.

Jessie Jack

born 1918   *interviewed 1992*

When I first came to the Shrubbery it was June 1947, but the Shrubbery had first opened in November 1946. Till then it had been the home residence of the Burberry family.

Before the National Health, patients were booked on a means test. People forget that. They paid what they could pay. But even when I first went there in 1947, the treatment was excellent - it really was.

When I first went there, patients stayed for ten days. Which is unheard of now! Though they were getting up and getting about. They were allowed to trot to the toilet and have a bath. They all had an afternoon sleep. It really was a smashing place to work in and for the patients as well. But then I think the war had taught us early ambulation - get them up and moving, rather than the old way - oh, the varicose veins! Do you know, they used to have a sandbag over their leg to keep it still! It was the worst thing that you could do. Get mobile is the answer. Get moving to prevent clots. But the babies were lovely. Little bundles.

You took them out to mum. 'Which one is yours?' 'Oh I don't mind, Sister.' I would take two up, they would have their wrist tags on. 'Which one is yours?' and sometimes they didn't know. Till you said, 'This one is yours, because of the wristband and this one is Mrs Jones's and you are Mrs Smith.'

Blanche Bunkle

born 1908   *interviewed 1998*

I had two babies at home, just with a midwife. John was born 1935, Tony in 1938. It wasn't easy, and then you got somebody to come and look after you. We weren't allowed to get out of bed, hardly, the first week.

With the third baby I went to a clinic. This big lady sitting there, round in Caston's Road. They tried to turn the baby because it was a breech, and they said, 'We'll get you away as soon as possible.' Well, I went home and I was soon in labour. Unfortunately, it was on a Thursday and my mother was helping in a church fête at St Michael's, so she came down and took the two boys back with her and looked after them while I was down at Winchester. That was very traumatic, though. My husband was away, and some of those ladies in that ward, they didn't want babies and one was having her thirteenth. Another one, they let her out of prison to have her baby.

Joan Metcalfe

I had four babies at home before the start of the NHS. For our eldest, we arranged for the doctor and the midwife to be there. The doctor's charge was eight guineas, the nurse cost £2.10s. As I was young and healthy, and there were no problems, we just booked the midwife for the next babies (anyway, the doctor just stood there while the midwife and myself did the work!)

The Isolation Hospital

Arthur Attwood described an account he received from Australia of a death of smallpox in 1758 at a Pest House in Chapel Hill, Basingstoke, at the time on the outskirts of the town. The Pest House, for patients suffering from contagious diseases, was then mentioned in a Charter of George III in 1784. When the railway was extended to Southampton in 1840 the Pest House and two almshouses had to be demolished to enable the railway bridge to be built. The railway company had to provide a Pest House close to the Cricketer's Inn off the Victory roundabout, a row of tumble-down, insanitary cottages, staffed by one 'nurse' who was paid a few shillings a week to feed them. In 1868 a public meeting decided to erect a new building for smallpox and other infectious diseases but the foundation stone was not laid until 1880.

In 1892 when the town found itself in the grip of the 'Scarlet Fever Visitation' the hospital had no resident nurses - if required, nurses were put on the train from the General Nursing Institute in London. By the end of June there were 30 patients in a hospital designed to take a maximum of 11 and a corrugated iron building was quickly run up in the grounds to take convalescent patients. However, by the time it was ready, the number of patients had mercifully declined and it was never used.

From History of Infectious Diseases Hospital by Dilys Eaton (edited)

The London and South Western Railway Company now planned to extend its station and goods yard on the land on which the hospital stood, so in 1900 a new brick Isolation Hospital was built on the Kingsclere Road, from plans by John Gibson 'who cornered the market in Basingstoke hospital designs.'

In 1905 a severe outbreak of enteric (typhoid) fever broke out, with 91 cases (13 deaths) between September and November. Again, the Isolation Hospital could not cope and six 'papier maché' huts were brought from Alton at a cost of £16,000 each and placed on brick piers, with connections for water, sewage and gas. While they were being set up, the old corrugated iron building was used at last.

Strongly-worded reports by Medical Officers for the Local Government Board and the Borough of Basingstoke blamed contamination of the water supply in Steam Dell off Reading Road. Even in 1895 the Borough's Medical Officer had written, 'Gentlemen, I beg to report Scarlet Fever has appeared in two places in the Town. I also beg to report several cases of Pustular Tonsillitis of severe form … this I have no hesitation in assuming is due to the water.' But it was not until after the 1905 outbreak that the Water Supply Committee was authorised to take steps for supplying the town from the new well at West Ham.

A report in the Hants & Berks Gazette for February 10th 1906, describes an action by the Corporation of Basingstoke against Herbert Andrews, who had refused to pay his water bill of 9s 4d for the quarter ending September 29th on the grounds that the water was contaminated. Was it really a Judge rather than a Magistrate who gave the Town Clerk such a hard time?

Defendant	*I was not supplied with proper water.*
Judge	*It has not got any whisky mixed with it? (Laughter)*
Defendant	*No, sir, it was sewage. I object to pay because it was contaminated.*
Judge	*Did you get any illness through it?*
Defendant	*I did not but a nephew of mine who works for me had typhoid fever through it.*

The Corporation would not admit that their water was polluted, but a public notice was produced from the Medical Officer of Health and the Town Clerk had to retract.

Town Clerk   The Corporation did issue certain notices to consumers of water asking them to boil their water because we feared contamination had taken place.

Judge   That won't do. They might just as well tell him to take a dose of castor oil. They have no right to poison him first and tell him that afterwards. Your duty as a local authority is to give a sufficient and proper supply of pure water to the inhabitants.

The following extract from the Report of Medical Inspectors of the Local Government Board on the outbreak of enteric fever in Basingstoke in 1905 shows the steps taken to prevent the spread of infectious diseases.

Borough of Basingstoke.
WATER SUPPLY.
NOTICE !

It having been found that contaminated matter has got into the Council's Well from which the Borough is supplied it is highly desirable that all water used for drinking purposes and for washing and rinsing domestic crockery, salad, etc., as well as Milk, should be boiled for not less than five minutes, until further Notice.

FRERE WEBB, M.D.,
Medical Officer of Health.

Town Hall, Basingstoke,
October 10th, 1905.

Albert Manday, Printer, 24, Church Street, Basingstoke.

The hospital provides for the reception of 40 patients, and in ordinary times, cases of three different diseases in both sexes can be treated in it. Each block has the usual ward kitchen and offices . . . In addition, the hospital grounds contain a block with laundry and drying-room, a mortuary and a Reck's steam disinfector, which is capable of giving a pressure of 40 lb to the square inch, and of maintaining a temperature of 230° F. In this connection I might mention that one and the same cart is used for the conveyance of infected clothing and bedding and for its removal after disinfection. This leads to unnecessary trouble in disinfecting the cart after the carriage of infected articles. The employment of two carts in the process of disinfection would simplify matters.

The hospital is connected with the town sewers and the town water supply is laid on to it.

On the east side of the Kingsclere Road, about 1¼ miles from the centre of the town, and a little over a quarter of a mile from the Isolation Hospital is a Small-pox Hospital. It is constructed of corrugated iron lined with match-boarding, and contains accommodation for 12 patients.

The Borough has a good ambulance carriage for the removal of patients suffering from infectious diseases. This is horsed by contract.

Ken Toop
born 1923   *interviewed 1993*

Some years ago I came across a building at Kiln Farm, Sherborne. It was being used as a house, I think it was, for turkeys or chickens, quite a big building, house-size. And I recognised it immediately. It was an old green, corrugated-iron, single-storey building. It had been the original Isolation Hospital, which used to stand on the Kingsclere Road before you came to Gudgeons' chicken farm and the Wellington

Terrace Park Prewett houses. But it became inadequate during epidemics for a town the size of Basingstoke, so the new one was built, where we lived. I've been round to the old building since, because I wanted to take a photograph of it, but unfortunately I suppose it fell into decay and it's gone now.

Dr Sandy Smeaton
born 1916   *interviewed 1998, 1999*

The wards of Isolation Hospitals were full of children and young adults with diphtheria and scarlet fever. Tracheotomies were common in the former and permanent kidney damage in the latter.

Hilda Applin

born 1907   *interviewed 1999*

You knew you'd got scarlet fever when you were ill. You got a very heavy rash and your throat and everything were like parchment. You were really ill. I had to have the doctor and he isolated me directly. Nurse Baker came to fetch me in an old ambulance.

Hilda Applin (circled) with fellow assistants at the International

There were over 100 up in the Isolation that Christmas, 1924. I went in there in November and I was still there at Christmas, of course. When they bathed you, they rubbed your joints with eucalyptus oil. The nurse used to sit on my bed and tell me stories about soldiers when she was nursing in France. But, do you know, the only medication I had there was half a cup of liquorice powder when I went in. And, with fever, my tongue and throat were like a dry desert, nothing to relieve it but cold water. There was only the one doctor, the County Medical Officer. He used to come in once and see you. But apart from that you didn't have a doctor come and see you.

The day I got up, I'd been in bed nearly three weeks and they wanted the beds for the night-time in the main block. I was scheduled to get up and go up to the convalescent block and I didn't even have a coat and I wasn't given a blanket or anything to wrap round me. That was outside. I had kidney trouble. I couldn't go to work for nearly six months. I reckon that's what caused it.

Do you know?

That the number of cases of Scarlet Fever notified during 1931 was 14.

That only one case of Diphtheria occurred during the same period, and no cases of Typhoid Fever were reported.

From the 1932 Health Week booklet produced by the Borough of Basingstoke

(Willis Museum)

Gwen Rumbold

born 1920   *interviewed 1992*

Both my sisters had scarlet fever. They went to the Isolation Hospital, which was in Kingsclere Road. They had to stay there a week or two, until all the rash had gone, I suppose. They came back with all their fingers skinned. They had purple nails. That was all part of the scarlet fever.

Even the parents were not allowed to go in the hospital. They used to look at them through the windows. When my sisters were in there, my mother and father used to go there. It was in January and the snow was up to the hedges. It was deep snow. No buses. They had to walk a couple of miles each way, just to look through the window. The caretaker's son used to run round the wards with lighted paper - there were open fires in the wards where the children were in bed.

Ken Toop

born 1923   *interviewed 1993*

My parents went to the new Isolation Hospital in 1923 and that was the year I was born. We stayed there until 1933. Dad was the gardener. Really he was a gardener of quite some competence. He'd worked in hot houses in Dorset. There was about two acres of garden at the Isolation Hospital. My father's work entailed the cultivation of all this ground, all by hand of course and the cutting of all the lawns, pruning of all the roses, rough grass cutting, hedges. Most of the green stuff and such things as he could manage went into the hospital for the patients' and staff use. And the other half of the job was ambulance driver, which took quite a lot of time.

Ken Toop's father

It was a joint job, as was common in those days, where the husband and wife were employed as one, and the wages were a joint wage. I would think Dad's wages were never more than about 35 shillings a week, about £1.15s. But of course there was no charge for the cottage.

Because it was a joint job, my mother had to work in the wards as ward maid. That entailed polishing the floors with these big long 'dummies', on a pole. All the wards up there - for diphtheria, typhoid, scarlet fever - were warmed by open fires, such as the warmth was. Another of my dad's responsibilities was to chop wood constantly, for kindling to keep these four fires lit, and part of my mother's job was to keep them stacked up during the day time.

When I was young, I used to accompany my mother all the time because there was no-one else to look after me. When she went up the wards in the morning I went with her, and I was with her all day long. I used to play with the patients - those patients that did recover and become sort of semi-convalescent and walk round the grounds. There were a lot of children detained there as well. I used to play with them. I don't think my mother was scared of me catching anything. I had inoculations, in the very early days of inoculations, and vaccinations of course.

I recall having mumps when I was at the Isolation Hospital Lodge, and that was painful. But I was very fortunate really. I suppose living among it through all those years when I was very young, almost from birth, and having the vaccinations done at birth must have given me some sort of immunity. And of course our water was quite good at the Lodge, when you compare it with a lot of other people's drinking water. Although it came from a tank, it was still quite good water, whereas lots of people's water came from wells. If it tasted all right, I suppose they'd drink it. They had no option anyway, did they?

Ken's father's job as ambulance driver was 24 hour cover.

He was called out at any time. Whenever the local doctor diagnosed diphtheria or an infectious disease, Dad was called out. And then he picked up a nurse from the nurses' quarters adjacent to the Lodge and they went off in the ambulance. And frequently in the day time I went with them and sat in the front with him, and the nurse used to come and sit in the back with the patient. It was an old Morris ambulance with artillery-spoked wheels. Many of the local people remember it, probably. It was a yellow colour. And we had that all the time that we lived up there. It was later changed for a white, more modern one but the original motor ambulance was a yellow Morris.

Because typhoid was caused by the impure water that came from inadequate drainage and sewerage systems, a lot of the cases we used to go to were from places like the Kingsclere Workhouse and the Basingstoke Workhouse. We used to get people who were on the road, like tramps, they used to put up in there and then they'd become unwell.

I can't remember any particular times of the year that were worse than others. But I've got lots of memories of farm cart tracks, round Hartley Wespall and Swallick Farm at Winslade, places like that which were quite inaccessible and it always seemed to be raining and muddy when we went, so I suppose the old man got called out more in the winter time really. This sounds nothing in a modern vehicle, but when you think that these old vehicles had narrow tyres and a lot of these old rutted tracks were almost impassable in the winter times, you realise what an awful job it was getting up there sometimes. We were called out in the middle of the night, anywhen, because the thing was you had to get these patients away from the surroundings in which they were.

Added to this was the fact that the public-health doctors had to make sure that there was no cross-infection with other members of the family and if there were any library books - which was rare - they had to be fumigated. When we used to get back to the Isolation Hospital Lodge, my dad had a big silver-plated sort of pump thing. I don't know exactly what was in it, but the routine was, after the patient and the nurse had got out of the back of the ambulance, Dad used to go inside and give this canister two or three pumps and then quickly evacuate and shut the door on it. I suppose that fumigated it against the next patient.

Dad was the only gardener and the only ambulance driver and my Mum was the only resident ward maid. There were nurses who lived in the house, and the Matron, but that was the limit of the staff.

Ken took notice of the way the hospital worked.

Sometimes the patients might be down to two, sometimes you might have 15, it was just impossible to say. On a Monday they used to make a point of it being a laundry day. If you can imagine, this place was built like a cruciform. It had wards on the ends of each arm and at the far end of one of them was a utility room with gas boilers and things. And this was the washplace where the washing was done. But of course there were no washing machines and things like that. All the washing for the patients and the nurses, all the sheets, everything was done in this laundry and it was all done by hand! And all the ironing. They had a large round table about seven or eight feet across, solid. And in the middle was a gasolier coming up, like a ring of a gas stove, and round it there was a cast-iron stand. And on this stand was a selection of flat irons standing upright against the gasolier. Loads of beeswax as well, lumps of beeswax scattered around. All the ironing was done on this. You used your iron with the beeswax - and all the nurses' hats had to be starched and nicely done, and you put your iron back in the centre and you took another one, and so you went on all the time. It was hard work, there's no doubt about that.

It was a continuing thing. When you'd cleaned the wards, lit the fires and done everything else, if you had time you went out and did some ironing, because it was always there to do. There was so much work that you just never had to look for anything to do.

When my mother and father were working, they had all the things to do at home as well, get the food ready and oil lamps lit. It was all oil lamps up there at first. When the gas came, it made life a bit easier. My mother still had to do washing indoors and my Dad used to dig our own garden and grow our own vegetables and all that sort of thing, so there was very little home life really. I never seem to remember seeing my parents sitting down, as it were.

There was no time off. You didn't have time off, in those sort of jobs, a joint job. My mum wouldn't have gone in at the weekend but if there was an urgent case that was admitted and nurses wanted a hand, obviously she would have given them a hand. But my dad was called out with the ambulance at any time, all hours, day or night, winter or summer. He might get called out two or three times in the day, he might go a fortnight and not get called out at all. But it was like that, because once you get a disease like that and it's in a family or you've mixed with children at school or something like that, it's liable to become widespread.

The people at the Isolation Hospital had visitors, but you couldn't go in. If you caught it you caught it, there was no half measures about it. You couldn't have a mild attack of typhoid. So you had to go in isolation and it was no good having an Isolation Hospital if people could have visitors, so there were definitely no visitors. You could only look through the windows. You weren't allowed to open them, they were locked inside, but you could stand outside and look through.

Isolation Hospital

The wards were quite large. You went in the central door and then you turned left or right to two wards. And, I would say there were about ten beds in each. As I recall, there were three isolation blocks, but each block would have had two wards so you could have had something like mumps in one, perhaps, or typhoid in the other one. All separately heated with open fires, of course. Plus all the open fires in the nurses' quarters and the matron's quarters. So my Dad's chopping of firewood in the morning was quite a horrendous job. And this was only one of his jobs. When you think!

Quite a lot of the patients died, a lot of young ones, a lot of children. But a lot got better, of course, and there's a lot of older people in the town now who were treated up there.

There was nowhere else to go. If you had any of the infectious diseases you had to go there. One authority wasn't interested in taking another authority's patients, you had to go to the Isolation Hospital where you lived.

Patients were so ill they didn't want to do anything. If you've ever seen anybody with diphtheria it's really, really terrible, they can't breathe. And a kid with scarlet fever was a frightening thing - not seen, luckily, nowadays

Many local people will probably remember the Lodge, because it was only during the redevelopment of the Ring Road that it was pulled down. It was quite a nice little Lodge, brick-built, with a nice little bit of garden, but it only had one small bedroom. So consequently my mother and father and myself all slept in the same room and when my sister was born, six years later, it was obviously too crowded. But having said all that, it was bearable, having regard to the conditions a lot of people were living under at the time.

I remember my time there quite well. I used to go along with my mother, whatever she was doing, and these fires in the open ward were a continual source of fascination. I went into a bank years ago to open a little deposit account when we first got married and there was a woman in there and she said 'Toop, not Kenny Toop?' I said, 'The very same'. She said, 'From the Isolation Hospital Lodge?' I said, 'Yes'. She said, 'I remember you. You used to light fires under the bed!' I said, 'Never, I never did that!' But, when my mind is refreshed like that, I can remember my Mum saying, 'Leave those fires alone'. I used to get a piece of paper and light them - a kid lighting a fire, and then I must have put one under her bed, to make smoke. My Mum, when she was quite advanced in years, remembered this woman when she was in the ward. She said, 'Oh, I remember her. She was a proper tomboy when she started to get better. She was out in the grounds climbing up the fir trees.'

Park Prewett and Rooksdown

Park Prewett and Rooksdown became known far beyond Basingstoke.

'The need of providing further accommodation for lunatics in the county has [resulted] in proposals which have a special interest for the town of Basingstoke. Park Prewett, a farm belonging to the Vyne estate, situate in the parish of Sherborne St John, has been acquired as the site for a new asylum, at a cost of £9000. It is intended to build upon the site accommodation for 600 lunatics and as the minimum cost per bed is likely to be at least £200 it will be seen that this undertaking will involve an outlay of not less than £130,000.'

Hants & Berks Gazette 6th January 1900

Mary Felgate

born 1912   *interviewed 1992,*

When the first wounded soldiers were brought back, I think they were up at Park Prewett Hospital. On sunny days they used to be brought up, perhaps by horse and cart, into the top Market Place. And they would be left sitting in wheelchairs in the sunshine to watch everybody going to and fro and shopping, and people used to go and talk to them. And I can remember one lovely sunny morning Mother saying, 'We'll go and take some roses down to one of the soldiers.' So Mother picked a bunch of our thornless roses and tied it up, and took me down there in my push-chair and stood outside what is now Lloyds Bank, which was Tyrrells the grocers. And she took me out of the push-chair, gave me the roses and told me to go over to the nearest soldier and give him this bunch of roses. And I don't remember what he said to me, but I remember he smiled and I ran back to Mother quickly because I was shy.

16.1.1920 Joint Asylum Visiting Committee: Sub-committee appointed for Park Prewett.

8 Jan 1925 The Staff also asked for a Loud Speaker Wireless Set to be provided and fitted up in the Club Room, adjoining the Recreation Hall. Resolved that this application be granted and that arrangements be also made for a Loud Speaker to be connected and used for patients' amusement in the Hall.

8 Jan 1925 'Lady Gardener Reported that Miss L.U. Jacottet had met with a cycling accident whilst proceeding home during the dinner hour and was being paid sickness benefit in accordance with the Committee's scheme. The Insurance Co. advised that there was no liability to pay compensation.

Notes taken from Park Prewett Mental Hospital Minute Book No 1

Ken Toop

born 1923   *interviewed 1993*

When we lived at the Lodge of the Isolation Hospital, the railway ran up to Park Prewett, and right alongside our house. Of course a lot of people don't realise Park Prewett was a medical hospital originally, and only afterwards it became a psychiatric hospital. The railway sidings went right alongside the Isolation Hospital, across under the road bridge, and a cutting went alongside our house, and about once a week an engine used to bring up three trucks of coal, because the whole of Park Prewett was fired by coal boilers.

In those days it was all locked wards up there. The asylum attendants - they didn't call them male nurses - used to wear a uniform to identify them if they were taking patients out, to show who was in charge. And those patients that were able to be taken out used to walk round the hospital, through what we called the Spinney. This was mainly beech trees, still only in their infancy, perhaps 12 feet high, they're massive now. There was a pathway right the way round the hospital. And it was quite common to see a long line of people with an asylum attendant going for this long walk right round the hospital for exercise, which was quite pleasant.

Across the road, also in Park Prewett, it was a hive of activity because there were the farm cottages - a lot of the patients that were able to be employed in Park Prewett worked there. It was a vast farm complex and stuff like cabbages and rhubarb and all that was grown there. Nothing was ever bought in that could be grown on the premises. All livestock too. They had pigs and all sorts of other things, chicken and anything like that.

There were several 'villas', separate houses, and even in recent times they were surrounded by railings. People said that was because the villas were for the more disturbed patients who couldn't be allowed in an open ward. We were fairly frightened of the patients because they acted in a frightening way. You're always frightened of anything which is out of your understanding.

I think until recent years they had about 1400 people in there. Although at the Isolation Hospital Lodge we were nothing to do with Park Prewett, we were completely separate, there were often people who used to be lost and stop at our Lodge to find their way - we've often had people stay there, small and cramped as it was. I remember in 1927 when I was only about five years old, during the very bad freeze up that we had, terrific snow drifts, we had a Jewish couple staying. They'd been at Park Prewett to see somebody and couldn't get back and they stayed overnight with us because the Kingsclere Road was blocked.

In 1939 most of the mental patients were evacuated to other hospitals, only 80 remaining, and Park Prewett Hospital was taken over by the government as an Emergency Medical Services (EMS) hospital, basically for the treatment of wounded soldiers, but also treating civilians injured in bombing raids. Some consultants were transferred there from St Mary's, Paddington, St Thomas's and Guy's. The American Section Hospital in Britain (AHB) ran an orthopaedic unit at Park Prewett, the surgeons exchanging gas masks for theatre masks and gowns.

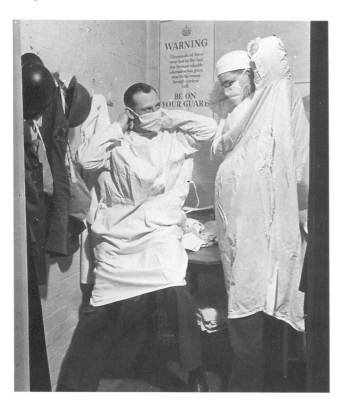

American Section Hospital in Britain: surgeons masking up for an operation, with gas masks and helmets on pegs

HRO 279M87/F2/14

Arthur Attwood

born 1916   *Gazette March 17, 2000*

One of the consultants, Dr Romanes, was a steam engine enthusiast and an owner of a steam traction-engine. He promised to drive his engine so that it could be seen from the spinal ward, which was near the main entrance. The engine duly arrived but with unpleasant consequences. It was so near the spinal ward that it began to fill with smoke. The doctor had to make a rapid retreat when accosted by the furious sister of the ward.

Susan Richmond

born 1924   *interviewed 1992*

There was so much going on there, with all the soldiers coming in and going out and all the young doctors. I was the Medical Superintendent's secretary in the EMS (Emergency Medical Service). There was General Scott, then Air Vice-Marshal Sir William Tyrrell and then Dr Thomas. They were appointed by the War Department.

Every time we had a Dutch soldier in, I used to have to phone Queen Wilhelmina's secretary and Queen Wilhelmina herself would come over from Mortimer and the Dutch soldier was brought down to her on a stretcher or in a wheelchair. The Duchess of Kent came, the mother of the present Duke of Kent . Her husband was killed in the early part of the War.

Professor Fleming visited the hospital to show General Scott his newly discovered penicillin. General Scott was very busy so I escorted Professor Fleming round the hospital and showed him where everything was. Eventually I brought him back and General Scott took him over.

We used to have marvellous pantomimes at Rooksdown, which was the facio-maxillary, the skin-grafting unit, under Sir Harold Gillies. The pantomimes were so funny, a great take-off of all the things going on in the hospital. They were mainly written by two orthopaedic surgeons, both called Ellis, who were very gifted, and most of the doctors took part.

It was a very happy time, a marvellous feeling, despite the War. We used to have big parties. We had a ball once a year in the big hall and once Sir William Tyrrell and I took to the floor to open the ball. I used to cycle up and cycle back again.

We had 2,000 beds. They weren't filled all the time but when we went back over to France on D-Day in 1944, we were a first transit hospital from the Normandy beachheads. They were bringing the wounded into Southampton and shipping them up on the trains. It was all beautifully organised. We had a self-contained railway line, up from Basingstoke station into Park Prewett, but I think we used that railway no more than two or three times because, luckily, the casualties weren't as bad as they'd anticipated and so in the end they used to come in a convoy of ambulances from the docks, driven by FANYs (First-Aid Nursing Yeomanry).

They all came in higgledy-piggledy, Germans, English, there were no guards, they were just put in the ambulance and those that could walk hobbled in and others came in on stretchers and wheelchairs. The Germans either stayed and were treated or went on into camps. They looked a bit scared because they couldn't believe that they could just come in like this. They were just treated as patients. And of course they couldn't speak English, which was always quite difficult, and very few people in the hospital could speak German.

But when you think of what we coped with in paperwork! There was a form for every soldier and we had to get all the particulars down in duplicate, because they hadn't got time from the beachhead and they were just shipped out as fast as they could. They were assessed and it was decided which patients could be moved on further. Every morning I made out the list of patients who were to be transferred, choosing the hospitals nearer to their homes. We shipped them out as fast as we could, ready for the next lot, so there was a convoy going out every day. If any naval personnel came in to us, they were transferred to Haslar or another naval hospital.

We had a contingent of doctors sent down from St Mary's Hospital, with nurses, a contingent from St Thomas's and a contingent from Westminster. And then there was VAD nursing, the Red Cross and the St John Ambulance.

Arthur Attwood

born 1916   *Gazette March 17th, 2000*

In its first seven years of its existence more than 4,000 patients passed through the wards of Rooksdown to enter life freed of the embarrassment of disfigurement. The vast majority of these were war casualties. The treatment was very complex and in many cases as many as 30 to 40 operations would be involved. Such treatment was given over lengthy periods. The hospital was headed by a team of six specialist plastic surgeons working together as a co-ordinated body. They were joined by a larger team of ancillary specialists working in their many and varied fields. The work was supported by a very devoted band of sisters and brothers.

Mr Frank Tovey

born 1921   *interviewed 1996*

Sir Harold Gillies did a lot of pioneering work. He developed a procedure for nose reconstruction that was adopted for use on patients with leprosy, He used to have a club for his patients and they used to have regular meetings at the Swan in Sherborne St John and traditionally it was known at the hospital as 'The Dirty Duck'.

He did all types of surgery, very largely on personnel who had severe burns and so on - plastic surgery.

Ivy Kneller

born 1918   *interviewed 2001*

My husband was plantsman up at Park Prewett hospital, in charge of the greenhouses, and when the new hospital was built, he was estate manager. We used to go to lots of dances at Park Prewett because he was on the social committee. They had a marvellous hall. People used to come from miles around to go, and we used to belong to the old time dancing group up there.

During the war it was used as a hospital and I used to help out there with the patients. Every Sunday we used to take out ones that had skin grafts and had long basket chairs to support them. We used to take them into the town sometimes, sometimes down to the Swan at Sherborne, have tea, then take them back. They were terribly burned, some of them, terribly scarred. They did wonderful work there.. Sir Harold Gillies, he was marvellous.

Sir Harold Gillies had treated many patients with facial injuries in the first World War, and when the second World War broke out, he set up his 120-bed plastic surgery unit at Rooksdown (part of Park Prewett Hospital, which had been opened for private patients in 1930, with prices starting at 2 guineas). This became one of the leading centres for plastic surgery. An instrument he designed is still used today, known as 'the Gillies'.

Rooksdown

Kathleen Laws

born 1918   *interviewed 2001*

Kathleen also helped to take the Park Prewett soldiers to the Swan.

The pub made the tea and the ladies provided the food. We went to a field nearby when the weather was good. We also made arrangements with the Waldorf cinema, who would take two soldiers at a time on Saturday afternoons. Once I managed to push my soldier to the cinema but on the way back I got as far as the Rising Sun, very uphill, and could go no further. Someone helped me all the way back.

Victor Price

born 1930   *interviewed 1992*

After D-Day they had special trains diverted through Basingstoke straight to Park Prewett and you knew those people inside those trains were severely wounded.

When I went to Park Prewett Hospital to deliver the newspapers, I just couldn't believe what I saw. The men there, they were young, the numbers of them with no faces, burned bodies.

I was allowed to go through the wards, no-one bothered me. I was just a little school boy - ex-school boy, you might say, with my satchel of papers and they just let me meander through; at the time I was selling **The Star** and **The Evening Standard**, which was a bit new to Basingstoke. And I saw the people that were just injured by bullets and explosions. Many of the burns patients were pilots. And although I was 14, I realised. This is what you called war, what those men had gone through.

The medical care was marvellous. In fact, that is where they had the unit for the burns. I think it was called the Water and Acid Bath, which somehow did marvels for them. You saw people with their arms wrapped round their faces, and the nurses told me they were having skin grafts. Where their faces had been burnt off, they were getting the skin from their arm to grow onto their face. They took it from all parts of their bodies, and I think they were lucky, they were pleased to be alive, but they must have suffered in the initial stages of what happened.

I visited there for the next two years. And I saw people get better, people disfigured for life. I think it stuck in me, that I thought I was unhappy, but these men - their lives weren't completely finished, but didn't they have a struggle ahead of them! A lot of them being single, obviously their chances of getting married were a bit extinct.

They came from everywhere, and I met some wonderful people. In fact, one of the chaps who wasn't burnt but had severe injuries lived in Basingstoke, and to this day I know him. This was the centre for the whole country, and not only this country but Commonwealth countries as well. Everyone who was injured to that extent or had that type of injury went to Park Prewett before they were put anywhere else. You must remember, we were only 45 minutes away from Portsmouth, so when the injured came straight back, this was it.

Charles Shirvell

born 1912   *interviewed 1992*

We played a number of times at the Park Prewett hospital, that huge hall up there, that's where the orchestra would play for the evening for patients. They needed a bit of patience too!

The backcloth has a Basingstoke scene

Barbara Broadbridge

born 1918   *interviewed 1992*

When I got the job at Prewett, first of all it was in the big main kitchen. I was helping with the officers' cooking. Officers were in one ward and also the hospital doctors, all the staff and matron. Well, I don't know that their food was much better but they had a bit more care taken with it, perhaps an extra cook to help. And so that was my job mostly, which I was glad of. We had a chef from London put in charge, another chef came, I think, from the Navy and there were about four or five cooks, mostly Welsh.

One or two of the villas around Park Prewett were used for some of the mental patients who were still there, and were workers. One looked after the bedrooms on our corridor, which was quite near the kitchen, and she would make a cup of tea in the morning and look after us if we weren't on duty until ten. Some days I think it was half-past five until half-past three. But the other times we came on duty half-past ten until half-past seven or eight, something like that. Every other day, I think we alternated.

So at times I went home for the night and then I could get back in the morning with a bus. Only about once, Christmas Day, I can remember walking home because there were no buses. And I think it was a very icy Christmas. I can remember walking home, because Prewett was the other side of the station, so I walked all the way. And it was so slippery it was really very awkward. Of course, the surface wasn't concreted or anything in those days, I'm sure, but I suppose being on a slope and I expect there was ice which had snow, and boys had been sliding most of the day to make it nice and slippery, so it was quite a job to get home. But otherwise it was mostly Venture Buses that brought me, which I was very glad of.

At the hospital if we were on duty - well, of course, air raids were mostly at night – we were supposed to get up and go down below to the tunnel which went all round the hospital under the buildings. The buildings were more or less in a circle, and the tunnel underneath held the hot water pipes, water mains, gas, electricity. It seemed a terrible place to be if anything happened with all the water, electricity and everything else, but that's where we were supposed to go for air raids.

I think soldiers quite often went nearer their homes if they were able to. But it was not a bad life for them here, I suppose. They weren't allowed out much, except occasionally into town, where they were always very visible with their bright blue suits. One or two of us from the kitchen would find partners and play tennis with them. We seemed to grab a tennis court that nobody was using - I think it was near where the Hospice is now.

Owen (Don) Blissett

born 1930   *interviewed 2003*

I replied to an advertisement in the then **Hants and Berks Gazette** for the post of Junior Clerk at Park Prewett Hospital. I was successful in my application and commenced at the hospital, at the age of 16, on 23rd September 1946 at the large salary of £70.00 per annum plus £29.00 per annum cost of living allowance.

The one proviso for applicants was that they had to hold a School Certificate and, as it happened, the results of the School Cert exams were published in the same paper as the advertised post. In those days the wheels turned quicker than the present day, as the job was advertised on one Friday, interview the next Friday, and I started work on the following Monday.

Initially I was set to work in the Wages Office with the late Stan Palmer. My first task was to write pay envelopes, in ink, (Biros were not the in thing in those days), each envelope was completed with name, pay number, gross pay, all deductions, and net pay. Certain salaries were prepared elsewhere in the hospital, the Officers' Salaries, so called, for senior staff by the late Bill Denne, and male nursing staff by the late Mrs Ethel Tindall. My second task was learning to use a typewriter, with

a large 'brief carriage'. This was a daunting task for someone who had never used a typewriter before; however, the experience has stood me in good stead in the years since then.

In 1946, when I joined the hospital, there were a number of soldiers still being treated for their wounds; however, they were gradually transferred to other hospitals, and gradually the old mental patients returned from their enforced evacuation.

The exception to the transfer of the wounded were those patients suffering from burns, who were being treated at the Rooksdown House Plastic and Jaw Unit. Rooksdown House was the pre-war private wing of Park Prewett Hospital, where accommodation and treatment, according to a brochure that I still have about Rooksdown, cost two guineas per week.

Job descriptions were unheard of, way back in 1946, so when the boss said, 'I want you to go and work in the General Office or the Stores Department,' you went, there was no saying, 'That's not in my job description.' As a result of this policy, I had spells in the General Office and the Stores Office; in the former one I was responsible for the daily recording and stamping of all outgoing letters, recording the admission and discharge of patients, the care of Ration Books, (food was still rationed at this time), which on occasions had to be returned to the Food Office in Basingstoke. The trip to Basingstoke to the Food Office meant that, in addition to my weekly salary of 38/-, I received 2d per mile for riding my bike there and back, a reasonable earner.

One incident that I can call to mind, when working in the General Office, was being dispatched by the Chief Clerk, the late Mr A. H Scrivens, to the Chief Male Nurse's office to get the measurements of a body, required by a Bournemouth undertaker. I was told that they were not in the office but that they were 'down the corridor'. Little did I know that those three words were to take me to the hospital mortuary, with a Charge Nurse, who lifted the lid on the coffin that was there and proceeded to measure the occupant for length and breadth. I can still visualise the shrouded body with a name label tied on its big toe, and can even remember the surname today. I suppose the Employment of Young Persons in Hospital Act had not been thought of then.

During my stint in the Stores Department, I was known as the 'Diet Clerk'. This meant the collection of the numbers of inpatients from the Chief Male Nurse's Office and Matron's Office, together with a list of any special diets, such as 'mince diet' and 'diabetic diet' and then performing the onerous task of calculating the quantities of provisions to be issued to the Wards or to the kitchen as the case may be. I say 'onerous' - food still being rationed, issues were calculated in fractions of an ounce, not quarters or half ounces, but more like a seventh of an ounce per day or every other day. One thing I do remember is that Marmite was issued to make a bed-time drink.

One escapade that took place whilst working in the Stores was the day when I was asked to get some empty boxes from the top of a stack - no problem. Unfortunately, I stood on the top of a 40 gallon drum of floor polish to reach the boxes. You can guess, the top caved in, and I went in, everyone laughed but me, it was 'good' polish. My trousers fell to pieces in a couple of weeks, and I've always said that I've given a polished performance ever since.

Mrs E Fawcett

born 1926   *interviewed 1992*

I worked at John Mares (clothing factory) and so did my mother and sister. We did the hospital uniforms. That was a blue uniform, and being near Park Prewett we sewed a lot of that. It was like a blue woollen material.

Mrs Kate Webb

born 1942   *interviewed 1995*

My parents worked at Park Prewett and met there before World War 2. During the war, Father was in the medical corps but he returned to Park Prewett after the war.

To start with, when my father came back from Scotland, part of Park Prewett was called Rooksdown Hospital. It was given over to general nursing for soldiers who had been burned in the war. There were a lot of very severe cases there. My father worked there for a while and there was a very important surgeon called Sir Harold Gillies. I never met him, but Gillies Ward in the hospital was named after him and

there is the Gillies Health Centre in Brighton Hill. I think they've got a Gillies Drive in the new part of the hospital grounds. They've actually knocked a lot of Rooksdown down now, which I find very sad, because I have a lot of good memories of Park Prewett since my young life was spent in and around there.

My father was working there with the men who were badly burned. Rooksdown Hospital was quite near to Wellington Terrace, which belonged to Park Prewett, and our house was right on the road there. And I remember, until I understood, being a little bit intimidated by these young men that would come out for walks, heavily bandaged, heavily, heavily scarred. They were recuperating and a Social Club had been started by the nursing fraternity, or perhaps the Park Prewett community, which is now known as the Wellington Social Club. That is quite a big social club now, but at that time it was just a little tin hut and as children we used to go banging on the back door, asking for bottles of lemonade or packets of crisps. These young men used to use this club, which was why they were walking down the terrace.

Extracts from the Magazine of The Rooksdown Club

The Rooksdown Club was formed in 1945, under the War Charities Act1940. Its aims were 'the welfare of patients and ex-patients, the maintenance of the fellowship begun at Rooksdown and the education of the public to accept the disfigured or maimed as normal.'

From the President of the Rooksdown Club, Harold Gillies

I can hardly imagine a more ill-adapted building for a surgical hospital than this old place, and the operating theatres are almost a joke. How is it, then, that we have had such a grand run for our money, and both you and the staff have been able to pull together and get the kind of results which you deserve? I think very largely it is what one might call the spirit of this place, which does not only mean the courage, hope and confidence of the patient, but also a little something else. It means a knowledge that everyone in the place from Elaine to James is out to serve you, and you are quick to evaluate the surgical efforts.

Heaven knows, we on the staff side have made plenty of mistakes. You cannot do this class of work without having disasters, or minor disasters. The very essence of this game is a fight between the blood supply of a part we are trying to make and the beauty of the result. If we had not got to pay any attention to blood supply, you would all be as beautiful as Robert Taylor and Hedy Lamarr. Then there is the mass psychology of a large number of humans with similar afflictions. You have seen it yourselves when one of you comes in with a comparatively minor condition who thinks it is the world's worst. He soon finds his correct level and his mental poise.

It is, I think, a little true that we react to a certain extent to the kind of face we have got, in contradistinction to the statement that our faces are the mirror of our souls. You know my bald head and lack of chin. Supposing I was to wake up with a large head of curly red hair and a big square jaw? Everyone would be so frightened of me and think me so fierce that I would begin to imagine I was the kind of character that one usually associates with such a virile type. To a certain extent some of you boys and girls are temporary failures, so you let your tails go down a little in keeping with the dud faces we have been able to give you.

However, we still go on learning not only about general plastic surgery, but about the particular individual in question, and you find these failures turn into good results. Not that we are ever content with our work. The surgeon who is can be labelled as one who is finished and of no use.

From the 2000 issue, reprinted from Rooksdown Pie, 1947

The Ortho Ward, Park Prewett - From Another Angle

John da Cuhna   *2002 issue*

John da Cuhna, a Lieutenant in the 23rd Hussars, 'had bumped into unfriendly Panzers in Normandy during operation Epsom, 1944, and was hit in the head.'

My departure from Park Prewett Hospital was as inauspicious as my arrival in late June 1944, both being in a railway ambulance train. However, I must say I was feeling a great deal better when I left.

Like that of many other men, my journey from the Normandy battlefield took me to a Field Hospital and thence, a few days later, by amphibious DUKW, through the surf and over the sea towards the open bow doors of an LST (Landing Ship Tank). Once in and over the ramp, my stretcher was slung up against the side of the vast hold. Being assisted by drugs, I cannot say when we sailed or what the weather was like, but it was a relief to reach Southampton which, I presumed, to be our port of arrival.

Disembarkation was not a matter for discussion. Our stretchers were simply loaded in pairs on to a platform and lifted by overhead crane out of the hold through the open hatchway. It was all done as gently as possible, but, as we all know, when one is in pain, any jolt causes added distress.

At Park Prewett, my destination was the Orthopaedic Ward in the main hospital which was manned by surgical and nursing staff from St Thomas's Hospital, London, with additional nurses from the West London Hospital. All were very different under the strict discipline of Ward Sister who behaved like a Colonel with an eye on promotion to Brigadier. After a couple of weeks or so I started to notice that some of the girls were really rather pretty. That was when it dawned on me that I was definitely going to survive.

A naval Surgeon Captain, probably a 'dug-out', puzzled me by stopping by my bed every day and looking at my notes. Then one day, he walked on by and never stopped again. When I asked the Staff Nurse why, she said he had discovered I was not a real (i.e. naval) Lieutenant, just an inferior Army person

After practising at the Bar, John da Cunha became a Circuit Judge and has now retired.

Staff of the Canadian Hospital at Hackwood Park

Brian Spicer

born 1928   *interviewed 1992*

At Hackwood House there was a Canadian hospital. We do get people back, who were patients there in the war. A psychologist came over from Canada, from Toronto, and he had been a doctor at the hospital then. Quite an elderly man who wanted to see it before he died, coming back to his old haunts.

Alf Hutt

We had the Canadian Hospital at Hackwood Park . My Grandfather kept pigs, I remember, and he seemed to do quite well doing a swap, I don't know if it was some of this pig meat but we used to end up with some canned supplies from one of the military sources.

St Thomas's House

The 1903 directory mentions an infirmary at St Thomas's House, Darlington Road, erected in 1878 for 'friendless and fallen women'. It later became known as St Thomas's Lodge and eventually housed a school for the deaf.

Lord Mayor Treloar Cripples' Home & College, Alton

> Later this became the Lord Mayor Treloar Hospital and College.

Although this hospital is in Alton, it belongs in this book because so many patients (and some nurses) came from Basingstoke. It was originally built by public subscription (and the help of the **Daily Mail***) in1901 for sick and wounded soldiers returning from the Boer War, but with the end of the Boer War it became an army hospital. In 1908 Sir William Treloar, Lord Mayor of London, opened The Lord Mayor Treloar Cripples' Home and College. During the First World War, it was extended with marquees to accommodate war casualties.*

Jo Kelly

born 1947   *interviewed 1999*

It had everything there, even its own railway station. During the First World War, a lot of the patients, the soldiers, came over on the hospital ships from France and then they came from Portsmouth straight into Treloar's by train. Special trains were brought in from Alton, up the branch line to the hospital. It was very much an open-plan type of hospital and so it then became a TB hospital, and later the orthopaedic hospital.

9.11.1909 Sir William Treloar submitted a letter which a boy had written to the Queen, on whose recommendation he had been received into the House, asking the Committee whether it would be prudent to publish same. Sir William Treloar reported that he had shown such letter to Miss Knollys, Her Majesty's Secretary, and Her Majesty had promised to send the children some sweets at Christmas. The Chairman produced a statement showing the average cost of food for each child, which was 4s 2d per week. After considerable discussion, Mr Lawson expressed himself satisfied that this was a fair and reasonable amount, as also did the other members of the Committee.

The Medical Superintendent's report was very forthright and practical. He pointed out the need for telephones, training in use of fire equipment, and the proper supply of clothing for children. The College Master reported, 'I regret I cannot say the Chaplain has won the affection of the boys.'

Reports were received on the Tailor's shop, the Leather shop, the Poultry Farm, the Garden, the Piggeries and the Milk Supply. On 30th November 1909 it was reported,

'The lads have formed a Dramatic & Literary Club.'

A booklet was produced on the Treloar Cripples' College, Alton. It covered Boot-making, Tailoring, Woodwork, the Reading and Recreation Room, Cricket Practice, the Games Room and the School Room, with the appeal 'Will You Aid Them to a Worth While Future?'

The booklet stated, 'We do not know yet what proportion of our assets can be allocated to the College. The Ministry of Health can demand a share, a large share, to pass to Government control with the Hospital in 1948. The exact sum remains to be negotiated. Recently the Ministry of Education has urged us to set up a school for physically disabled boys and girls.'

The Lord Mayor Treloar Hospital and College by G.S.E. Moynihan (Paul Cave) was published In 1988 to commemorate the 40th anniversary of the National Health Service and the 80th birthday of the Lord Mayor Treloar Hospital and College.

Notes taken from Minute Book

Barbara Green

born 1921   *interviewed 2001*

Barbara Green was interviewed at her home in the Deane's Almhouses in London Street, just after her 80th birthday. She trained as a nurse at Lord Mayor Treloar Hospital.

We worked from eight o'clock to seven, or eight to six. We did a very, very long day, and our lectures were done in our Off Duty, which was two hours a day. We had one day off a fortnight, half a day a week. It was all very hard work. You didn't have much fun. You could have a boyfriend, but if you became engaged, you went. That was the end. This is why you'd see all the old Sisters in the ward, they knew their ward inside out, because they were there every day, except on their day off. And they stayed there till they died, or until they retired. A bit like being a nun, a vocation, you were married to your job, so you didn't expect to go home each night. Just during the war, you were allowed to be married. And if a nurse was caught talking to a porter - or larking about with a porter - she was gone the next day. You weren't allowed to fraternise with porters, because that was a bit below you. Nurses were looked up to then. I don't think they had many poor nurses.

They certainly didn't when I went to Treloar's, because they all had an allowance in every month. I didn't get one, I might add, but they did.

I started full nursing just before the Second World War, when I was 17 ½. In the first year of the war, there were some Australians at Alton, and they sent an invitation for us to go to a dance. Matron came down, during our Friday sewing day. That was when we had to mend our uniform, and if we hadn't got any mending to do, the Home Sister used to tear it so that we did! Matron said, 'I've had an invitation for you girls to go to an all ranks dance, but I have turned it down, and told them that I will send my maids, certainly not my nurses.' That was very hard.

The little juniors started down below and worked up, which is what they don't do today. They go to college and train before they even go in a ward, I believe. When you were a junior, you stood up every time a Staff Nurse passed by - or even someone who had been in your school if you were junior to them. And Sisters, oh, you wouldn't sit down with a Sister passing you by - you stood up. And if Matron walked in the room, of course, naturally you stood up. It was very much like the army, I would imagine. Very disciplined; which is what is lacking today. I mean, no Christian names - you wouldn't call one another by a Christian name. No, we were all called by our surnames. The doctors were all 'Sir'. We didn't call any doctor other than 'Sir'. Right up to my retirement, I always called them 'Sir', in any case.

At meal-times the juniors sat at the table, in order of seniority and the little maid would bring your food, on a plate, served up by the Home Sister at the end. Almost always she'd start at the bottom of the table, the most junior, and then you'd have to wait for the one at the top of the table, the most senior, to pick her knife and fork up before you could pick yours up. So sometimes your meal got pretty cold.

There was coffee-time at ten. We used to have bread and dripping, beef dripping, and we all loved it, and a cup of cocoa. But there was also some cake there if you wished. And then lots of stodgy stuff, rice puddings, and bread puddings. It was wholesome food, but you wouldn't say it was wonderful.

On night duty, we had a hot meal in the morning, before we went back to the nurses' home to bed, and I remember one poor girl sitting with her elbows on the table, very tired, and the maid came along and said, 'Sister would like to know if you would like two saucers to put your elbows on.' So she knew very well, 'Sit up or else.'

We had to do a lot of cleaning. And at night we used to clean out the annexe, where the bathrooms and the sluices were. The bedpans had to be washed, by hand, with soapy water, and polished and hung up, put up on a rack. And we had to go round cleaning. One Sister was very tiny, so when we finished we used to carry a chair over and she'd stand on the chair and rub her hand across the top of the door, and if there was a little bit of dust you had to do the whole lot again. And there was only one of you doing it, because you were the junior.

The treatment for osteomyelitis was to put the leg in plaster and leave it quite a few months until the maggots had really eaten it clean. When the plaster came off, the wound was as clean as clean, and healed up beautifully.

Peggy Perrett

born in 1922   interviewed 2002

I contracted polio when I was three years old and I wasn't able to walk until I was seven. The day that I, apparently, first contracted it, I was at a family wedding and I couldn't stand. My mother carried me about all day. When we got home the next morning, Sunday morning, she took me in to the GP in Basingstoke, and he said I had infantile paralysis and a dropped foot, and he would see about getting me into hospital. But I wasn't taken into hospital until I was ten, that was Treloars'.

There were two sides to the ward, girls at one end and boys down the other, with the Sister's office between, Sister Hadley.

They did the operation, and I wasn't allowed out of bed. I had a chilblain on my finger, and I had to go down for light treatment. I used to go in a tunnel that had 36 bulbs in it.

We used to have a teacher come for half a day each day and we had maths and any other subject that they wanted to bring in. We also used to have a band, given instruments to

play. We used to make up rhymes about the nurses and the practitioners etc, and we used to have pictures once a week. One of the men that used to do the odds and ends, we called him 'Bronco' and he used to come and have a cine-camera, and the babies in the bottom end of the ward used to be brought in and sat on the bed with us, the ones that could look after them.

We only had visiting on a Saturday and a Sunday. The parents were allowed in to visit us for an hour and a half, but that was all you were allowed. You didn't see your parents again until the next Saturday or Sunday. There was one time when we couldn't have visitors because there was a bit of an epidemic of some sort. We weren't allowed to keep the things our parent brought us. My mother used to have to write my name on the eggs that she brought me. My parents had to pay for me.

When it was the summer time, we used to be put out onto the verandah.

Treloar's verandah

This means not just the patients but the beds! Not too much trouble with the ordinary hospital beds, though even these were of iron, but patients in traction or with body plasters had big heavy beds that took iron bed frames - and needed four nurses to push them. They were even pushed out at night.

Many of the photographs in the Treloar's archives in the Hampshire Record Office show the importance the hospital placed on getting the patients out in the open air as much as possible. For fêtes and outdoor events beds were pushed out not only onto the verandah but onto a big field in front of the hospital, with flags and balloons fluttering overhead.

Some of the children there had rheumatoid arthritis and they were put in traction at times, and they tried all sorts of things to help them. One girl had been in there seven years. They had a wooden building where they put the girls who had lupus. And when you went in, you first of all went into Observations, and that was individual. Although, the second time I went in, they put me in with three boys at the end of the block. And I always remember one of them saying to me, 'Why don't you have a bottle?' Because I had to have a bed-pan every time. I had to go back in 1934 and have the same thing done. Although I was only in three months that time and payment was only eight shillings a week as opposed to ten.

The Marine Hospital

After that I went through life quite well. I learnt to ride a bike. I used to go dancing in my teens. I learnt to drive a car. There was nothing I couldn't do that anybody else could do, except that I couldn't hop on the bad leg. If I played hop-scotch, I had to hop on my good leg.

The hospital had a Seaside Branch at Hayling Island.

A good account of Treloar's is given in 'The Lord Mayor Treloar Hospital and College' by G S E Moynihan (Paul Cave Publications 1988). It contains many photographs, including these two smiling girls.

Two young patients

George Doel

born 1918   *interviewed 2001*

George Doel tells how he met Kath, his future wife, in 1938.

When I first met her, I thought she'd broken her leg and was walking about. I didn't realise she had a calliper and a big boot on till I saw her the next day in daylight. She'd caught polio when she was five and I think it was at Alton that they gave her a calliper. What was visiting time? Once a month out there? And her mother couldn't afford to get out there to see her. It used to cost a small fortune in those days for a woman like Alice, just what she was earning, housekeeping and what have you, to catch the bus on a Sunday to go out to Alton.

After we were married she had a major operation at Henry Gauvain's at Alton, when they transferred the blood circulation, because she used to get chilblains in her bad leg and they used to be terrible, she used to be in pain. Henry Gauvain's was part of Treloar's, a big country house. It was named after the top orthopaedic surgeon in the old days. And when they took her over there for the operation it frightened the life out of me, because they had no lifts in there and the wards were upstairs and the operating theatre was downstairs and they had to stand each side of the stretcher and lift it over the banisters, and there's a 16 foot drop if they turned that over! I used to stand there, old heart in your mouth, but Kath didn't know much about it because she was a bit dopey, drugged up a bit. Mind you, it was a marvellous place.

They said that they'd separate the nerve that wasn't feeding the blood supply down to her bad leg and they'd join it up with the blood supply to the right leg and see how it went. She was in bed for six months. Made life a bit tedious! I had to farm the kids out.

We had to pay for everything ourselves in those days before the NHS. I'm talking about 1943. I used to take Kath to London for her callipers and her boots and it was £15 for a pair of boots and £15 for a calliper, and that wanted some finding. The only assistance I ever got was when I belonged to the HAS, since I joined the railway, and we used to pay threepence a week and they used to help pay the hospital bill.

The calliper was a full length one, hip to ankle, out stiff. It was only since the National Health Service that she had callipers that used to crack in the middle so that she could bend her leg.

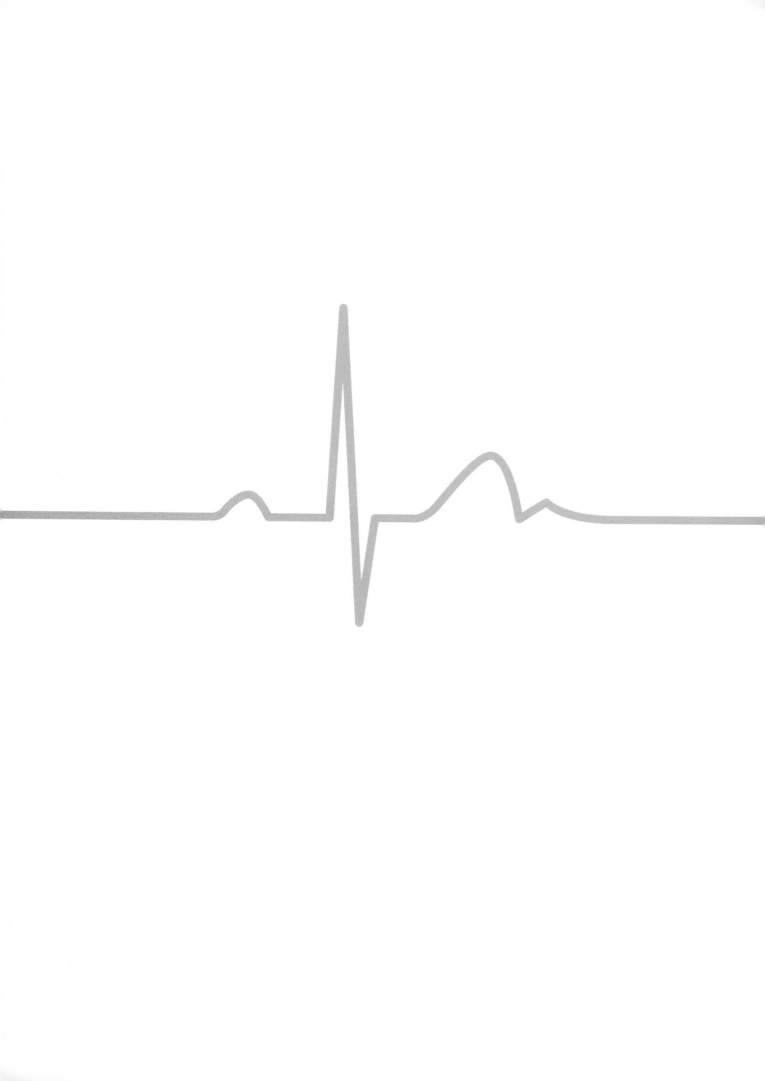

'On the National Health'

Basingstoke's medical needs grew with the town's further expansion. In 1952 the Atomic Weapons Research Establishment (AWRE) was set up at Aldermaston, creating many more jobs and building housing for its employees. A major upheaval in the town was the 1960s redevelopment to house 'London overspill', with a drastic rebuilding of the town centre, new housing estates and a Ring Road. The greatest gain from all this was the building of a new hospital, which continued to expand and is now planning to bid for foundation status. As the town grows more and more, it is also affected by other medical advances: the new GPs' contract, Primary Care Trusts, and Basingstoke's prestigious medical facility 'The ARK'. Now let Basingstoke people tell their story.

It made a difference

Hilda Applin

born 1907   *interviewed 1999*

The National Health made a lot of difference. People made a lot of use of it, and some people were greedy. I know someone who went and had new dentures and two pairs of glasses. She said the optician was rude and told her she didn't need them but she said she was entitled to them.

When you went to see doctors, there was a room for private patients and a room for National Health ones. Private patients often went in ahead of you when it was your turn. Oh yes, there was a difference made. It depended on the doctor. Sometimes a prescription was written out before you'd finished talking to them. I had to take Nan, my mother, once and she hadn't gone over to National Health and the receptionist couldn't find her name because she was a private patient. The receptionist said, 'Well, she shouldn't be here' – with the National Health patients. Nan said, 'I knew it wasn't right. I knew I shouldn't have been with them.' When Dr Potter persuaded Nan to go on the National Health, I think it came

The Hospital Ball in 1948

on her pension. She was reluctant because she thought he wouldn't come if he wasn't being paid. 'You'll please yourself whether you come or not.' That didn't go down well.

They called being National Health, as opposed to private, 'going on the panel' - that is, the doctor's panel.

Dr Sandy Smeaton

born 1916

interviewed 1998, 1999

The new National Health Service changed everything. Patients were encouraged to join a doctor's list. This was something quite new. Previously, people were free to go and see any doctor they pleased at any particular time. But when the Health Service started, people came and asked if they could go on your list. The panel system before then only covered the working man. The Health Service brought in the whole family, so there was quite a big intake of patients. There was no private treatment as such. The population in general were covered. It was quite incredible really, a revolution in medical care.

Doctors

'Potter and Co' (3 New Street)

There was a six-man practice where the French restaurant 'Bistro Je T'Aime' was until recently.

Dr Sandy Smeaton

born 1916

interviewed 1998, 1999

Potter was an Edinburgh graduate and not a bad chap in spite of that! His first name was Harry, but he was always referred to as H Radford Potter. I never got to know Leslie Housden, but he was reputed to be 'good with children' and he later stood for Parliament as a Liberal, unsuccessfully. He became an adviser on parentcraft to the Ministry of Health and wrote a book on 'The Art of Mothercraft'. Keith Williams was a good doctor, quiet and unassuming, and much respected in the town. Cobb 'specialised' in ophthalmology. Weston was an asthmatic who had been taken on during the war, as he was unfit for military service. Douglas Watt joined Potter & Co. in the autumn of 1949, having been in practice in Salisbury (Rhodesia) for a few years after the war. Tony Bowen-Jones was a quiet, rather introspective Welshman, whose wife had been Alexander Korda's continuity girl at one time. He was a very obliging and dependable anaesthetist and over the years all of us had much to thank him for.

Jo Kelly

born 1947   *interviewed 1999*

As a child, I saw quite a lot of my family doctor. He was Dr Radford Potter. Every time I walk past the *Pierre Victoire* [later the *Bistro Je T'Aime*] restaurant and I see the bay window, I remember when it was his room, the front room, as he was the senior partner. I had quite a lot of operations as a child, so I seemed to spend a lot of time going round there, because whenever I came out of hospital Dr Potter always wanted to see what had happened to me. So my mother would have to take me round. But he always had his own way of doing things. He must have been the most terrible doctor to keep in line. Doctors' receptionists are usually able to keep them in line and they are a good 'buffer' too. My mother used to feel quite embarrassed because we'd go in and sit in the waiting-room, just have arrived, and he'd come out and say, 'Oh hello, Nellie, come in.' And you'd see the receptionist saying, 'Dr Potter!' and there'd be a whole room full of patients. I can remember, you kept your head down and you shuffled in, because if he called you in you had to go. We were never kept waiting. But there was always a very big full waiting-room.

Dr Potter (far left)

He was also very good at coming out to see patients in their homes. My mother always used to say that you would hear stories of him before the NHS: when there were poor families in this town that had got young children, not only did he waive his fee but he would supply anything that they needed. So if there was any medicine to be bought, he bought it. If they needed extra food, he would provide it. It would be sent round with the man who did the gardening and who drove for him sometimes. He would turn up on the doorstep of their house with a basket of food. Dr Potter was one of the old school of doctors!

He kept pigs.

His house was in Cross Street and backed onto Church Square. It had orchards and he kept pigs. It was one of the places that was damaged when the bomb fell in the 40s, so he moved out of town.

Dr Bowen-Jones

Jo Kelly

born 1947   *interviewed 1999*

The other doctor I really remember as a child was Dr Bowen-Jones, the father of my school friend, Lizzie, who lived just round the corner from me in Winchester Road. It was next door to Jim's Chinese Chippie, which was a shop in those days. And I used to go round to Lizzie's to play. In fact, we dreaded it during the summer holidays because his view was that young girls should catch any sort of childish ailment while they could. So he would go out to visit a patient - a child - and come back and say that child had measles. He would come round and collect me, and Lizzie and I would go and play with this child in the hopes that we could catch measles. So we were taken to play with children we didn't know at all, that had got measles, German measles and mumps. He had talked my mother into thinking that it was a very good idea but the thing was that I never seemed to catch them! But Lizzie always went down with them. So poor Lizzie hated it because her father would make her go out and catch all these terrible diseases. That's the real thing that I can remember about Dr Bowen-Jones.

Winton House and 14 Winchester Road

Winton House was a huge Georgian-type-fronted house, now Panacea Ltd, IT Specialists. It had a two-man practice, Dr Treth Rowe and Dr Montgomery. Later they moved to 14 Winchester Road and Dr Burrell and then Dr Hugh Hamber and later Dr John Williams joined the practice.

Zena Labanowska

born 1921   *interviewed 2003*

I think it was in 1948 we moved along from Winton House to 14 Winchester Road. The practice had grown. Dr Burrell had become a partner and he lived in the bungalow attached to the surgery. We had a big waiting-room for the patients and Dr Burrell and Dr Rowe had their own consulting-rooms. There was a living-in receptionist, in a flat above the surgery, and she worked in the little dispensary and was there to take telephone calls. I went in at a different time then. It was different from popping in to Dr Rowe's house. So I used to go before surgery and take dictation. Now I was secretary to the practice.

There's a huge three-storey office block there now, completely rebuilt just in the last few months. It wouldn't be recognisable now.

Dr John Williams

born 1939   *interviewed 2002*

The surgery in 14 Winchester Road had probably the coldest waiting room that has ever been designed by anybody. It would have fitted very well for an undertaker's chapel of rest. It had a marble-coloured floor going up the walls.. We only had two consulting rooms, but sometimes we would use a consulting room upstairs, which was really just a converted bedroom in this little property. Basically there were two consulting rooms, a little area in the middle where the notes were kept, and there was a sink, where urines could be tested.

Dr Sandy Smeaton

born 1916   *interviewed 1998, 1999*

Treth Rowe had the ruddy complexion of a farmer, which was not misleading, as he had a small-holding at Hannington where he bred pigs. He was a recognised authority on the subject and would go off judging several times a year. He was an astute physician and looked after the geriatric wards at Basing Road Hospital.

Cross Street and 1 New Street

Dr Sandy Smeaton

born 1916   *interviewed 1998, 1999*

In 1949 I was looking for a practice and I settled to come to Basingstoke, the attraction at the time being that this was a small, friendly market town, with a hospital run by the general practitioners, and a maternity home with about 15-20 beds. This, plus the general practice, seemed to me just about the ideal place. So I came and joined Dr Kelly.

Each practice worked from its own premises, not in any way purpose-built, but converted houses. In the case of Dr Kelly, the surgery was really part of his house in Cross Street, which was very old and had no damp course and kept going down steps because the ground slopes down. You could go from the surgery into the kitchen. Later, to make this Number 1 New Street, we opened a little door leading to the surgeries at the back, which were the old stables.

New St doctors' surgery

It was very much a cottage industry then. I suppose it was haphazard by modern standards. I think the average surgery in those days would have a desk and two chairs, a couch, a wash-basin and a small autoclave to boil and sterilise syringes and needles. The waiting-room had about a dozen assorted chairs, totally inadequate much of the time.

Doctors at work

Dr John Williams

born 1939   *interviewed 2002*

The two key doctors in Basingstoke, when I came here in 1966, were Dr Burrell and Dr Smeaton. They were involved in all the medical politics; they were on all the medical committees, and they tended to represent Basingstoke down at Winchester.

Dr Burrell and Dr Smeaton

On my first day when I joined Dr Burrell's practice in 1966, I got a phone call from Gill on the internal phone from our house next to the surgery. 'Eileen Bowen-Jones has said that we are going there for lunch today. You have to be there for lunch at one o'clock.' I said, 'My first day! I want to know what is going on, what I'm doing!' She said, 'Mrs Bowen-Jones has asked us to lunch. We will be there!' A royal command! So I was there, where we were welcomed into the town; that was a reflection of the way you were welcomed into the community by people.

Surgery waiting-rooms were well-named! You waited...

> **Dr Michael Williams:**
> Dr Bowen-Jones made an enormous contribution in the field of obstetrics and anaesthesia at The Shrubbery.

Dr Sandy Smeaton

born 1916   *interviewed 1998, 1999*

Our surgery at 1 New Street started at half-past eight in the morning. No appointments. First come, first served, very much so. They would go in officially from nine to ten, and at two minutes to ten the waiting-room would be full, because anyone coming up before ten o'clock would be seen. They were queueing out in the street sometimes. With a bit of luck you'd finish about eleven o'clock. This was Monday to Saturday, plus each evening in the week six o'clock till seven (which might be nearer nine o'clock). And then Wednesday afternoon, Saturday afternoon, there were extra surgeries for

country people, about a five-mile radius - Dummer, Herriard, all the villages round about, coming in by bus.

They came in the door along the passageway into the waiting-room on the left, and there were chairs all round the wall. You came in and you put your head through the receptionist's window to tell her your name and she got out your card. Then you took the chair nearest the door. A part-time receptionist answered the phone and dealt with record cards during surgery times, morning and evening.

> When a patient went in to the doctor, everyone shuffled up to the next chair.

Dr John Williams

born 1939   *interviewed 2002*

At 14 Winchester Road the front door was opened from a quarter to nine to a quarter to ten and then the lock was dropped and anybody who came after a quarter to ten wasn't allowed in. Patients who were going out after a quarter to ten were shown out by the one receptionist-manager-administrator for the practice, who would take the patients to the door, undo the Yale lock, open it, push them out and, if anybody was standing there, say, 'Surgery is at a quarter to six,' and the door was closed again in their face. Or 'Go round to the hospital.'

The waiting room would be absolutely full of people. There were no appointments, it was first come first served, so people would start queueing down the surgery path at eight o'clock in the morning. When the benches round the walls of the big waiting-room were full, people stood.

When they came in, patients would go through and tell the receptionist they were there. She would get the notes out and they would say, 'I want to see Doctor X or Doctor Y.' And then the notes would just come in on your desk, so you would be getting through these notes and suddenly the door would open in between patients and the administrator-secretary would come in and she would roll out about five or ten sets of notes onto your desk in the order in which they had come, and you would realise you had a whole pile more to see. At the end of morning surgery, you would collect your list of visits that she had taken, and she would give you the notes for those, and that would be anything from ten to forty in the winter. I could do forty visits per day.

The idea was to always finish morning surgery by a quarter past ten. I think the speed with which people came through was quite phenomenal in those days. Much quicker than now. They would say, 'I just need a line, doctor,' meaning a certificate. 'I've been off two days, I need a doctor's note. I didn't want to bother you, but I need a note, otherwise they won't accept...'

We used rubber gloves in those days for examining patients, and at the end of morning surgery rubber gloves would be peeled off and left in the sink, and the assistant would collect all the rubber gloves and wash them out and you would see them hanging on the line outside the window, to be used again, once they were dried, for later surgeries. You would sprinkle some white chalk into the gloves and on your hands, so you could get your rubber gloves on again. The rubber gloves were re-used and re-used, and without being sterilised in any way. They were just washed thoroughly in soap and water.

On 21st March 1966 we introduced an appointments system; we were the first practice to do so. We had a lot of flack. They'd say, 'I'm going to have flu in October. Can I make an appointment now, doctor?' or 'I gather I've got to plan when I'm going to be ill.' But eventually, of course, people came to accept it and all the other practices, within the next year or so, had gone over to having appointment systems.

An unusual patient

Dr John Williams
born 1939   *interviewed 2002*

When I first came to Basingstoke in 1966, a patient walked in and I said, 'What can I do for you?' 'I want 2 lb of cotton wool, doctor.' 'Sorry?' 'I want 2 lb of cotton wool.' He just wanted a prescription for 2 lb of cotton wool, which would be one big roll of cotton wool. I asked him what he wanted it for. It turned out that it was for something on his leg that he was bandaging up with cotton wool. By then I could smell what the leg was like. So I sent him round to Hackwood Road Hospital, to be seen by the Sister in the casualty department, and had the leg looked at after morning surgery. When I got up there, I was faced with a very irate Sister.' Have you seen that leg?' she said. I said, 'Well, of course I haven't.' 'You come and see it.' And I was faced with a leg that had a hole in it that was six inches long, four inches wide and two to three inches deep, in the back of his calf. A huge great hole, weeping, festering, smelling disgustingly unpleasant. What we did was to put the leg into an old bread bin, I think it was, that we filled with normal saline and just soaked away all the muck and the cotton wool that was stuck to the festering wound. What he had was a really serious varicose ulcer and by treating it, by cleaning it properly, putting a proper dressing on it, bandaging the leg properly, it took us something like six to nine months to heal that ulcer, but we did actually get it healed by then. Because it was a varicose ulcer, and not an arterial ulcer, it wasn't particularly painful, and as long as he kept it well padded up with cotton wool (he was living by

himself) he wasn't worried about it. If we hadn't cured it, the likelihood is that it would have become really unpleasantly infected. He might well have developed a septicaemia and died of that. Or, alternatively, it would have become so infected that it would have damaged the arterial supply, and he might have had a massive haemorrhage.

Hospital visits

Dr Sandy Smeaton
born 1916   *interviewed 1998, 1999*

We didn't have the facilities in our surgeries for any procedures other than simple straightforward examinations. Any other procedure, we would refer the patient up to the hospital and follow them up, and carry out whatever was necessary in the hospital. Every day after surgery, one would go up to the Hackwood Road Hospital, where a patient might have an X-ray or you might get the help of an anaesthetic from a colleague. Then one would go on to the Shrubbery to see someone who had been delivered the previous night. Then perhaps one would get in a visit or two before lunch-time, and often visits in the afternoon - unless it was an ante-natal clinic. Visits would range between ten and thirty a day, depending on the time of year.

Dr John Williams
born 1939   *interviewed 2002*

So you'd do morning surgery, go to Hackwood Road, have a quick cup of coffee, meet other doctors, see the patients in the accident and casualty department, people you'd sent round, anybody who had been in the previous 24 hours from your practice. Dorothy Paul was the radiographer up there, and you would send patients to her for X-rays. One day a week each practice covered the casualty department out of hours. On a Wednesday it was our turn.

Ted Knight was said to be a very senior and experienced radiographer, a great 'character' and often a wise adviser to the GPs. He often helped Mr Turnbull, the vet, by doing x-rays on dogs or cats that had been in accidents.

Night calls

Dr Sandy Smeaton
born 1916   *interviewed 1998, 1999*

My wife, Cicely, answered the phone and dealt with record cards outside of surgery times, at nights and weekends on call. We lived 'over the shop' really for ten years, 1949-59. We had no mobile phones in those days. If I went out on a night call (which was not infrequent; if you went to bed before midnight you were always disturbed) the only way Cicely could communicate to me that I had another call, was to leave the light on in the hall and this would save me parking the car and so on and coming in to find I had to go out again. And then, after some years, they got this little bleeper that would let me know I was wanted, but it wouldn't tell me whereabouts. Of course nowadays a doctor carries his mobile phone and he can be contacted anywhere at any time. But at that time it was the Cicelys of this world, who contributed a vast amount without any remuneration.

Dr John Williams

born 1939   *interviewed 2002*

When I first came here, the method of working was that you did a week on and two weeks off, so you were on duty every night for a week except for your day off. The next week you would be off every night. However, being the junior partner, I covered one partner's night off one week, and the next week I covered the other partner's night off. So there was never a week when I wasn't on duty at least one night.

Partnerships

Dr John Williams

born 1939

interviewed 2002

My predecessor had come in 1959 and had been offered a partnership in the practice, and was on seven years to becoming an equal partner. So his share in the profits of the practice would slowly increase, but it would be seven years before he would become an equal partner. By the time I came in 1966, it had become slightly easier to find a practice, so practices were looking to give better terms, so I came on five years. Two years later, we appointed an extra partner, because by then Basingstoke was expanding and doctors' lists were going up, and we couldn't cope. We needed another doctor, and we appointed him on three years to parity. Nowadays people are going into almost immediate parity in practices

Church Square

Dr Michael Williams

born 1930   *interviewed 2001*

In the early 1960s Dr Potter's practice moved into a new building which later became the Benefits Office. This was an

Church Square

early example of a purpose-built surgery, demonstrating many architectural novelties - and mistakes! It was built some ten years before the first local Health Centre at Bramblys Grange. It was actually in Mortimer Lane, but Dr Potter wanted for old times' sake to recall the site of his old house in Church Square, bombed during the Second World War. We were a big, wide-spread practice, with a radius of ten miles. I can remember travelling 19 miles to a call in the middle of the night. Potter thought for a long time that with such large numbers it wouldn't be manageable to run an appointments system; nowadays, with hindsight the appointments system has become very much part of the fabric of general practice.

Dr Richard Turner

born 1946   *Interviewed 2005*

The practice list size was approximately 19,000 in the early 1960s until 1987 when the partnership acquired a branch surgery in Lychpit. The practice list then grew to approximately 21,000 and the number of partners increased to 10.

Dr Margaret Page

born 1940   *interviewed 2004*

After doing the usual house surgeon and house physician jobs at the Royal Free Hospital in London, I did midwifery and gynaecology jobs in London and Portsmouth, then a year of anaesthetics in Portsmouth and six months in paediatric medicine. Then in 1968 I answered an advert in one of the medical journals for the post of assistant in a general practice in Basingstoke. In those days there was no formal training for general practice, unlike the present time where there is a structured programme lasting at least two years. I was informally interviewed by some of the partners of the Church Square practice and the job was mine - no signing contracts and suchlike! Dr Bowen-Jones was the senior partner - or maybe it was Dr Watt initially - with Drs Alan Gibberd, Donald Munro, Michael Williams and John Teall completing the practice. I was the only female practitioner at that time.

I remember sitting in with a couple of the partners for possibly three or four surgeries to get the feel of general practice and then I was on my own - training completed! Of course, I could and did always ask for advice when it was needed.

As the assistant, I was generously provided with accommodation, first in a semi-detached house called 'Rubella' (the medical term for German Measles!) and then in 'Grove Cottage' in Skippett's Lane. It was a delightful Edwardian cottage on the edge of a cornfield in those days; it was truly idyllic and I very much enjoyed living there. Sadly, after the construction of the motorway, the cornfield was replaced by a warehouse, part of an industrial estate.

I met with exceptional kindness from all the partners at whose homes I regularly lunched - in those days there seemed always to be time for lunch, unlike the present time where a lunch break has more or less vanished. Mrs Bowen-Jones was a remarkable lady; having worked in the film world as 'continuity girl' to Sir Alexander Korda, she now gave valiant support to her busy husband, as did the other wives, manning the telephone, quite unlike the present day where surgery staff field most of the calls. I really enjoyed my weekly lunch dates and the delicious meals that were provided.

The practice area was extensive and I especially appreciated being assigned home visits in the countryside in places like Preston Candover or Dummer and occasionally even to stately houses like Hackwood Park and The Vyne, where I remember there was a patient on kidney dialysis. Night visits at that time held no fears and many times I recall cheerfully setting off into the darkness, with no anxiety of being accosted by car thieves or drug addicts.

The practice secretary (or maybe she was called a manager even then) was a cheerful and charming lady, Mrs Mary Crewe, and I remember a lovely elderly gentleman - probably a retired accountant - who carefully wrote out our monthly payslips by hand!

I met my future husband while working in Portsmouth and we were married in 1970. Our wedding gift from the practice was a set of beautiful Worcester porcelain ovenproof dishes and a casserole, which are still in use today, evoking memories of those happy times. Our early months of marriage were spent at Grove Cottage, with my new husband commuting by train to St Thomas's Hospital. His subsequent appointment as a Consultant Surgeon in Portsmouth in 1971 meant that my early GP days in Basingstoke sadly had to come to an end when we moved into the Portsmouth area, where we still live.

But I have very many happy memories of my formative years as a general practitioner in Basingstoke.

Bramblys Grange

Dr John Williams

born 1939   *interviewed 2002*

The County Council came along with a suggestion that the facilities in Basingstoke were inadequate, which they clearly were, both for our practice (Dr

Bramblys Grange Health Centre

Burrell's) and for Dr Smeaton's practice, and that we should move into a Health Centre. Health Centres were very much the flavour of the month in the mid-late sixties, so Dr McDougal, the Medical Officer of Health in Winchester, came up with the County Architect to talk about the concept of building a Health Centre on some land behind what was Bramblys Grange, There were four doctors in each practice. We described what we wanted, then we met again about a fortnight later, and the architect came up with a plan. This was to put all the eight doctors in consulting rooms at one end of the building, and all the notes at the other end of the building, and the waiting area in the middle. So we said, 'I don't think you were listening last time because we are two separate practices, and we don't actually work together. We work separately; we will work in separate ways; we will bring our own staff, when we move in.' One of the doctors, David Side, said, 'What are the dimensions of the building?' and the architect gave them. We arranged to meet again in a fortnight's time and the architect came up with another fairly useless plan. David Side produced some graph paper and said, 'This is what we are looking for.' And the architect said, 'Gosh, can I have that?' And that was Bramblys Grange. Dr Side, effectively, designed Bramblys Grange.

The Charter for General Practice, which came in in 1966, made a great difference to the viability of all this. The government now repaid rent and rates on buildings, to allow GPs to have much better premises and get reimbursed. (In the old days, of course, if you had more expensive premises, it came out of your own pocket.) And also it paid 70% of the salaries for staff that the doctors employed. This was considered to be part of GPs' pay. The concept would be that GPs earn, say £40,000 a year, of which £20,000 is reimbursement of expenses for staff, rates and everything, and £20,000 is what you take home with you. So, now in 1968 we could look at the Health Centre and think, 'It doesn't matter what it costs us from the rent point of view, because we are going to get all that back, and we can have a treatment room, we can employ a nurse and, yes, between the two practices we can pay the 70%; it's actually 35% each, and we can actually pass stuff over to her, and although we still have Hackwood Road, it will be much more convenient to be able to use a nurse within the building.' So General Practice started changing with the advent of the Health Centre, and at about the same time, the 'Mini' opened. [see page 94]

We started in Bramblys Grange with one nurse shared between the two practices and ended up with both practices having a full time nurse working within the building. By then you had a District Nurse and a team working with you. In our case at Bramblys Grange, with five doctors, we had two District Nurses, that's fully qualified Sisters, two what you might call Staff Nurses and two Care Assistants - so the District Nurse had a team of six. We had two Health Visitors. We had a Practice Nurse that we employed full time in the treatment room and we had a Health Promotion Nurse, but effectively she was a nurse who was really moving into this new field of nurse management of illness, she would manage the diabetics and the asthma patients to a strict protocol. She would review patients with asthma and review patients with diabetes on a regular basis and I'm sure that's extended now since I retired, for reviewing hypertension and reviewing coronary artery disease. But there are strict criteria for what she has to look for and what she has to do - nurses do that sort of thing very very well, probably better than doctors do.

In a way it's going the full circle, because when I first came to Basingstoke we would do all these sort of things in Hackwood Road Hospital because we had access to them. Then we moved out, as it were, of the hospital into the Health Centres and then we started sending everything to the main hospital and then the main hospital said, 'We can't cope with all the demands on us,' and pushed it all back towards General Practice again. And GPs need to acquire different skills for doing different things.

Zena Labanowska

born 1921   *interviewed 2003*

In 1970 we moved over from 14 Winchester Road to Bramblys Grange because of the influx of people from London when the practice was growing and we needed much larger premises. Health Centres were very much the vogue at that time.

I think I was the first practice manager in Basingstoke. The Health Service was looking differently at all medical matters and practice managers were unknown. I went to Eastleigh and London on practice managers' courses and Dr Rowe said, 'You go up there, Zena, and tell them what it's like to be a practice manager!' My duties grew and I had to deal with wages and all the things appertaining to staff. I used to sit in when the doctors were interviewing for employees. Whereas once there was just me, now there was myself, and the receptionist outside, two Sisters in the treatment room as well - everything just grew so quickly. Now I worked as a normal day-time job and finished before half-past five.

There was no dispensary at Bramblys Grange. There were two different practices sharing it at the time. Patients had to go to the chemist's to get their prescriptions made up.

Private patients rang up for an appointment with their doctor and were seen out of surgery hours.

With the Health Service there was much more form-filling and do this and do that. Hands were tied more. You were kind of being ruled from afar – the doctor wasn't just running his own surgery, as it were. As the Health Service has grown, so there was no more the homely single-handed practice. Filing cabinets suddenly appeared, now there were far more patients, people could come more easily, they didn't have to stop and think, 'I can't go to the doctor's, I can't afford it.' And the practice grew, as people were moving into this area more.

I retired from Bramblys Grange in 1986. The practice gave me a lovely party, all staff and all doctors were there. And they gave me a silver salver, which had every one of the doctors' signatures on it, even Dr Rowe's, who by that time was no longer around. And a handsome cheque as well. And now in my own little study I have the desk that was Dr Rowe's desk originally in his consulting room.

Church Grange

Dr John Williams

born 1939   *interviewed 2002*

When we'd moved into the Health Centre at Bramblys Grange, the County Council wanted to pull down the old Bramblys Grange building, Tom Thornycroft's house, so the Church Square partnership moved from Church Square into the second phase of the Health Centre building. I have to say

without enormous enthusiasm from the two practices in Bramblys Grange at the time, because we knew there wasn't going to be room for car parking. Between the two practices in Bramblys Grange already we had about 20,000 patients and Church Square had 20,000 patients, so we were suddenly looking after 40,000 patients in the same car parking site. It just didn't work.

The problem with Church Grange and Bramblys Grange is purely the car parking and the expansion of what general practice can do - the need for more rooms, which you can't provide on the site.

Dr Michael Williams:

The demise of Hackwood Road Hospital and in particular its GP casualty department by the end of the 70s meant that a lot of the work done there after morning surgery, and other accidents, had to be transferred to the new hospital's A & E Department. Paradoxically, this situation was aggravated, despite the provision of sizeable 'treatment' rooms in the new Health Centres, by the lack of adequate operating tables and resuscitation facilities, with the consequence that even the highly experienced anaesthetists amongst the GPs were advised not to continue this work in the Health Centre.

I think there would be no advantage in the two practices combining. When I retired, Bramblys Grange had set up a practice in Chineham. We set up one doctor and as Chineham expanded we took on more and more, so by the time I retired we were a two-end practice, with five doctors in our Chineham surgery and five doctors in Bramblys Grange working as one practice of ten doctors. Once HantsDoc came in, there was no advantage at all in working as one practice on two sites. And in fact they've split up, partly because they were developing in different ways, they were working in different buildings, one was changing things and the other would say, 'We don't do that? Why do you do that?' 'Well, because it suits us.' 'Well, we don't do that.' And suddenly, 'Why are we bothering to discuss it? They'd rather work alone. We can work on our own. It doesn't matter any more.' So they've split up. And I think two or three other practices have done the same sort of thing. The advantages of size are purely administrative. In a way one GP looks after 2,000 patients. If you have a single-handed doctor he's got to provide all the facilities for 2,000 patients. Once you've got above four doctors you either need to double the number, so you've got four, eight, twelve, sixteen, or you might as well stay as four. There's not a huge advantage in having five doctors instead of four, six instead of four. You have your treatment room, you're getting to a point where perhaps it isn't big enough, you need more nursing time to be put in in the one day, you need two nurses, so you need a bigger treatment room - but the whole concept is of size and value.

Dr Sandy Smeaton

born 1916   *interviewed 1998, 1999*

A second Health Centre at Bramblys Grange was a recipe for chaos, and one would have thought that such a concentration of health care on one small area was undesirable. Presumably any adjacent land was too expensive to buy for car parking.

The Hackwood Practice

Dr John Williams

born 1939   *interviewed 2002*

The Hackwood Practice used to be Dr Smeaton's practice. They moved from Bramblys Grange down to the corner of Essex Road. Previously, in the 1960s, with places like Popley developing, it had been argued that every person should have a doctor within pram-pushing distance, but on the whole I think patients would rather visit a well organised setting than they would have lots of little doctors working in two or threes in different corners of the estate.

The Chineham Practice

Dr Keith Ollerhead

born 1958   *interviewed 2003*

Our practice only split off from the Basingstoke practice a couple of years ago. I started here in 1989 and we were then with the new contract - the Government introduced fund-holding and we became fund-holders in the fourth wave of fund-holding. We were still one large practice. The really instrumental thing in changing our future was the introduction of GP co-operatives - HantsDoc meant a real improvement in working arrangements. We had developed on two sites. We'd got the centre of town, a health centre, and here on the edge of town, we initially moved into a bungalow which was on the Reading Road, which was extended to form a small surgery - I was the third doctor to join the practice, working from the bungalow, and by the time I joined they already had the plans well advanced to build this purpose-built surgery across the road, next to the church, Christ Church, and then in the years after that the houses were built all around the surgery, so we're now in the middle of houses but when we first moved here we were surrounded just by the woods and the church next door.

Changes in general practice

One change was the relationship between GPs and consultants

Dr Michael Williams

born in 1930   *interviewed 2001*

The 25 years between the middle 60s and the late 80s were the best time to have been in general practice, before the intrusion of management and bureaucracy and politics and while the main hospital was becoming fully established with not only consultants who were appointed to that hospital but

a resident staff of junior doctors. The relationship between consultants and the GPs is still good, but it isn't on the same footing as it used to be in the early 70s.

Something that has disappeared almost entirely is the domiciliary visit. In its heyday, in the 60s and 70s, if I had a problem as a GP one of the consultants would come and see the patient with me at home. So the consultant would see the background and know what the difficulties were, and the advice he gave the GP might save having to send that patient to hospital.

There was a particularly close friendship between the Basingstoke GPs and the Winchester consultants. I would ring one of them at his out-patient clinic at Hackwood Road to ask if he would do a domiciliary visit to one of my patients. 'I'll finish my clinic at midday. Shall we meet here then? Your car or mine?'

Now, even though the consultants are in Basingstoke, with the main exceptions of the geriatricians and the psychiatrists, they are not asked and don't expect to be asked to visit. The GPs might still ring them up if they wanted help, but if they thought a case should be admitted they would ring the Registrar or the House Officer at the hospital. Unfortunately, as beds have got fewer and waiting lists longer, there might be some resistance, 'I haven't got a bed.'

I remember Dr Graveson, the neurologist at Winchester, coming to visit one of my patients on a Sunday morning. The patient was stone deaf and the doctor spent three-quarters of an hour writing down questions to get a full history of the problem.

Mrs Cicely Smeaton (wife of Dr Sandy Smeaton)

born 1921   *interviewed 1999*

If there was a domiciliary and one of the consultants was coming from Winchester, they would come up after surgery was finished and it was often nine o'clock, ten o'clock before Sandy would come in and eat. So you didn't have a main meal then, you had it at mid-day.

Clinical Assistantships

Dr Michael Williams

Dr Radford Potter, who retired in 1964, used to direct his young partners to take up a 'medical hobby'. Over the years this led to GPs being officially appointed to Clinical Assistantships in particular fields to help the Winchester Consultants at their Basingstoke clinics, much in the way Senior House Officers and Junior Registrars do in hospitals today. For instance, John Teall specialised in dermatology, Sandy Smeaton and I in ENT (ear, nose and throat), Alan Gibberd in paediatrics and Tony Bowen-Jones in anaesthesia.

GP trainees

Dr Sandy Smeaton

born 1916   *interviewed 1998, 1999*

In the 1960s or 70s the Government decided to fund a GP trainee scheme, whereby recently qualified doctors were attached to selected practices for a year. The scheme proved so popular with the trainees that there were not enough 'Training Practices' to meet the demand, and Don Burrell and I were asked to accept trainees. I am sure we would not have been considered if we had not been working in a Health Centre. The scheme was later changed to offer the trainee two years in hospital - six months in four different departments - followed by the year in general practice. It provided the hospital with a steady supply of well-motivated junior staff and the rotation could include the less popular departments of casualty, ENT and psychiatry. From the practice point of view, the partners were able to have a good look at the trainee before offering a partnership; it is not in the least surprising that there are many ex-trainees in practices in the Basingstoke area.

Patients' expectations

Dr John Williams

born 1939   *interviewed 2002*

The pressures on General Practice in the 1990s became intense, to do all the paperwork, all the administrative work, all the new things that were brought in. The thing that's probably caused the biggest problems is the rising expectations of patients, with the need for proper explanation, the 'worried well', the whole concept of rights, and 'It's my right to have everything I want when I want it'. I'm not criticising people for that, because they have been encouraged to expect it, but it left the GP taking longer and longer over consultation, and I am sure nobody should be doing consultations of less than ten minutes these days. Whereas we did five minute appointments when I started an appointments system, and we would very happily expect to see 15 patients in an hour, which is less than five minutes. By the time appointments had been going for 20 years, you were beginning to drop your appointments down to seven and a half minutes and really knowing you ought to do ten, but then you wouldn't have enough appointments to offer your patients to fit in all those who needed to be seen. So there was always this conflict between looking after a large enough number of people, dealing with the patients in the time, and dealing with people's expectations, and the need to have a proper explanation.

There was a lovely article in one of the papers recently. A woman had gone to her doctor with breast cancer and the doctor had said, 'You need to go and see a surgeon. The surgeon will tell you what the options are.' So she went to the surgeon and he rightly told her what the options were. She went back to the GP and said, 'Don't send me to somebody like that. When I go to a hospital I expect to see somebody who will know what to do, and will tell you what he is going to do. He will know what is the best treatment for me, and I won't be left to make the decision for myself.' The next patient came in and had been to another hospital and was complaining that she had seen the surgeon who had said, 'You need a hysterectomy.' And he hadn't discussed the options with her. They are both right and they are both wrong. And that wasn't there in the 1960s; that wasn't there at all. You

were probably too God-like. 'Do this.' 'Why?' 'Well, because it's the way it's done. I'm a doctor. I've been trained to know this. This is what I'm telling you.' You did it in good faith; it wasn't a question of a megalomaniac doctor. Most of us were doing what we genuinely believed were the best things for the patients. But the thought of the patient disputing with us what the treatment was going to be was totally incomprehensible to most doctors in the 1960s. By the 1980s it was changing and by the 1990s it was completely different. I think now it's a very different world altogether.

In many ways a lot of the doctors of the 1920s and 1930s knew they couldn't treat all the illnesses, so they spent a lot of their time reassuring their patients. By the time you had got to the post-war period with antibiotics, you were expected to be able to treat illnesses, so medicine became a much more mechanical, physical treatment of the thing, and the concept of illnesses being what's called multifactorial, partly anxiety, partly physical, partly family history, the whole concept of what it was that made people become ill, was being investigated. Ballint's book in 1958 was a seminal book, really, in exploring that, and there are still doctors who meet regularly, called Ballint groups They meet together to discuss the problems they have experienced with their patients, and the psychological effect of the doctor, the patient, and the illness on all three, the interplay between the three, because of course the effect the patient has on the doctor, and the doctor's perceptions of illness and what he brings to it play a part in how he handles it.

When you start teaching General Practice, you talk about the four people who are present in a consultation. There is the doctor and the patient, and there's the doctor thinking what he is not saying to the patient, and there's the patient interpreting what he thinks the doctor is saying to him, and all those four people present in any one consultation. 'How are you, doctor?' ('By God, you look terrible. You look bored stiff and miserable. I hope you are going to be concentrating properly on what happens to me.) 'Come in, sit down.' ('Oh, My God, it's not you again!') These are the four people who are present in this situation. Lots of books have been written on it. All proper General Practice has to be holistic medicine; you have to be treating the whole person, not the illness. It applies just as much to somebody with advanced terminal cancer as it does to somebody who has got an anxiety state.

If you have got advanced cancer, what are your problems? All right, there are the physical problems of the cancer, maybe the pain, but there are also anxieties, what's going to happen to your family when you are not there, or whether you have prepared things, or whether there is unfinished business, you know, in the past, which has never been resolved between people. In the hospice you will see an enormous amount of this, the nurses spend a huge amount of time dealing with family problems that have not been resolved, which are getting in the way of the person dying in peace. That's the psychological concept of medicine. And you have to balance that against recognising the physical detail.

There are new ways of helping understanding. Many people when they go down to see an oncologist, or a cancer specialist, are so frightened they don't really take in what's being said to them. I remember a patient with quite serious cancer coming back from Southampton, where he had seen a specialist. He'd brought back a tape of the consultation and a tape recorder and he was able to play it through with me, so that I could hear what he and the specialist had discussed, and I could explain to him things that he hadn't understood at the time. We had the chance to listen to it again, and for me to answer any queries he had about it. That was something that was happening quite a lot; I think it still goes on.

Medical records

Dr John Williams

born 1939   *interviewed 2002*

When a computer goes down, General Practice stops, literally. And you can't prescribe for anybody, because all prescriptions now are written on computer-generated prescription paper. You don't have a prescription pad the way you did, virtually every prescription that is done is done from the computer and if you do one out of hours you have to go in and put it into the computer. More and more practices are going what is called "paperless"; everything is on the computer. Every letter that comes from a hospital is scanned straight into the computer and when patients move you get about two miles of paper, because they print out everything that is on the computer. Of course, the computer back-up is tremendous.

But we are still using what are called Lloyd George folders, and these are the folders that were introduced with the National Insurance scheme that Lloyd George introduced in 1911, those small oblong folders you see GPs using. Those are called Lloyd George folders, and they are still used by most practices. It is astonishing that they haven't changed. There was a move to go to A4, but in fact A4 wasn't that much more successful in many ways.

Storing records is enormously difficult; it's one of the problems of the future, really. Ideally everything should go on a card, and the patient takes it everywhere they go with them. That's the logic; you have your own 'floppy', almost, and you go in to the doctor, and at the end of the consultation he says, 'Here's your updated floppy. Take it away with you. If you see another doctor, you can feed that into his computer, if you move away.'

If somebody comes to Basingstoke and registers with a Basingstoke practice, the Basingstoke practice notifies the local Health Authority. In our case it was always Winchester. The card goes to them saying, 'This person has moved from Derbyshire to Basingstoke. This was their doctor and their address in Derbyshire.' Winchester writes to the Derbyshire Health Authority and says, 'This person has now moved to Basingstoke. Would you contact Dr X in Derby and ask him to return the notes to you?' Those notes will be returned from him to the Derbyshire Health Authority, from the Derbyshire Health Authority to the Winchester Health Authority, from the Winchester Health Authority to the new chap in Basingstoke. It used to take six weeks unless you'd made a special request and then it would depend on the original GP responding quickly.

At the moment they are going over to the system of having Hospital Trusts and Primary Care Trusts which will be responsible for organising the general practice services.

The treatment room

Dr Keith Ollerhead

born 1958   *interviewed 2003*

The nurse in the treatment room was introduced in one or two practices in the 60s and 70s and became pretty well universal in the larger well-organised practices in the 80s. But they were very much seen as a GP's assistant. And so they would help out with things like minor ops or for the insertion of coils. They would do dressings after treatments either here or at hospital, and they would perhaps start doing things like their baby clinics on their own, where they would do all the injections of the small children. But nowadays the nurses have extended their role so that they actually provide triage, they actually take the requests for today's appointments in many practices and they actually talk to the parents or the individual, see whether they do need to be seen today, whether they can be given telephone advice and whether they need to see a nurse or whether they need to see a doctor. And in the practices that are running this in Basingstoke they have found it a tremendous help in being able to cope with the demand for same-day appointments.

In our practice at Chineham this happens to a limited extent, but through the local Primary Care Trust (PCTs) - what was the Health Authority - we have supported it and on a more formal basis in some of the centre of Basingstoke practices, at Hackwood, Church Grange and Bramblys Grange.

GP contracts

Dr Keith Ollerhead

born 1958   *interviewed 2003*

In 1990, the Government imposed a new contract on GPs and as I began to look for a job in the summer of 1989, everyone was very worried about what the new contract would mean to their income and whether they could afford to take on replacement doctors, and there was a real scarcity of vacancies, and so I had to look far and wide. It was around the time of the Norman Tebbitt 'Get on your bike' and I got the latest copy of the *British Medical Journal* and started at A and applied to Aveley in Essex, Beaconsfield in Buckinghamshire and Basingstoke in Hampshire, and then I thought that was three good jobs and that would do for this week and got an interview for all of them.

Because the new contract was imposed on doctors, they were very upset by the changes that were made in it. And I think it's fair to say, here in 2003, that there are still a lot of doctors who feel extremely aggrieved about the changes that happened at that stage about the way GPs were paid. The proportion of pay related to the number of patients was switched, so they got far less for just being there and far more per patient. So there was an encouragement to work with a bigger list, to earn more, and obviously to get really good quality it's better to work with a smaller list of patients and to be able to give them more time. And therefore those practices who historically had had smaller lists and had done reasonably well under the old contract missed out under the new contract and felt obliged to increase their lists and therefore felt under more pressure.

The average list size is now around 1,800 - at that time in the late 80s it was well above 2,000 - and the incentive to go higher was quite a real pressure on GPs and therefore they felt the double whammy of higher expectations from each patient and having to cope with more of them. Particularly in a growing area like Basingstoke.

The only recognition within the system for different requirements is that for people below 65 there's a flat rate, 65 to 75 is a step up and 75+ is a further step up, a recognition that obviously on average older people need more time, have more illnesses and more tablets and medication that need checking. But it doesn't take account of other groups with special requirements. Particularly here in Chineham we have a very large number of under fives, and they often have a lot of illnesses; they have parents who came to Basingstoke and left their extended families behind and haven't grannies or aunties who are experienced at dealing with small children. So there are a lot of very isolated nuclear families here who rather quickly come to the doctors with a lot of minor illness and expect to be seen after a very short wait. So there's tremendous variability and pressure to see people who need to be seen today. And when you've already got a very busy day, the pressure to see five or six extra people really can have its grinding down effect.

Another new contract for GPs was introduced in 2003, the day after this interview.

Fund-holding and PCTs (Primary Care Trusts)

Dr Keith Ollerhead

born 1958   *interviewed 2003*

To explain fund-holding, the previous, Conservative, government wanted GPs to take on the budget for the purchase of care for the patients registered with the practice. This was basically for planned elective surgery, like hernias, hip replacements, for medication, and for running the practice and it was rather less than half of the total spend on each person because the Health Authority was still responsible for purchasing the emergency care and for a whole series of specialist procedures like liver transplants and heart transplants,

Once the budget was set for a group of patients it was very difficult to change it. So for an area like ours, where year by year the list increased, you got extra funding for the extra patients that joined the list, on a pro rata basis. But if you didn't get the base line right it was extremely difficult to re-adjust it. We wanted to be sure we got the base line right, so we only joined the fourth year of fund-holding. We did it for two years and we were quite successful in getting rapid access for our patients - particularly for things like physiotherapy, which could be done at the surgery, both at Bramblys Grange and at Chineham, so the patients didn't have such a long wait and didn't have to go to the physio department at the hospital. Perhaps a quarter of my time was spent number-crunching, so that was time when I couldn't be dealing with patients. We also had to have two or three dedicated staff who were counting the numbers of out-patients and the numbers of operations, recording them on our computer system, querying when we were charged for people who weren't registered with us - it was very labour-intensive.

Then the Government changed and they announced that fund-holding was ending and they introduced the Primary Care Group which took over 100% of the care for patients, both elective and emergency. I became the Chairman of the Primary Care Group, working as a part of the Health Authority. There were five 'PCGs' in North and Mid-Hampshire, the old Health Authority area: Andover, Winchester, Basingstoke and North Hampshire, Hart and Blackwater Valley. Over the years those have amalgamated and there are now three PCTs, Primary Care Trusts. The Health Authority has gone and there's now the whole of Hampshire and the Isle of Wight Strategic Authority, based in Southampton. Our PCT in Basingstoke covers Tadley, Basingstoke, Alton, Bordon and Liphook, a population of about 200,000.

Primary Care isn't just General Practice, with its GPs, nurses, district nurses and health visitors. It includes all aspects of care from the other associated professionals like pharmacists, dentists, optometrists.

Dr Richard Turner

Born 1946   *interviewed 2005*

Church Grange and Lychpit surgeries have always provided a comprehensive service to their patients and had no difficulties implementing the first new contract in 1991, which developed the opportunities available with fundholding. We have just successfully finished the first year of the second new contract in 2005.

The partnership has always enjoyed a very good relationship with the local District Hospital; there has always been direct access to physiotherapy, X-ray etc. and also to the Postgraduate Centre in the new ARK, offering weekly lunchtime meetings as well as various courses and talks.

We hold or have held appointments to local businesses, including Wiggins Teape, AA, Sainsburys, De La Rue, Surtech, ITW (Fastex), Winterthur Life and the Civil Service, as well as various insurance companies. From time to time the practice is involved in clinical trials and carrying out executive medical examinations for local companies.

We are a forward thinking and innovative practice, but unfortunately currently constrained by rather poor premises which we've outgrown and regrettably the PCT is currently £9.3 million overspent, so the chance of us moving premises in the next three years is very small. Our current plan is to refurbish our existing premises.

At the end of 1992 as part of a DTI initiative, a management consultant visited the Practice and the partnership was assisted in developing a strategy for the future and enabled a system of portfolios for individual partners in important areas of practice management. We have a regular weekly business meeting and also regular clinical meetings. It is our intention still to maintain a personal list system. We recently set up a company called Cedar Medical, to develop new medical Practices within Basingstoke in a franchise-type mode which we feel will be a necessary development as Basingstoke will continue to grow significantly over the next 20 years according to the local and regional plans.

HantsDoc

Dr John Williams

born 1939   *interviewed 2002*

With the advent of the co-operative, the out-of-hours service, HantsDoc, the whole concept of general practice has changed. HantsDoc came in in the 1990s because it was becoming increasingly difficult to find new doctors to come to an area where doctors actually did all their own on-call within practices. Doctors would start getting anxious and worried on a Monday or Tuesday, because they were on duty for the next weekend. By the Monday morning you would have one doctor who was getting worried because they were on next weekend, one doctor who looked absolutely shattered because they had just done the whole weekend and probably by the end of the weekend they had got irritated with what seemed to them to be unnecessary calls, and so they had had a row with two or three people and they were so frustrated by all of this that it just seemed that the moment had come. Co-operatives had started in Kent and Lancashire as experiments in the mid-1980s and suddenly they became very much a concept. However, most of the GPs in the area didn't think that it would be a good idea to share off-duty time with all the other doctors. Partly because they did not believe that all the other

doctors were good enough. Some of the practices, particularly the very good practices, felt, 'I don't want him seeing my patient.'

I was very involved in this. It was the last thing I did before I retired, and we got doctors down from other co-operatives to talk to the GPs in Basingstoke, and I said to them, 'Look, you know, we can't be that different from the doctors in the rest of the country and we are not going to get new doctors coming into Basingstoke if everybody else goes for systems of out-of-hours and co-operatives and Basingstoke is still trying to work in the old fashioned system. So we've really got to think about this.' So they said they'd try it and the fascinating thing was that some of the doctors that were most against it, within six months were saying, 'It's wonderful. I do a six hour stint twice a month at a weekend. I work really hard the whole of the six hours and I see patient after patient after patient, and then I am free. Instead of sitting around at home thinking, 'Shall I cut the grass? Yes, I think I will.' Then the phone goes! Then you are cross because it's gone just when you were just going to do something else. Most people seem to think it works pretty well. We put a lot of work into setting it up, a very, very intensive six months before it took off.

'Shall I cut the grass? Yes, I think I will.'

The doctors who go out don't have access to the patients' notes, but they never did. By the time I retired I was one of ten doctors with two surgeries, one in Bramblys Grange and one in Chineham. When you got called out at night the chances of it being a patient you knew were really pretty small, and of course you didn't go into the surgery and get the notes because if somebody rang you at three o'clock in the morning and said, 'My child is terribly wheezy. I'm really worried about him,' you went to see the child. Gradually as computer systems improve, the doctor going out will be linking up with the practices. When we set up HantsDoc, we had a system whereby doctors could notify HantsDoc of particular problem patients with particular illnesses. So if somebody was dying of cancer you would come in to do your session in the evening, you'd be given details of, say, half a dozen patients, 'These are people who are particularly ill, so if we hear from them…'.

Dentists

Jeffrey Dodd

When the National Health Service started, the British Dental Association (BDA) advised dentists not to enter, because there were no safeguards. At that time there were three qualified dentists in Basingstoke and there were two that would be known as '1921 dentists', because dentistry only became a closed profession in 1921, so anybody practising dentistry before then was automatically allowed to continue, whether they'd any qualifications or not. The three qualified dental surgeons in Basingstoke agreed to take the BDA advice. However, 80 to 90% of dentists joined the service on the first day. Any dentist who did not join on that day was penalised by deducting a set amount from his pension when that became due. I had this sum deducted each year from my pension, that is 25 years, since I retired. Fortunately the sum has never been increased since 1948 and therefore is no longer too onerous.

The BDA's advice proved correct. After two years the government had only to place a document on the table of the House of Commons to reduce the fees paid to dentists and they did this on at least two occasions. No debate, no dentist could do anything about it and this went on until there was a Royal Commission under Pilkington, who was a glass manufacturer in St Helens. We didn't come out at all well from that Royal Commission. We all said it. When Enoch Powell was Minister of Health, we didn't get much help, I can't remember exactly why or how; and later on, when the Conservatives were in opposition, McLeod was very helpful to dentists but, as soon as they won the next election and he became Minister of Health (and this is second-hand), when the dentist committee went to talk to him, he said, 'Gentlemen this is not the right time to ask for an increase in fees.' And one of the dentists said, 'Well, Mr Minister, when is the right time?' He said, 'Last year.' And the other time when we went to see the government to try and get some more money, the Labour party were in power, Callaghan was the Prime Minister and he said, 'Gentlemen, you represent 1,500 votes and have no political clout, so you're not going to get any money.'

So I was really very angry about the whole situation but in the end I decided I was just going to do my work and if they paid me - or, goodness, if they didn't pay me - well, there was nothing I could do about it

When the National Health Service came in, there was an immense amount of work.

Two-thirds of the population of Basingstoke had full upper and lower dentures which they'd had for over 20 years, when they should have worn them for ten years, largely probably because they were not all that well off and didn't think they could afford the fees. They all turned up.

As far as the patient was concerned, it was entirely free. And that system never works. When I was a dental student at Leeds Dental Hospital, patients came there who couldn't afford to go elsewhere basically. We always charged them sixpence, whatever we did, because the people who ran it didn't think it was right that they got it free. If people get something free, that's the value they put on it.

I think it changed slowly, as soon as the National Health came in, because people began to realise that they didn't want to lose all their teeth when they were young. So, as far as I was concerned, it was very good. And the last time I saw any young people, about 15 years ago, I saw a very big improvement.

I think it is hopeless now because, basically, the patient pays all the fees. I didn't think it was right when they didn't have to pay anything. For a long time they paid a pound towards the cost other than for dentures (they paid more for them). I think they got it about right when they paid half the fees. Now they pay at least nine-tenths of the fee. There were also the people who came along who probably had dentures anyway, and said, 'Well, we don't believe this can be any good if it's free, but as it's free we might as well have it.' There was that attitude as well.

And one of the troubles with the dentists is, the government never paid us properly. And, unless you were willing to go to South Africa or Rhodesia or Canada, there was no alternative for 80% or 90% of dentists. What was annoying during the first two years at the start of the Health Service was that the *Daily Mirror* and other tabloid newspapers went on about dentists being millionaires, which I wish was true

I did very little private work because I found, well, there's only one way of doing it. I couldn't say, 'If I'm only paid half the fees I think I'm entitled to, I can't do the work half as well as it needs to be done.' And also, there was some resistance from people with a lot of money. I had a stockbroker patient, who was a personal friend of mine anyway, and I think in the Labour Government the top rate of tax got up to something like 80%. And he said, 'Well, they're taking all my money I earn in tax, so if there is something I can get back out of the Government, that's what I'm going to do.' So you didn't win on anything, you see.

But, from what I can see, there are a lot of dentists now who are saying, 'I'm not going to do any National Health work because I don't think the fees are any good.' But, as you more or less pay nearly all on the National Health, patients are more willing to say, 'Well, I'm going to pay a lot whichever way I do it so I might as well do it privately.'

Jeffrey Dodd was in practice in Basingstoke for 27 years.

Over that time I didn't see a lot of changes in the techniques I was using until more or less the time I retired. Well, the equipment became rather different. By that time, about seven years before I retired, I had a partner. And it made us very poor for three years, paying all that money for the equipment. But I'd been in the army, serving overseas, I'd pedalled out a lot of cavity preparations on a treadle machine. And then the new thing came in for drilling cavities. Instead of being worked electrically, it was worked by compressed air. It had been used in America for years and six were imported by an American dental firm in London. I think four went to the teaching hospitals and I got one of the others. I was just about the first dentist to have one. It was very time-saving, because it did the job a lot more quickly. And I think there have been various modifications and improvements since, but basically it is what's used now.

In the last ten years there have been a lot of new materials. And there's quite a lot of nonsense talked about the old ones. They're talking about 'mercury poisoning'. My father, who was a dental surgeon, filled teeth with amalgam all his life, and lots of people older than him did as well. It was a standard thing to use mercury amalgam.

About the time of the start of the National Health Service, the technique for deep root treatment was already there. I've got a tooth which had a root treatment done between 1940 and 1942 and it's as sound as it was then. Root treatment was not done on the National Health very much because the National Health wouldn't pay for it - well, they paid for it, but doing a successful root treatment can take an awful long time.

When I did fillings and so on, drilling teeth, I would mostly inject a painkiller.

I think probably the anaesthetics have improved but didn't change a lot. The biggest change I saw in my time was the high-speed drill coming in. And of course, instead of sitting your patient in a chair and standing up all day, we got chairs that went flat and we had the patient flat on their back. Some of them didn't like it at first. Particularly there were some ladies who didn't like being put flat out. But it's a lot easier to relax if you're lying down flat out than if you're sitting up, grabbing the chair. I was probably one of the first to do that but everybody does it now. I only know one or two people who still have patients sitting up.

I've always felt that to do crown and bridge work is very exact and it's got to be spot on. And unless you do it all the time every day the chap who does, say, one crown every two months is not going to be as good at it. I was referred to a consultant in, I think it's called 'conservative dentistry' and he does really nothing but crowns. He comes to Basingstoke, perhaps one day a week and he's based at the Mayday Hospital in Croydon. But there are very few of these consultants about.

I had a dental laboratory and I employed a dental technician to make dentures. Very few people do now. And I think they're not as lucky as I was, to have a chap on the spot and to be able to say, 'Come and look at this, I want you to do this, this is the problem.' Well, if you just take impressions and send them away, you can't find out the things he could tell you. But I suppose it probably isn't economical to employ your own.

I employed two girls and a technician. I wasn't on my own for very long, because there was so much work to do. I had an assistant dentist for quite a long time. I had difficulty getting them because the Government limited the fees you could pay them. Jobs for assistants were much the same everywhere and there were far more jobs going than there were assistants wanting the jobs. They were not very interested in coming to Basingstoke, particularly when it became a New Town. They could go to Bournemouth or Torquay or somewhere more attractive and get the same sort of salary.

I could always ask for advice, not necessarily from other dentists in Basingstoke. Reading had a very good section of the British Dental Association and I used to go there. It helps to have contacts with colleagues in the profession.

Bobby Pearce

born 1924   *interviewed 2002*

When I qualified in 1951 there were 148 dentists that wanted assistants. I went to see half a dozen and I couldn't relate to them at all. They were offering me flats above the surgery, use of a boat at weekends, all this sort of idea to entice me to go, but I took Dulcie with me and almost inevitably we said, 'Don't think so,' and then one day I had a note from a chap about Dr Peter, a dentist in Bounty Road, Basingstoke, who desperately needed an assistant. Well, it was what I was looking for in that I didn't want to work in pin-striped trousers and dark jacket. I would much prefer my sports jacket and informality. I felt that I wanted to be a family dentist, and Basingstoke had about 14,000 population, I think, then.

When I first arrived I was shown where the toilet was and where to hang my coat, and then the dentist said to his No 1 girl, 'Now, you will look after Mr Pearce, won't you, because I'm going off to the hospital.' So he vanished. This was my very first job and I was given a list of 32 patients and a list of dental suppliers and off he went. Which was rather being thrown in at the deep end. If I had got a problem, we had Rooksdown House plastic and jaw unit round the corner, and the dental surgeon was Norman Roe who I had known at Guy's, so I could ring him up for help, but in the event I didn't need to. Dr Peter was away for seven weeks before he returned, looking very fit and able to stand up comfortably.

We settled in very happily. The dental practice was well organised, it served a complete range of patients: agricultural workers, factory employees, office staff, tradespeople and professionals of all disciplines. One odd quirk was that we weren't on mains electricity in Bounty Road, but on 100 volts because it was made locally so we had to have most complicated transformers to get it up to 240 to enable us to use X-ray machines and dental drills.

Then I set up on my own in Victoria St, about 1955, because I wanted to be a completely National Health practice, but Dr Peter and I still gave anaesthetics for each other's patients as necessary. Doctors never came unless there was something very wobbly, but I could call the consultant anaesthetist in if necessary.

Then I became the dental surgeon to Park Prewett for one full day (two sessions) a week. And then for the Hackwood Road Hospital and the Basing Road Hospital, until I retired in 1980. Then I changed to two full day sessions at Basingstoke Hospital, dealing with prosthetic problems and teaching dental students.

Many weeks I went up to the Rugby Club on their Tuesday training night and I'd line up eight Rugby players. I had some pre-formed Rugby shields but they had to be individualised in that you put some gunge in them and held them in their mouth for a moment, asked them to keep their teeth closed together. I started at the end of the line and when I got to the end, number 1 would have been cooked, so I was able to hook

out the denture, trim off the excess of the material that I'd put in, put it in a little plastic bag and say, 'Now leave it till tomorrow,' because it takes 12 hours to set properly. I did this regularly until everyone was fitted, then I would go back to check them all again in a month's time.

I've loved being a dentist. All fillings are similar, but the owners of the cavities are very different, some needed cajoling, some needed encouragement, some needed a severe talking to - so it was a delightful job, so rewarding that at the end of the day you could look at a mouth and say 'I've done that,' a satisfaction that I can't imagine that even a doctor can obtain - they became lots of friends, they came regularly, and there is nothing I would rather have done. I always knew people from their teeth better than their names or faces.

In my General Practice, I was booked to capacity every day.

Jeanette Patterson

born 1938   *interviewed 2001*

It was after I moved to Basingstoke in 1980 that I got a job as a dental nurse. I saw a part-time job advertised, and they said the dentist was willing to train, if you didn't have any experience. I'd had experience working as a volunteer in hospital when I lived at Fareham (in those days you were allowed to go in and wash patients and make beds and so forth, and as my sister was a nursing sister in charge of one of the wards there they were always looking for volunteers). I'd also got book-keeping experience and I'd done receptionist duties before. The dentist did train me, and I started doing the dental surgery assistant's course. I learnt an awful lot; he didn't actually have a general anaesthetic list, but later on, when I moved to another dentist, because I needed a full-time job, the second dentist did. And I learned to take X-rays, I learned to help recover people - this has all changed very much because you're not allowed to do that now. I was with that particular dentist for seven years.

A dentist today

In 1990 the Government made a new contract with dentists for National Health work, but found it cost too much and imposed a reduction in fees. Another contract is due to be agreed in 2005, and practitioners are concerned that the same thing will happen again. Continued lack of finance in the NHS is an ongoing problem.

Today there are frequent reports in the newspapers about the lack of NHS dentists and the long queues of people wanting to join a new dentist's list.

CHEMISTS

Doug Warsop

born 1917   *interviewed 2001 and 2002*

Nowadays, to be a pharmacist, you go direct from A-levels to university, at about 18, get a Bachelor of Pharmacy degree and then do 12 months' experience in a pharmacy - that's in a shop or in a hospital, or even perhaps in a manufacturing place like Eli Lilly. Having served that time, you become a Member of the Pharmaceutical Society.

In about the 1950s, the lovely old coloured jars you used to see in pharmacies, with Latin names on them, began to disappear. Then you put drugs in the bottles supplied by the manufacturer, with a date on, and of course you didn't mix an old bottle with a new bottle, so the old bottle had to be thrown away after the expiry date had passed. I know of one chemist who was under instructions to use the new method and the old jars were no longer required, so he actually took them into the back yard, threw them against a brick wall and smashed them up. Well now, of course, these jars are on sale in antique shops for pounds.

Now containers are used once and afterwards thrown away. Some tablets are supplied in little blister packs and some have got 'Monday, Tuesday, Wednesday' stuck on and that's to make it easier for people to remember whether they've had the tablet for the right day. Some people have suggested that a pharmacist should go in to old people's homes from time to time to make sure these old people are taking the medicine at the right time and in the right quantity. But of course if a pharmacist is going to spend his time doing that, who's going to pay for it?

Doug has seen many developments in the kinds and uses of medicines, and the way people get them.

The whole history of medicine is changing. Quite a range of antibiotics have been found and in the modern pharmacy you get lots and lots of bottles of tablets, chemicals and antibiotics and such like for specific illnesses. And, instead of the pharmacist having to mix up these medicines and things, he's probably taking things off the shelf already made, manufactured, thoroughly tested by these big companies.

When new medicines are developed, the Government's Committee on the Safety of Medicines oversee all the research and they make the decision eventually as to whether or not the drug is permitted. And then, of course, it's only on prescription to start with. And the doctor has to have a yellow card and if you go back and say, 'Doctor, that medicine you gave me does so-and-so to me,' he's supposed to put it on the card and send the card back to the Committee on Safety of

Medicines and they will build up a little case as to whether the drug is safe to use. And, of course, if the doctor starts reporting deaths, there's going to be a big investigation then and the drug might possibly be withdrawn

Through the period after the War, medicines were divided up. There were those you could only get on prescription, and go to the chemist's to get it dispensed. There were medicines that you could get through the pharmacy - that's very often when they asked you questions, like 'Who's it for? Have you taken this before? Are you taking any other medicines?' Assistants on the counter have been trained to ask all these questions. If they have a doubt, they should then call the pharmacist, who might come and say, 'I think you'd be better off going to see your doctor.' And then there were other medicines that could be sold by anyone. The supermarkets were growing rapidly and began to sell more and more medicines, cosmetics, films and cameras and all those sorts of things and that was taking away the trade of the little pharmacist. I'm sorry to say that some of the pharmacists really just couldn't compete because they weren't getting paid as much for dispensing. More and more people are going to supermarkets now and some of the supermarkets are employing a pharmacist themselves.

At the moment you've got Boots and Superdrug: they're very powerful. They've got big shops and they can bulk-buy and they can afford to do things better. But Lloyds are coming up very fast and snapping up all the little shops that are closing down, and of course they're expanding all the time.

I believe Boots now offer to collect a prescription and dispense it for you and Lloyds advertise on the television to say they will collect the prescription. And there is a chemist who will collect prescriptions and go to the house and so on. I knew a pharmacist who used to call into an old people's home to see if there was anybody in there that wanted a prescription and so would take the prescription away and bring it back dispensed in the evening. So that's quite a nice little service.

The Pharmaceutical Society look to see how many chemists there are in a certain area so you don't overcrowd an area with pharmacists. But in the rural areas a doctor might still do his own dispensing. He probably has an assistant who does the work, but the doctor is taking full responsibility

The pharmacists must keep records of everything, particularly of dangerous drugs, of course. That's another problem these days. I know one or two shops have been burgled, people just looking for drugs.

Another new thing is the National Health Service Direct phone line. It's a 24-hour service. It's mainly run by nurses, and they're well qualified. If there is a query they might say, 'We'll ring you back.' And for a mild illness they might tell you to go and see a pharmacist. In fact I've got a recent publication, *Community Pharmacy Referral*, that tells the pharmacist how to deal with anyone who comes in from National Health Service Direct.

The Government is trying to encourage people to use the pharmacist more, to take the pressure off the doctor. If the doctors are very busy, you might have to wait two or three days to have an appointment, but the pharmacist is available any hour of the day without an appointment. Some areas are building Health Centres, with opticians and dentists as well as doctors.

I just wonder what the future will hold. Even now, doctors are using computers more. And I think the time will come that, when you go and see a doctor, he will put your name in to the computer and tell it what is wrong with you. Then the computer will come up with a list of drugs that you could take for that condition, but it will remind the doctor that you are allergic to certain drugs, that you are taking something that would react with the new proposed drug, and eventually the doctor will look at the bottom line to see what medicine is available. It's possible in the future he might have all the drugs he wants upstairs in the stockroom, the computer will select the drugs he wants dispensed and they'll come back down a tube, and you walk out from the doctor's surgery with a bottle of medicine without having to go to a pharmacy!

Eli Lilly

Eli Lily won 2nd prize in the 1953 Carnival

Of the British company's 522 employees in 1962, almost 200 had worked for it more than 10 years; 78 had been Lillyites for longer than 15 years; and 22 for longer than a quarter of a century. These are impressive figures, especially when one considers how many of those 522 jobs had come into existence relatively recently. Now they say at Basingstoke that if you've been with Lilly five years you'll be with Lilly for life.

Unpublished history of Eli Lilly p 53

Eric Godden

born 1925   *interviewed 2001*

Eric Godden had worked at Eli Lilly and Company before the war (see pages 18-19) He joined the RAF, became a navigator and trained as an accountant. After the war, he came back to Eli Lilly as a cost accountant. He found things had changed a lot, with many more people working there. In the mid-1960s he was involved in the installation of a computer.

A special air-conditioned room was prepared for the computer. Representatives from each division were trained in computer systems, programs, operations etc. It was to be a Honeywell Main Frame computer so training courses were attended at Honeywell in Brentford. It was decided to first of all use the computer for materials control and production planning and sales analysis so responsibility for each area was allocated. Investigating procedures, writing systems for them, programming and installing took quite a lot of time. An automatic typewriter, which was uncommon then, was purchased and this stored information, making things a lot quicker, and also cut out copies that had been needed before. Once written, systems and programs had to be tested. I probably lived the nearest to the premises so I would tend to go in late evening and work a number of hours while the computer was free, testing programs and checking that they worked. Computer results were compared with manual results and generally the computer results were correct.

The chemical plant and the capsule plant did shift work, so they were occupied at night, but as far as the main building was concerned, this was unusual. I know when I was working in the computer room once, the night watchman came round and assumed we'd forgotten to switch the lights off and did so, leaving me in darkness. Night watchmen patrolled the building every hour.

Doug Warsop

born 1917   *interviewed 2001 and 2002*

The NHS did affect our production and staffing. Before the NHS came in, drugs like Sodium Amytal and Seconal Sodium were only available for private patients, who had to pay for their medicines. Afterwards, the medicines were available for anyone. I think the sale of our capsules, for those two products, shot up to something like 300 million a year. I'm not quite sure of that figure but it was quite a tremendous jump from the few million that we produced under the old scheme when people had to pay for it.

In the capsule-filling department, we had to get extra machines to cope with the amount of work we were turning out. During the war and just after, we used to get the capsules from America. But I think it was around about the 1950s, we had our own capsule-making plant, where we manufactured these capsules which we then used for ourselves, and also sold to other companies who were putting their products into capsules.

Capsule sorting, 1966

Capsule sorting, 1989

Around 1960, we opened up a special area near Bagshot, Windlesham. Earl Wood was the name of the place. That's where we started doing our research, and we were quite independent from what they were doing in America. If they came up with an idea, then they would bring down the samples to us at Basingstoke and we would manufacture, perhaps, a small quantity and then they would take the tablets back to carry out their research and eventually it would go for clinical trials.

It was round about 1962, I think, when the managing director retired. Then we had Americans coming over. They were bringing new ideas and changing things somewhat. It did not affect me in production, fortunately. I suppose they brought the contraceptive tablets, which we made for a while. We had to take special precautions then. Because we did have one or two cases where men were manufacturing the tablet in normal basic conditions, and they began to develop breasts. These particular fellows were losing interest in their girl-friends. They were taken out of the department and moved to an area free from contamination. I think they quickly returned to normal. We did make these tablets in a special room, isolated from the rest of production. In the same way, we eventually produced penicillin in an area away from normal tablets. Later on, further antibiotics were done in a separate area.

I got involved in all sorts of tableting and a little later on I was involved in packaging as well. So I looked after the whole thing, including the liver plant, which was put up in the 1950s. Raw liver was recommended as a very useful cure for anaemia and we made liver extract. We produced the dried powder in capsules, which were very easy to swallow. A large quantity of liver would be minced and put into a big vat, boiled up with water and the volume would be reduced with evaporation under reduced pressure. It was dried, and the powder would be dried and again powdered further, eventually filled into capsules and one or two other ingredients added. We used to create quite a smell in the place. There was a lot of cleaning to be done afterwards! You couldn't leave traces of liver around. It was all ox liver. That was a problem we had with making capsules, whether the gelatin came from pigs or cows. You had to be very careful when you exported to a country that didn't believe in eating pork. For a little while, we tried to switch away from gelatin and use methyl cellulose, but we found the capsules did not dissolve quite as well as gelatin, so we dropped this idea quite quickly. Then eventually Vitamin Bl2 came along and they thought that was better than liver.

Eric Godden

born 1925   *interviewed 2001*

We began to make liver products, where we bought in raw liver which had to be processed and eventually made into a powder and the powder filled into capsules. I think the liver came from London, probably Smithfield. It was an anti-anaemia product - a little easier to take as a capsule than as raw liver! The only thing was, processing it was rather a smelly operation. Everyone in the factory knew which day it was! It went through quite a long process, not just cooking, it was pressed and filtered.

And then as well as 'Lextron' there was another product called 'Bilron' made from animal bile, which was also a bit smelly. The liver plant was right next to the canteen, for some reason!

More changes in the 1960s and 1970s

Doug Warsop

born 1917   *interviewed 2001 and 2002*

About 1962 or 1963, I think, the Thalidomide scare came about, where Distillers were making a drug that was for morning-sickness and they found that certain pregnant ladies had misshapen children, no arms or legs. Of course, the drug was immediately banned, and then Distillers had huge claims for compensation. So they decided that there were certain hazards in the pharmaceutical industry and they just decided to rely on their gin and whisky, which were safe products to make, and Eli Lilly took over the pharmaceutical side of Distillers and called it Dista. Then we did rationalisation. They had a better injection area than we had, so our injectibles went up to Liverpool and some of their products came down to us. We manufactured some of Distillers' tablets down here.

Then came chemical manufacturing in the 1960s. We were making a range of products in the chemical factory, which was a separate building from the main manufacturing area. So we made Acetohexamide, which is very good for mild cases of diabetes. Then we were making a product which was similar to Codeine, called Dextropropoxyohene. That was a pain-killer, which was incorporated with Paracetamol to make Distalgesic, which was very popular. Then, more recently, going into the late 1970s, Boots were making Ibuprofen, used for rheumatism and arthritis at that time. We played around with the molecules and eventually came up with Benoxaprofen which was kinder to the stomach. For a while it was very successful, then came a bit of a problem later on, with the rate at which it was excreted by old people. All our tests were done on young people working for the research centre. And it was found that if you took the normal dose in the morning, by the following morning all traces of the drug had completely disappeared from the system. So they were quite happy about that. The only side effect we did find was that certain people on the clinical trials developed photosensitivity, a rash in the sunshine. So doctors were warned to be on the look-out, and if a patient did get a rash, they were taken off and put on something else.

In about the 1970s we had government inspectors coming round and 'Good Manufacturing Practice'. Before that, you just relied on the company to do the right thing. Eli Lilly, fortunately, always had a good reputation.

Everything became automated and controlled by computers. Take the tablet machines. They became completely enclosed and machines could be adjusted automatically by the machine and samples taken at intervals, measuring size and weight, with a print-out showing the results. Everything was dust-enclosed, so the machine was running silently and fully controlled. Then the tablets or capsules were put in one end and the machines filled up the bottles, put the labels on and packed them. It was all automatic, controlled, completely different. So, where we used to employ a lot of mentally- and physically-handicapped people doing the simple repetitive jobs, those jobs were no longer there, and we needed a minimum number of people just minding these machines.

I've seen many changes over my years there. So the happy days of rows of girls singing have disappeared. We still maintained a company that was free from control of unions, because we had one or two unions sending along representatives. They allowed them to come and talk to the people, but when it was all over, I think the people thought, 'Well, we're not paying anything to Lilly and we are getting all that the unions can offer us plus extra: extra holidays, free hospital treatment through the BUPA scheme.' So I think everybody felt really satisfied. Then, of course, we had a pension scheme where people did not pay anything, non-contributory, but when they retired they got a pension. It was a very caring company and it still is.

We used to have groups come from the various doctors' practices, nurses and all these Sisters, to see what we had got. In fact, they were amazed at the equipment we had in our health department. We had straightforward equipment for weighing people, measuring lung capacity, eye testing, and ECG. People could go into a sort of telephone kiosk and sit there with earphones on, and music would be played at various concentrations and levels, and they could decide by signaling whether they could hear or whether they could not. They used to do tests for cholesterol. Some of the people in the medical practices envied our nurse, who was in charge there. People working in the Chemical Plant used to get checks every 12 months, but eventually the Chemical Plant was closed down because it was probably cheaper to get the drugs made elsewhere. The Capsule Plant was sold to the Japanese. I think the American boss, who was in charge of the whole world set-up, thought he could do a deal with the Japanese. So about six sites that used to make capsules like us - France, America and Australia - all these plants were sold to the Japanese in the late 1980s or 1990 perhaps.

I retired in 1982 after nearly 40 years, when all the things were beginning to change.

Derek Anthony (then Communications Manager, 2003)

I don't think our relationship with the NHS has changed very much over the years. Doctors still prescribe our products and pharmacists still dispense them. The two big changes have been in the greater regulation of our products by government and the greater involvement of patients in deciding what treatment is appropriate for them.

Since the 1960s we have had to obtain a licence from the Medicines Control Agency before we can introduce a new medicine. This tighter procedure was introduced in response to the thalidomide tragedy of the early 1960s.

During the 33 years I have worked in the pharmaceutical industry, patients have taken a more and more active interest in the treatments they receive. This has meant that pharmaceutical companies now have to provide much more information about their products to doctors, patients and patient support groups. The advent of the internet has greatly speeded the move to more informed patients.

Val Cole

born 1940   *interviewed 1995*

I was on the penicillin so I packed the penicillin tablets. We worked from eight o'clock in the morning till a quarter past five and my wages were £3.5s. A lot of money, wasn't it! The conditions were good. It was a nice place to work. I did like it.

Then, because I worked with penicillin, I got allergic to it, so I landed in Southampton Chest Hospital for about five weeks, ill. We didn't have a chest hospital in Basingstoke. It was just a little old Cottage Hospital in Hackwood Road. So they moved me - I had to leave Lilly eventually because I was allergic to the medicines.

Opticians

Mark Offord, FBDO

born 1940   *interviewed 2005*

My career in Optics started in Newbury in April 1957 as an apprentice Dispensing Optician. There followed a three-year course in both Visual Optics and Ophthalmic lenses, including a three-month stint on the manufacturing side of the business, making both frames and lenses.

Compulsory registration of both Ophthalmic and Dispensing Opticians had recently been introduced; everybody was able to have an NHS eye examination, also to be supplied with NHS frames and lenses. Charges for these items had been made since the early 1950s: £1.6.0d for lenses, £1.2.6d for frames; these gradually rose. A small number of private frames were available, some designed to take NHS lenses; others, such as rimless and upswept frames, were completely private.

In my particular company, Clement Clarke, the testing of sight was undertaken by Ophthalmic Medical Practitioners, OMPs.

Cataract operations entailed a two-week stay in hospital, followed by the wearing of extremely strong prescription spectacles. Contact lenses, hard plastic, were just coming into general use in the early 60s. Varifocal lenses had just been invented.

Moving to Basingstoke in 1969 to open a practice in the new development, I began to see changes coming in, though we were still not allowed to display prices in our windows.

More fashion frames began to appear, designer names such as Mary Quant. Big businesses began to move into Optics with the relaxation of the publicity rules. Woolworths, British Home Stores, Boots all opened Optical outlets, Boots becoming the new owner of Clement Clarke, among others.

The 1970s saw the abolition of the universal free NHS eye examination and the end of NHS frames and lenses, followed quickly by the de-registration of Dispensing Opticians and the introduction of 'over the counter' reading spectacles. With the decline in the numbers of OMPs, Ophthalmic Opticians, now known as Optometrists, began to work both in partnership with and for Dispensing Opticians.

Change gathered pace with a great increase in the fashion element of spectacle wearing, with Calvin Klein and many others, both famous and not, joining in. Price wars are now the norm, with 'buy one, get one free' (BOGOF) plus millions spent on TV advertising.

The introduction of soft disposable contact lenses, weekly and daily, increased the market for contact lens wearers. Cataract operations are now done on a day patient basis, ocular implants are used with almost perfect vision straight away.

Computers now, of course, are an integral part of all optical life, from the manufacture of both frames and lenses to sight testing equipment; soon the human element will not be required!

Vickers

Les Picket

born 1940   *interviewed 2003*

I had an accident at work on a Saturday. I split my elbow. They took me into the Hackwood Road Hospital, and it was stitched up. On the Sunday it all swelled up. I was sent to Heatherwood Hospital in Ascot onto a hyperbaric machine to have treatment, because they I thought was going to lose my arm. I had gas gangrene. There were only two of these machines in the country. One was at Heatherwood, to be on a tour of England and demonstrated and the other one was in a big hospital in Cambridge. It was like an oxygen tent.

You had to put your arm into the machine. It was like getting into a big glass tube and they pumped pure oxygen through and it just sent everything out; I did it for every day for a week, two hours at a time. I since found out the machine was actually made in Basingstoke by Vickers. In fact, if I had not had the use of that machine I would have been one-armed by now.

Health services, Clinics and First-Aid

A medical officer

Dr Tom Roberts

I think I am the longest-serving doctor (not practising in medicine) in Basingstoke. When I first came to the town in

1961, the Cottage Hospital was staffed by the GPs but the consultants came up from Winchester.

My office moved from the Market Chambers to a 'terrapin' building in the War Memorial Park. I was there until the NHS was reorganised in 1974. My title changed three times and I became the first Director of Public Health.

The town was about to go through a great upheaval; that was why I had arrived. It was only about three months after I arrived that the Town Clerk, the late Mr Roger Purvis, issued a memorandum to all of us, asking us to put down in order of priority what we thought should be in the town plan. It did not have to be from our own discipline and I put down a market, a hostel (for the people that would come to build the town), a crematorium. They were all passed. The hostel, Nelson Lodge, was built up by the old fever hospital.

The crematorium was in the first town plan but, the planners being what they are, it was dropped. It was going to be up the road, over the railway bridge, by Tesco's at Chineham, where the old sewerage farm was. They never bothered to look at the rules and regulations. You cannot build a crematorium just anywhere. It has got to be 100 yards or so from the nearest house. Then there was this argument on what constituted the boundary. Was it the boundary of the furnace? Or was it the boundary of the land? It died a dead duck and now years later it has opened near Dummer, 40 years on.

What I did not like was the way they were putting up hundreds and hundreds, in fact 1000 to 2000, houses each year. I remember writing in one of my reports that they were putting up houses and conveniently forgetting the infrastructure. People live in houses but they need shops to go out to buy things from and they need a transport system to convey them to the shops and work. All that was very late in arriving, they are still getting there.

The working relationship with the local GPs wasn't all that close, because Community Health Services were in the remit of the County Council. The County Council did not believe in having anything to do with the Borough, - no partnerships then, oh no, no. The hospital services were with the old Cottage Hospital. Some went to Treloar's and some went to Winchester. Park Prewett was purely a psychiatric hospital by the time I arrived. Until the Mini-hospital was built, hospital services were rudimentary. There were a few operations and a few out-patient sessions.

I always used to have a good dig at bureaucracy in my annual report. You could write virtually anything in that and not get the sack. The office of MOH was a very powerful one. All right, you could be sacked if you stole or anything like that but, regarding your work, you had to be sacked by the Minister of Health. The Council could not do it.

District Medical Services

Dr Michael Williams
born 1930   *interviewed 2001*

Before the Health Service there was a tripartite division; you had the hospital services, general practice and the district medical offices, the welfare services. It was only when the Health Service started that they became gradually linked up. The District Medical offices were at Bramblys Grange. I think this was in the early days of the Health Service, before they were amalgamated with the Children's Services. I don't recall much rapport between them and the GPs, but for many years my father, Dr Keith Williams, was the Public Vaccinator and did all the smallpox vaccinations there.

Dr Sandy Smeaton
born 1916   *interviewed 1998 and 1999*

In 1949 the County Medical Officer of Health was responsible for many aspects of community care, and employed his own doctors, dentists, midwives and nurses. For the most part they worked quite independently of the local GPs. The doctors were all women, dealing with infants and school-children, the dentists also dealing with school-children. The midwives were involved entirely with home confinements and the nurses with domiciliary care.

A District Nurse

Elizabeth Anderson
born 1921   *interviewed 1995*

When I got this job on the District, there were two District Nurses. One did all the north side of Church Street, up Chapel Street, under the bridge. The other one did all the south side. I started as half a one, but I'd only been there for about half a day before somebody went off sick and I was pitched straight into it. No District training, no nothing. I was given a dress round my ankles and a funny little hat and a black bag and told to get on with it.

In those days they took anybody who had the qualifications of a midwife and the qualifications of a State-Registered-Nurse. I had all the qualifications but at that time I didn't have my Queen's Certificate because I had never envisaged going into District Nursing.

We had to do everything that you can do in a hospital but at home, with the support of your little black bag. As you didn't have half the accessories that you would have in hospital, you had to do an awful lot of improvisation, turn

chairs into bed cradles and all sorts of things. When the Red Cross was revamped, we used to get all our backrests and our bedpans and our bottles on hire from them. You used to go round with commodes in the back of your car. And if you could get them in, you could never get them out again! They used to come to pieces and all sorts of funny things happened with them, with the lids and things rolling down the hill, down Kingsclere Road, much to the amusement of the bus drivers. The drivers never got out and stopped. But they didn't run them over, which was something.

I used my own car because they used to have these horrible little Minis that were always breaking down and, anyway, I hate small cars. I used to get quite a good petrol allowance for it. I should think we covered about 30 to sometimes 40 miles. It depends how far out into the country you had to go. You used to go into the surgeries in the morning and the doctors used to give you the jobs to go to, like removing sutures, doing dressings, bed-baths. They were the bane of our lives.

It used to take you ages when you got out into the country to find these places, because the maps were all haywire, out in the rural areas, when you're down a cart track somewhere, going to the cottages. And then when you got there they'd say either, 'Oh, he's died,' or 'He's gone into hospital,' or something or other, so it was a wasted journey. Still, in good weather it was gorgeous.

You started about half-past eight because we'd have as many as four or five diabetics who had to have insulin and you had to start pretty early in the morning so that you'd get them all in before they had their breakfast. Then you'd get in there and find somebody was not so good, or in a coma. Well, that sort of put you back, as you can imagine! You were supposed to finish at four, but you didn't always. Sometimes you finished at one. If you knew you had something to repeat in the evening or in the late afternoon, you stayed in town. If not, you went home but you were always on call and, you can bet your bottom dollar, as soon as you got inside that front door the phone would ring and it would be an emergency and you'd have to go out and deal with it. Somebody had a haemorrhage or something or other. And so, back you used to go. In my day you were never off duty except when you had your day off or your weekend. And I've worked sometimes with a patient right up till ten, eleven. But you didn't mind because that's what you were there for. And they needed you.

Then things began to change.

It was much better when we were appointed to a doctor's surgery. I had Church Square doctors. I had four doctors and the other nurse had another four. And we sort of divided up the other doctors as they came along, assistants or trainees.

By then we had about eight nurses on the District. They did away with the Queen's Nurses then, somewhere round about 1958.

Mostly, you used to get patients coming home from the hospital and some of them had to have dressings done. Some were so bad that you had to go twice a day. We used to get strings of sutures and the inevitable enema. And general tidying them up, making them comfortable. If you could get them out of bed, you'd sit them in a chair. Later on in the afternoon, you'd go back and put them back to bed. Officially we didn't do any cleaning, although I spent one Christmas unbunging somebody's drains. And we didn't really do any cooking. But you weren't just a District Nurse. One dear old man said to me, 'You know, I don't look upon you as a nurse.' He said, 'You're more, you're part of my family.' You know, he meant it. And that's how you felt when you got into the house. A lot of people used to say, 'Ah, thank God you've come!' And you were appreciated. I had a lot of marvellous memories of people. Sadly, most of them have departed this life. But it was a very rewarding job.

Afterwards, they started to bring in assessing patients, which was very difficult and tricky because you didn't know how much of it you could really do, how much of it was really needed. But you always gave them the benefit of the doubt. You had reams of paperwork, four pages to assess one patient - their sleeping habits, and how many times they had to get up in a night, and that wasn't so bad, but there were ridiculous things like how many stairs had they got? Had they got a downstairs loo as well as an upstairs loo? Well, those sorts of things didn't make a patient comfortable.

Our whole idea was to keep them up, mobile, so that you didn't get the dreaded word 'bedsores'. Or a sort of general cabbage-like state. You used to encourage them to do things for themselves as much as possible - well, we did, I don't know that that ever got through to the hierarchy.

Things started to improve when the hospital had more wards and they moved from Hackwood Road, which was really a minute place, up to where it is now. But previously, the 'Mini' – where the Maternity Hospital is – that was the General Hospital for a couple of years, and then they moved into the big hospital when it was finished. It was all lovely and new and clean - marvellous.

It didn't really take some of the strain off us, the fact that there was a big hospital and more room, because they needed a lot of nurses and an awful lot of our work was with geriatrics. And they used to assess them and sometimes you just could not cope because you only had the patient's husband or the family to fall back on, so they had to go into hospital. Well, now, of course, they only keep them in hospital about a fortnight. In those days they stayed in for a time and they might die in there or they might get that much better and give the poor wretched family a rest. And then they came back. A respite stage.

Then the hospital brought in day cases, people with varicose veins, hernias: they'd go in in the morning and have the operation and then they'd stay there until they came round and they weren't haemorrhaging or anything. And then the ambulance used to bring them home. Well, you had to be there to welcome them home. I mean the poor relatives were in a terrible state; they didn't think they could cope but they had to. And then you'd settle them in and make them comfortable and the next day you'd go back and take them onto the books. But when you get three or four of them coming back, it's a bit tricky. It was like a recovery ward because some of those patients weren't really with it. They were still suffering from the effects of the anaesthetic.

Basingstoke's redevelopment had an effect.

We first became aware of what was going to happen in Basingstoke in the 60s. And then it sort of came down like a ton of bricks on us. But it certainly did improve things, because of course then we had this terrific overspill from London. But this didn't increase the staff.

Then they started 48-hour delivery for the midwives - they'd go in with their patients, in to the hospital, deliver them there and then they'd come out, back again to home. It took it off the home deliveries but they still had to keep these patients followed up, each 10 days or something.

The redevelopment of the town in the 1960s affected our workload quite a bit - I should think another 60 or 70%. Because before that you would only do the Borough, the urban patients. We always said in the old days, if you went out to a patient you asked them, 'To whom do you pay your taxes?' And if they said, 'The Rural District,' you said, 'I'm so sorry. I've got the wrong house,' or something. It was ridiculous. But they had a triple thing: nurses, midwives and health visitors, embodied in one person out in the villages. And she might have a couple of villages to do. And you didn't tread on anybody else's toes - oh no, that was not done! But when we were allotted to the doctors' surgeries, you went wherever the doctor's patients were. And I happened to have doctors that had been in Basingstoke quite a while. And they had patients as far out as Cliddesden and down beyond Farleigh Wallop and then they'd go out beyond Oakley and up to Upper Wootton and Ibworth. And all the way out into Sherfield and Turgis Green. Which is quite an area to cover. And we had quite a lot of patients in Basingstoke on the vast new estates.

When the doctors moved into Church Grange, they had ten doctors, plus three or four assistants and trainees and part-time people. The parking was appalling. We shared a building with people like Child Welfare. Bramblys Grange surgery was attached to us and they must have had about eight doctors. But we never had a lot of contact with them, though occasionally we used to have to relieve on the District for them.

We had a terrific number of clinics, immunisation clinics and child-health clinics. We used to do the immunisations every Wednesday afternoon, great lists of the babies, and the pre-school children. We would never do it unless you had a doctor in the surgery and a health visitor there, because most of them wanted to see the health visitor as well. They used to have as many as 40 sometimes. They used to start at two and we were on our knees by the time four o'clock came - screaming babies. We had a very busy life. And we were busy in the Community, as you say now, because you don't talk about a District Nurse, it's a Community Nurse.

I go about nowadays in the town and I can't forget a face. I don't remember names but I never forget a face. And these people come to me sometimes and say, 'Weren't you Sister Anderson?' And I say, 'Yes.' 'I thought you were. You used to come to Mum.' Or 'You used to come to Dad'. And then you'd be thinking, 'God, who is it?'

I retired from the District 12 years ago. And then I thought, 'I can't sort of stop like that.' So I went to Bell & Howell, did a year of industrial nursing. That was an eye-opener.

What did she feel about the way work had changed?

Well, I think, to be quite honest, there was so much bureaucracy attached to it, you felt as though you could never get on with the job. Because there was always, 'You must do this this way.' 'You must do this that way.' 'Change this and that.' And oh, the paperwork! Well that's not what nursing's all about. Community Nurses are saying that they won't strike, because of the patient, but they do feel as if they're going to stop filling in forms and all the paperwork. Now you see they've got little portable computers.

The nursing didn't change. It was a jolly good way of treating people. So many people wanted to be treated in their own homes, which is understandable. It was only until you couldn't cope with them, when they were falling out of bed or they were so heavy you couldn't lift them and move them. And of course you always had this spectre of bedsores. Up in the hospital they used to have terrible post-operative abcesses, stitch abcesses, and nobody could ever put their finger on the cause of them. One surgeon gave up and said, 'For heaven's sake, send them back to the District Nurse and let her see what she can do with them.' And we managed to cure many of them because it was one-to one. We had scrupulous guide-lines laid down about how you approached these things.

Six seven years before I retired we had pre-packed instruments, pre-packed syringes and pre-packed dressings and all those things which we used to get from a depot, the doctors would write the 'scrips' up and you'd get them for them, or the patients would get them. And we used to get the syringes from the Ministry of Supply. Whether you got all that you asked for was another matter. But all things like disinfectants you got from the Health Service. And great big bundles of incontinence pads, which we got from underneath the Church Grange surgery.

I started nursing when I was 16. It must have been about 1934. I wanted to be a doctor but circumstances were against that so I went in and did the next best thing. I went into nursing. And I never rued the day.

Penny Parsons

interviewed 2005

Penny has been a hospital nurse, a Medical Rep, a Community Staff Nurse for the Loddon Trust and is now a District Nursing Sister.

I love Community Nursing because you are much freer, with more autonomy, you don't have a vicious Ward Wister or a vicious Consultant looking over your shoulder as you do something, you have more room to make your own decision. And I love going to meet people in their own home, you can see how they function in their own home and you begin to understand the person as a person and not just a person in bed 15 with acute appendicitis.

Until 1994, when the Community Care Act came in, District Nurses had largely been doing Personal Care, washing and dressing and looking after people in their homes and what was the Home Help was there to do the housework. At the point I joined there were still some District Nurses who would go out and wash somebody's back. Why just their back I have no idea, but because they couldn't reach their backs we'd go out and wash them and we were still doing what we'd call Social Baths, people who just needed a bath. Quite quickly that stopped. District Nurses were no longer doing Personal Care, because it was deemed that you did not need to be a qualified nurse to do that and it was taken over by Social Care and Social Services. The only time we might get involved now is in the very late stages of a terminal illness when, because of pain and perhaps moving people, you need to be a qualified nurse because you can move them more sympathetically. That's been a huge change, the level of care that we now take in the Community; we're looking after some incredibly ill people in the Community, when 10, 15 years ago they would have been in hospital or in some other setting and so our skills are becoming more and more sophisticated all the time.

Sometimes people's expectation of what is available in the Community doesn't match the reality of it. People have to pay for Social Care, and District Nursing is free, There are two possible areas of friction for Nurses in the Community. I often say when people are terminally ill, 'We understand that it is your express desire to stay at home throughout your illness, and we would help you to achieve that in every way we can; however, sometimes symptoms and your condition necessitate you going in, because we cannot offer you a 24-hour service, much as we'd like to. So there may be a time when we say you'd be better off going into hospital or the hospice.'

The other area, which I wholeheartedly support, is the introduction of our Zero Tolerance Policy, set down by the Trust, that Community Staff will not be subjected to abuse of any kind. So we have the right to say, 'I'm sorry, because of x amount of risk factors, that we have assessed, we will not come into your home.' We now have the backing of our Trust and our manager to make us safer in the workplace. That can cause conflict because people still have the mindset that Doctors, Nurses, Specialist Occupational Therapists, Physios, will put themselves in any situation because they have a Duty of Care to do it and sometimes people do not understand that their home, they themselves or whatever, has been assessed as being too much of a risk for staff to visit.

The greatest pleasure I have in being a District Nurse is when people say 'Oh, thank you very much for doing everything you can'; it's a feeling that you've helped improve their lives in some way. Whether because you've cured their leg ulcer or you've made them become self-caring, looking after their own illness, whether it's diabetes or arthritis. And it's also knowing that the family appreciate that you've gone that extra mile in keeping people at home when they may have, ten years ago, been in hospital.

To give you some idea of the grades of staff in the Community I'll start from the sort of bottom up - and forgive me, girls, if any of you read this!! There are non-qualified staff who are very important to the team. They do things like going out and taking blood pressures and some have been trained to take blood tests, they do eye drops and they do simple dressings. Often when a wound has got to a stage where it is nearly healed, a Health Care Assistant will go out and do the dressing. Once they have been supervised by a qualified member of staff, they are deemed to be competent to do that task; it is much more task orientated.

Then you come on to the qualified - but generally newly qualified - Staff Nurses, who may not be very experienced in the Community, and they will, often under the auspices of the more experienced staff, perform more complex care than the Health Care Assistants, so they may well take on the more complex wounds, they may help people sort out their medication, for insulin and things like that. Then G Grade Sister - or the Charge Nurse it could be if it was a man - is the manager of the team, and has the responsibility of ensuring that 'the correct skill mix' goes in, so that an appropriately trained, qualified and experienced member of the team performs the appropriate task. Often terminally ill people have multifactorial aspects going on, so it may be appropriate for the senior person, often the District Nursing Sister or the Senior Staff Nurse to go in, assess, regularly reassess, monitor and evaluate.

Not only is she responsible for that, she is responsible for looking after the roster of when people are on or off duty, she has a responsibility to make sure that the paperwork is all up to date and that people have received the statutory training. We like to encourage people to do additional training, to keep them interested and motivated. The Trust views the G Grade Sister, or Charge Hand, very much as the manager of the team who has the clinical lead as well but is there to manage the whole team overall, whereas Senior Staff Nurse is not so much involved in day-to-day aspects, like doing appraisals or recruiting staff, but will often be there for clinical expertise.

The National Average is about 70 people per District Nursing Sister's caseload. Some of those people will need to be seen twice a day, others will need to be seen, say, once every three months for routine catheter change. Two new people on a caseload could double your work because of their needs.,

As far as I know, all District Nurses are employed by a PCT (Primary Care Trust) and we are contracted by a particular practice or surgery to work for them. We are accountable to the doctors, because we are supposed to be working in partnership with them, but our actual managerial responsibility is with the North Hampshire PCT.

People get referred to us in numerous different ways; often the hospital had a patient coming out of hospital and they find out which GP the person is registered with and contact the District Nurse. Often the GP will directly refer somebody because they realise their needs can only, now, be met in their own home. It can sometimes be the patients themselves or their carers or it can be a Care Agency that are performing the Social Care but realise now that there is a Nursing need.

We work in partnership also with Consultants, Physios, Occupational Therapists, Continence Advisory Service etc. because we should be offering what this Government calls 'a seamless care', in other words the patient is not supposed to see where one part of the care finishes and another part begins. Because the patient is with the GP, the GPs still have a great say, not in the nursing care itself but in the way that the care is co-ordinated. They can often be the Gatekeeper for many services, get the admission, get them referred to other services that we can't. But sometimes it feels that the sway of power is still with the GP.

The skills the District Nurse has now have developed significantly. Research and, practice have moved on, When we first started treating leg ulcers, back in the Dark Ages of the early 1990s, we literally just stuck dressings on top and hoped for the best because we didn't understand what the underlying cause was. A leg ulcer is a symptom of an underlying problem. Now we have developed much more sophisticated ways of diagnosing and treating it and you have to have additional specialist training for the four layer compression bandaging system, with regular updates. If you get the compression bandage too tight you can cause arterial insufficiency and severe problems to the leg. We also have Doppler training, assessing the arterial and venous workings in the leg to diagnose the problem, to make sure you are treating it appropriately.

We are doing chemotherapy in the home - we just wouldn't have thought about that 10 to 15 years ago. Managing people with central lines, drips that go straight into the heart, looking after those lines, flushing them once a week, or giving them regular chemotherapy, putting it up, putting it down. Now the latest shift is looking into managing people at home with the Chronic Disease Management, often very complex care and needs. I think they'll try to make us much more holistically- rather than disease-orientated. I was trained to do venopuncture and when I first started in the Community that was quite a rare thing, but now our Health Care Assistants are doing venopuncture as well.

The District Nurse, as part of her training as a Health Visitor, has also been trained to Nurse Prescribe, which means that she can prescribe from a limited amount on the National

Formulary, largely for dressings and other simple agents, like simple pain killers, and some laxatives. I've done the Extended Nurse and Supplementary Nurse Prescribing course, which means I can prescribe from a much larger range from the National Formulary, which is being continuously updated and I can prescribe some antibiotics in certain circumstances and a bigger range of painkillers. I can prescribe freely within the limits of a care plan written up by the doctor, so it's a three-way agreement between the doctor, the patient and myself. It may be prescribing things like diuretics, for a patient in heart failure. The only drugs that you can't use for a care management plan under Supplementary Prescribing are Scheduled Drugs. I believe that is being looked into but it would necessitate a change in the law, the 1968 Medicines Act. I can truly see that with Chronic Disease Management part of my additional training - another six months, a degree level module - could be better utilised than it is now.

There is a time of change at the moment. I went to a conference on 'Modernising District Nursing, Liberating the Talents of District Nurses' attended by people like myself, a District Nurse, a clinician on the ground, and by Managers of the service, so we were looking at it from two different levels. The managers of the service were saying, 'Yes, the District Nurses have got to change, because we've got to meet the ever-changing health needs of the population, to be more proactive and reactive.' The ordinary District Nurse, like myself, was saying, 'But how do we manage this, how are we going to achieve this with no additional training or no additional staffing?' So I think there is a dichotomy of feeling. I feel that District Nursing is forever evolving and if we have to take on Chronic Disease Management to prevent people being readmitted to hospital, we have to skill ourselves up to meet those needs. However, there will always be those other traditional District Nursing rôles, people are still going to be terminally ill, people are still going to become diabetic, even more so and need training in their diabetes. People are still going to have leg ulcers, people are still going to need Continence Assessment, particularly as an ageing public, so what I refer to as a traditional District Nursing rôle is still going to be there. I think we will need to learn to adapt to meet the changes coming along.

A Specialist Continence Adviser

Valerie Bayliss

born 1954   *interviewed 2005*

Valerie was appointed to a new post at Basingstoke District Hospital, where she set up a Clinic, but later she moved into the Community as a Specialist Continence Adviser and was able to liaise with other Community staff.

In the early days I felt worried that many people must be giving out information that was not particularly evidence based, just what they thought. Certainly in latter years we have discredited quite a lot of the information that was given out at that time. There was a Continence Adviser not very far away who told everybody with a catheter to have 4 grams of Vitamin C every day and the doctors were prescribing it and the patients were buying it. Four grams of Vitamin C is a huge amount, if you had a cold you wouldn't take any more than a gram. It cost a lot of money and when they actually looked into it there was no evidence base for it, it didn't do the patients any good at all. So there is a real moral responsibility within me to know that what I'm telling people is accurate. We should be able to say, 'This is the research that backs it up.'

Now we can look up Forums on the Royal College of Nursing's website for all sorts of specialities, where you can not only talk to colleagues and find out who's doing what but actually look up the research that underpins it as well, so you don't have that awful isolation any more. While I was once the only Specialist Nurse in the Trust, now there are probably 30 or 40 Specialist Nurses in Basingstoke alone, with all sorts of rôles, dealing with leg ulcers and wound care and breast care and lymphodaema, which is the swollen arms after a mastectomy.

Specialist Nurses were a cheap option, but they were also somebody from a different background; whereas the doctors were taught to analyse and diagnose and treat, we also had a caring component to our rôle, which is becoming far more autonomous still. The European Working Time Directive says by 2009 all doctors mustn't work any more than a 48 hour working week and there is no extra money in the pot and there aren't enough doctors in training anyway to replace those doctors that are currently working more than those hours. So they are encouraging the use of Specialist Practitioners, Nurses and PAMs (Professionals Allied to Medicine, such as Physiotherapists and Occupational Therapists) to cover a lot of the tasks that the doctor used to do. Now HCAs (Health Care Assistants) do urine testing and take blood pressures and take temperatures and pulses and supervise intravenous infusions if they are trained to do it. They tend to be trained on a task-by-task basis, as well as studying for NVQs (National Vocational Qualifications) so some Health Care Assistants can do quite complex jobs. But we're going to be desperately short of staff, because where are we going to get all the nurses from? If we're taking over part of the rôle of the doctors because we haven't got enough doctors, somewhere there's going to be a gap.

I think people will look at nursing differently in years to come, more professional than vocational, with more of a career structure. But it was a shame they got rid of the State-Enrolled-Nurses because they were good, practical bedside nurses. We still need people at the bedside.

The management gets restructured in the Health Service about every five years and most people don't take a lot of notice, though it does change your job title, it does change your grading, it does change your salary a little bit one way or another. I've been a Staff Nurse, I've been a Sister 2, I've been a Sister 1, I've been a Number 7, I've been an I grade, I'm going to be an 'Agenda for Change' band. It doesn't actually make any difference to what I do but they do like to have a reorganisation now and again. I've been managed by Matrons, I've been managed by Nursing Officers, I've been managed by non-nurses.

But what made the difference to how we deliver care is not management change but the acknowledgement that we need evidence to underpin practice. That has improved patient care and even saved money, because if you've proved that a certain piece of care doesn't work you won't do it any more and if you've also proved that a certain piece of care will work, you do do it. When I first trained, people used to have leg ulcers from their ankles to their knees and I can remember putting honey and oxygen or egg white and oxygen on them. Leg ulcers were very expensive in terms of people's time because the nurse would go week after week after week and they'd just break down again. But they've discovered now it's not just what you put on them, it's how you bandage them, so they've got this layered bandaging system, which actually heals leg ulcers.

Thirty years ago, if somebody had a cholesystectomy and they had a drain in, you lifted their drain bag six inches for three days until it was on the top of the bed and then they took the drain out. We just did it because we were told to. You wouldn't do that now, you would not take a piece of action without thinking through why you were doing it. I think that's why Specialist Nurses have evolved, because we've shown we're capable of providing the sort of level of service that the patients want.

Once patients wouldn't have questioned what we did. I can remember slapping the most bizarre things on people's wounds and it could have been strawberry jam for all they knew but they'd never question it, whereas now people know what's being done to them and why and what is the best treatment. Now at least most people can go into a consultation saying, 'I've read this on the internet, can you give me your opinion?'

The Family Planning Clinic

Dr Gill Williams

born 1939   *interviewed 2002*

The doctor who trained me in family planning told me that when she went into a family planning clinic at Portsmouth in the 1950s, people threw bad tomatoes at her - which seemed archaic to me.

When we came to Basingstoke in 1966 there was a vacancy in the Family Planning Association clinic which was held in the old Bramblys Grange. The Family Planning Association was a charity, and the chairman in Basingstoke was Mrs Queenie Roberts, the wife of a solicitor in the town. I took a Friday afternoon session once a week. The children's dental clinic was on the ground floor and we were on the upstairs floor, and the smell of ether pervaded the clinic by the end of the afternoon. The doctors and the nurses were paid but all the other helpers were voluntary. I think they were

called lay workers. And they all wore hats and they weren't ordinary hats, but elaborate hats you'd wear for a wedding. It was terribly formal and old-fashioned.

The very first day I did a clinic, one of these lay workers came up to me and said, 'I hope you won't give the patients any advice until they've done their duty.' I said, 'What do you mean?' And she said, 'Well, until they've had their children, of course.' This was 1966! We were actually allowed to give family planning advice to married women even if they hadn't had children, but we weren't allowed to see unmarrieds. We could see pre-marital women, as long as they had their wedding arranged.

The Family Planning headquarters were very powerful. You had to go on courses and the training was excellent, very advanced for the time. We were taught how to teach, and we were videoed teaching - this was the 1960s/70s - so that we could see our mistakes. At one training session the Director drew a sieve on the blackboard and he said the patients were overflowing the sieve because we weren't seeing enough patients and it was our job to get them through the sieve for advice. I said that the patients didn't want to go through the sieve and weren't coming for advice because they couldn't see their need. That argument still rages today.

Bramblys Grange house (see page 6) did have the old house atmosphere. It had an amazing staircase. It was rather like Chineham House was, in those days, big rooms and very high ceilings. And I think there were sash windows, and bare floorboards. The heating wasn't terribly adequate and the sound-proofing wasn't very good. And we just had a screen that was falling over and it was all fairly primitive. In the very early days at Bramblys Grange, the patients wore stockings, they used to have to sit in the corridor in a line with their stockings, rolled down to their ankles so that it was quick for the doctor. These things come back to you.

When I started, the methods offered were just condoms and pessaries, diaphragms or the rhythm method, but it was mostly the diaphragm, so the women took charge of the contraception. The coil - IUCD - had a long history, going back to days in the desert when they put stones into camels' uteri. But it gradually got more sophisticated. I think it was first used in England in the 1930s but didn't become popular until the 1970s. Later, copper IUCDs were introduced and were much smaller, and eventually progestogens were put in the devices, so hormones were released gradually. And of course all the stock - the caps and condoms - we had to carry a lot of stock and we always had to lock it away.

Sometimes there were people walking up and down outside, deciding whether or not to come in. At first family planning advice wasn't given on the Health Service. It was all private and the patients paid. But of course when I started it was just beginning to change with the advent of the pill and then the Abortion law. The pill changed everything. We were constantly busy. The Family Planning Association bought 8 Fairfields Road and ran the clinics from there and started up a Youth Clinic for unmarrieds. There was a wonderful retired missionary, Dr Snow, who had worked in India all her life, and when she retired she lived at Privett, and she used to run the unmarried clinic. When the clients did marry, they used to bring her pieces of wedding cake. She was most amazing. She was a tiny little person, lots of fun. And a very sharp voice. But she was wonderful. She taught me so much. I gradually took over the youth clinic from her.

In 1974 family planning was taken over by the Health Service.

The Family Planning Association couldn't agree the price with the Health Service for 8 Fairfields Road, so they really went in opposition. Some people still paid and some people went to the Health Service clinic, which was run above Church Grange surgery, because by that time Bramblys Grange (the house) had been demolished and Church Grange and Bramblys Grange (the Health Centre) had been built. Dr Burrell's practice asked me to do locum work, and then I became a partner in 1975 and did a lot of gynaecology and family planning, because I was the first woman doctor in that practice.

The Health Service opened clinics elsewhere in the town, first in a council house in Oakridge and then at Chineham House in Popley. The health visitors would bring some of the poorer people. There was a lot of counselling involved in family planning, and with the poorer people we very often had to persuade them to use family planning. There was a domiciliary service. Dr Isobel Gibson used to go round to people's houses. Gradually vasectomy counselling came in and the Family Planning Association did that, with Dr Chris Everett doing the operation. He eventually bought the Fairfields clinic and ran it himself as a private venture, and then they bought a house in Skippetts Lane.

The doctors like me did the counselling for couples, which was quite interesting. Somebody took a knife to me once. His wife had dragged him along. And occasionally you'd get people whose marriages were breaking down and it would come to light as you counselled them and they'd have a humdinger of a row in front of you. People came requesting abortions, which as a Christian I found very difficult. And then the British Pregnancy Advisory Service started up a clinic. I think they had premises in Church Grange. Dr Isobel Gibson worked for them. Patients were referred to London and Bournemouth for abortions.

There was a positive element too

Of course we were also involved in helping people who wanted babies. You could do the very first sort of steps, on keeping a chart of their cycle, sort of thing, but not very much - I found that very frustrating but of course once I went into general practice I could do more.

The initial consultation would be fairly lengthy. And also people did come for second opinions from their GPs, with discharges, aches and pains, and later they'd come for routine smear tests, which caused quite a lot of annoyance with the GPs because they started being paid for doing smears, so if it was done by someone else that was not a good thing. I trained quite a few of the GPs in family planning in their time as trainee GPs. In my era they used to come mainly to the Popley clinic for experience in putting in coils. And I think most GPs were family planning trained.

The Baby Clinic

Dr Michael Williams
born 1930   *interviewed 2001*

There was a children's welfare clinic held at Church Cottage. My mother was one of the volunteers who helped at these sessions. Dr Hilda Hunt was its delightful and very popular children's medical officer. There were very few women doctors at that time.

Betty Godden
born 1927   *interviewed 2001*

I've helped at the Baby Clinic for 18 years, since I gave up teaching. Miss Alice Hunt had helped there for many years, probably since she retired from teaching at the High School, where she had taught me. As she worked on her own, I asked if I could help and eventually I went every week for many years. Miss Hunt gave up when she was about 90 and she lived to be one hundred.

The best change has been the scales. When I started there were two sets of scales which had a scoop to put the baby in and a set of weights, the constant changing of which made them very insecure for the baby. The newer scales are electronic, they register the weight automatically and can be changed from pounds and ounces to metric weight at the flip of a switch. I think the electronic scales were partly funded by the money saved through selling cups of tea to the mums.

I had to give up weighing the baby with the old weights, it was too much for my back, so I did the register. One volunteer registers the babies and the other records the weight of the baby on their record - the mother always puts the baby in the scales. We feel we are helping because it does free the health visitors to talk to and advise the mothers. We had one or two mums once come from another clinic, who commented that at the other clinic the health visitors had hardly any time to talk to them, as they were so busy doing everything.

At one time we could sell different powdered milks and vitamin drops. Now they can only buy it at a reduced rate if they have tokens or Family Credit.

It's entirely up to the mums how often they visit the clinic. They don't have to come, but normally they come during the baby's first year. It then slopes off. Some come back a little later because they are expecting their second child and wish the toddler to get used to seeing other babies, which is a nice idea. At one time, we had nine mums who had their first babies about the same time. They'd come week after week and enjoy the gathering, making an afternoon of it. We were concerned that if all the second babies arrived together the clinic would be full with nine toddlers and nine mums and babies every week. That doesn't happen very often now. The clinic was held upstairs for years and mums had to leave their buggies downstairs - if not padlocked, they could be stolen. The style of buggies has become so much larger recently and, the clinic being held in a ground floor room, it soon gets overcrowded.

I don't think the babies have changed; but the attitude towards them has. Feeding on demand is the in thing, whereas a generation back babies were fed at six, ten, two and six o'clock on the dot; now if a baby opens its mouth it has to be fed. One of my hobby-horses - children wanting everything on demand. The mother can't exactly be blamed, because she's been advised to feed the baby whenever it asks. So they grow up expecting to eat and drink exactly when they want to and to do what they like when they like!

The mums generally find help and reassurance at the Baby Clinic and enjoy coming, and it's not only mums who come - many dads who can get time off work more easily bring the baby, and in some cases it's always the grandmother or the grandfather that regularly attends.

The St John Ambulance Brigade

In 1952 the County Ambulance Service took over responsibility for running an ambulance service for the town, but members of the Brigade continued to act as attendants. The Brigade met at the old Oddfellows' Hall in Victoria Street until the building of their own St John's Hall, May Place.

The Red Cross

Kathleen Laws

born 1918   *interviewed 2001*

I've been a volunteer at the Red Cross for 20 years now. Before I went there, it had been at Chute House and before that it was at the Haymarket - well, not the Haymarket, the Grand, I think it was then. But it's been up at Bramblys Grange ever since I've been there. My job is just issuing medical aid stuff: wheelchairs, commodes, bedpans, raised toilet seats, bath seats, walking frames. The only thing you have to have a doctor's certificate for is the wheelchair. That's for insurance purposes. Everything else you just come in and say what you want - if we've got it! That's the trouble, these days. The Red Cross only supply wheelchairs and walking frames now. All the rest of the stuff comes from a place called JDS at Gaston's Wood. And the idea is very good, the idea is you fill in a form when you issue the stuff, you send it to JDS and they see what you've issued and they're supposed to replace it. But I'm afraid that doesn't work. At the moment, because it's the end of the year, they start a new year in April, we've only got one commode up there, well that's not much good for anybody. We haven't got quite a lot of the stuff that we should have. Everything that comes back to us has to be sent back to JDS to be cleaned. We used to do it but we're not allowed to now. And we send it back with another form, so they should replace that, you see.

I like the job because you meet people. I quite look forward to it. I think a lot of them come up there to have a chat and talk over their troubles, they come up there and tell you their life history. Occasionally you get somebody very rude but most of them are pretty good. But the only trouble is the

wheelchairs, they're only allowed out for three months, supposed to be, but once people get hold of them they don't want to let them go and we have to keep on ringing them up and trying to get them to bring them back. Sometimes they bring them back with good grace and another time 'Oh, no, no, we're not using it. It's out in the garage'! You know. I get a bit stroppy. I think, 'Well, they should think that there's other people wanting it, shouldn't they?'

When I first started, there was a Miss Balfour and a Miss Pilkington at Winchester and a van driver. You used to order what you wanted, on Wednesday, and it came every Friday. Well, now, there are far more people working there and you order something on the Wednesday but it only comes a fortnight Friday - if they've got it, which nine times out of ten they haven't. There is a Red Cross at another centre in Basingstoke, the Gillies Health Centre on Brighton Hill. If we haven't got anything we ring up Brighton Hill and if they've got it they can let the people have it. We work together but they seem to get more stuff - well, I don't think they do as much trade as we do.

In 2005 Kathleen Laws received the Band of Honour for 23 years service with the Red Cross.

Joan Bull (left)

born 1921 *interviewed 2001, 2003*

I did 17 years with the Red Cross; even when I worked away from Basingstoke, I still kept it going. I started as a VAD, did the exams for First-Aid, Nursing and Welfare and I was a Section Leader quite soon, then Assistant Commandant, and then Commandant and then Group Leader. Every weekend, practically, you were on First-Aid duty. We used to go to Farnborough Air Show, that sort of thing.

When the Queen carne to Basingstoke, principally to see the new AA building, I was asked to go as a representative of the Red Cross. All the various organisations were situated down the bottom of the town. I was near the Bata shoe shop, about where the Sports Centre is now. And the Queen came, but I - me, who's always liked talking and so on and so forth, and done lectures and everything for the Red Cross, was struck completely dumb! So the Queen said 'How are you?' and I think I said, 'Very well, thank you.' 'You must be kept very busy.' 'Yes,' and looked at her with an inane grin on my face. But she was very sweet and very approachable.

Hospitals

Nurse training

Rita Phillips

born 1942   *interviewed 2004*

When I started nursing, there was a two-year training for State-Enrolled-Nurses and a three-year training for State-Registered-Nurses, as they were then known. You were a full-time student nurse and a full-time working nurse, which is very different from training today. We went through a formal training with tutors, in the classroom with lectures and presentations and homework and we also had the job on the wards, looked after by mentors and Sisters and senior staff. Then you would be eligible for promotion from Staff Nurse to Sister, from Sister to Matron or whatever.

You worked and you studied at the same time, but you got on-ward experience whilst you were training and I think that's invaluable. At the Hampshire Clinic we do have student nurses from the NHS. Some of the nurses in the first, second year, come here to do a six-weeks' placement and there's so much they haven't seen. I just think they miss out a little on that hands-on experience. There's nothing quite like remembering the first patient who dies. There's nothing quite like remembering the first patient who vomits all down you. It's something that you don't forget.

I think modern day nurses also miss out on the care that we always used to have as student nurses. We always had a Home Sister who looked after us. If you weren't well she would be there for you. We weren't allowed out late at night. We had to go to Matron on a Monday morning to ask for a late night pass and we were only allowed one late night pass a week. You had to be in by ten o'clock and by the time you'd got out of the cinema and run up the road to the Nurses' Home you'd be late, so you never saw the end of the film. It wasn't really worth while going to the cinema. But they cared for you and you knew where you were. There was always somebody that would listen to you, and you were protected from late nights, not getting enough sleep.

We had to get up at five o'clock in the morning to be down for breakfast at half-five, and we had quite a considerable distance to walk from the Nurses' Home to the hospital, but we had to be there for five-thirty, for breakfast. And because the Matron was Scottish, it was porridge with salt on. And we had no choice. We stood and stood until she came in; it was 'Good morning, Matron.' 'Good morning, nurses.' We then had to say grace. We then sat down to our bowl of porridge with salt on that would 'see us through the day'. And we thought she was taking care of us.

We had to go to lunch when she went to lunch. We'd all stand and wait for her to come in. We'd say grace. We'd all sit down and have our lunch. And woe betide you if you didn't eat it, because how could you work on an empty stomach? 'Why aren't you looking after yourself?' And we laughed and we moaned about it but at the end of the day the discipline was no bad thing. And I think that's sadly lacking today. It's very different today.

Nurse training these days is more gearing nurses to be managers, to be specialist nurses in their field. I think a lot of the values of older nurses have gone, the standards are different; it's very sad, but I think it's a fact of life, 'That's somebody else's job and not quite mine.' We used to have nursing auxiliaries, we used to have State-Enrolled-Nurses, we used to have State-Registered-Nurses, and it was very much part of the whole. We talk about looking after patients holistically, but part of that holistic look was around nutrition and the basics. And in those days Sister would always serve lunch and you would stand and queue up as the nurse to see what Sister was going to give Mrs Smith in Bed One. She's on a light diet and you'd be given boiled fish, creamed potato and maybe two or three peas. And then it would be your responsibility to take it over and feed the patient and bring it back to Sister to let her know that she'd eaten it. Because if she hadn't eaten it, that was a worry, and we'd need to look at how and what we'd give that patient to build her up, to make her strong, to get the nourishment she needed. And I think these are the things that get overlooked now, sadly.

Mr Frank Tovey

born 1921   *interviewed 1996*

The idea of 'Nursing 2000' was that nurses would be more or less trained in college throughout their training with odd spells on the wards, whereas before, of course, they worked on the wards and went to the Nursing School from time to time, so they had a 'hands-on' experience. I think that gave rise to a much better type of bedside nursing, but it is quite true that, with the development of techniques, one did need a more sophisticated type of nursing for intensive care units and for special treatments. The idea of 'Nursing 2000' was that nurses would be in college and just spend spells in certain wards to get experience, but it meant that we did not get the 'bedside' nursing - the shaking up of pillows and making sure the patients were comfortable, that I was really used to. I think this has resulted in too high an educational level being required for nurse training, so that girls, perhaps, who have no high educational qualifications but have got the care for patients, what I call the 'bedside care', have been unable to meet the educational requirements and we have lost them to nursing. But I am not really qualified to talk all about this

Valerie Bayliss

born 1954   *interviewed 2005*

You get a diploma now and it only takes you a year to convert it into a degree.

The Shrubbery

Dr Sandy Smeaton

born 1916   *interviewed 1998, 1999*

The Shrubbery Maternity Home was well-established by 1949. Apart from an outside stairway as a fire escape, there had been no structural alterations. There was no lift. The labour room was a small upstairs room with the nursery adjacent, the other bedrooms had become two- and three-bed wards, the conservatory had four beds and the billiard room could accommodate six beds, when not in use for staff parties at Christmas. On average, there were about 20 beds, but in later years the bed-occupancy seemed to depend on demand. Particular credit was due to Miss Bainton, the Matron, and her midwives for a very good service under what would now be considered very primitive conditions. It must be remembered that sterile supplies and disposable syringes were still some years away.

The Shrubbery

My predecessor, Dr Kelly, did not do obstetrics, so his expectant mums were seen by the midwives and only saw a doctor in an emergency, probably in labour and late at night. When I arrived in 1949, I started my own ante-natal clinics at the surgery and deliveries in the Shrubbery. At the Shrubbery, patients were under our care throughout and we had total control of the treatment. There were six or eight doctors coming in each day, looking after their own patients. The nurses had to adhere to instructions laid down by each individual doctor, and it surprised me that there were never any upsets with staff or the matron. No one did more for the smooth running of the Shrubbery than Dr Bowen-Jones, who was always available for emergency anaesthetics at any hour of the day or night. We were all very conscious that the nearest Consultant unit was 18 miles away in Winchester.

However, there were still quite a lot of normal home confinements. These were mothers who for some reason didn't like the idea of going into a maternity home. They much preferred to be at home. The pressures in the end, I think, came partly from the husbands who found themselves in this very awkward situation of sitting downstairs, smoking or whatever, waiting to hear what was happening upstairs. so the husbands generally tended to favour the mum going into the Shrubbery, where they handed over their wife to the midwives with a great sigh of relief. Understandable, I think. The pressure also, I think, came to some extent from the doctors, who found that, if there was any mild complication or forceps or an anaesthetic required, this was much more easily dealt with at the Shrubbery than at home - because at home the lighting was never all that good.

'They used to say some girls went straight from the Shrubbery (Girls' High School) to the Shrubbery (Maternity Home)!

'No gooseberry bushes or cabbage patches in Basingstoke; babies here were born in the Shrubbery - more refined!'

Jessie Jack

born 1918   *interviewed 1992*

When I was at the Shrubbery, staff came and went. There was one night Sister and one relief, so this meant there were two night Sisters, they would have had four staff on at night. If someone had to be transferred to Winchester, a member of staff would have to go with them. Eventually there were more than two night Sisters when the bottom floor opened and there had to be a staff midwife upstairs and a Sister downstairs, where the labour suite was.

There were 14 beds when I first went there, 32 beds was the ultimate. The old billiards room became another five- to six-bedded ward. We often had ante-natal patients with blood pressure, in for a long stay or in for a rest before having their babes. But that became a ward and of course then the labour suite was built.

The day staff covered from 8 am to 9 pm. We had a half day a week and a day a month off when I went there. They wouldn't do it now, would they? The night staff worked from 9 pm to 8 am. Later, when I was the boss, I did a round after I had taken the report with the night staff and said goodbye to the patients that were going home that day. Then I would go down to the clinic. The junior staff would give out the breakfasts, whilst the senior staff would be bathing the babies. The babes would go out for a 9.30 feed; some mums fed them and some didn't. All the feeds were supervised, especially those that were feeding their own. The bottle-feeds were straightforward but the mums needed help when they were breast-feeding.

At ten o'clock, the mums had coffee. In the early days, the babes were back in the nursery, but eventually we found the mums liked to have them all day long and it meant you could introduce demand feeding. The bottle-feeders seemed to last but when the mums were feeding their own, unless you test-weighed them, you didn't know how much they had had. So then we let them all demand feed; this meant that when they were hungry and were sniffling we let them feed. It seemed to work. Some staff were against it at one time but then they realised you didn't have crying babies if you let them demand feed. After lunch, it was the two o'clock feed. When it ended, you took the mums' pillows, leaving just one, and they went to sleep on their tummies. They used to go out like a light.

Now visiting time was three o'clock, so they had an hour's sleep. Visitors would come up to 4.30. We didn't have open visiting. It is a bit more difficult when the doctors are doing their rounds. An afternoon visit, then the husbands in the evening. If for any reason the husband was not around, then the mum or someone could visit in the evening. And then they had tea. They usually had tea whilst their visitors were there, then supper and the 'ten-o'clock feed', so they were all tucked down by 10.30. The babies all slept in the nursery at night.

That's mainly the nursing side. In the early years the mums got up, but you had to keep a check on their tail ends and all that, so they had bedpans, but after 24 hours, eventually they were all trotting about and having a bath, dealing with themselves. This was nice for the staff.

The cleaning of wards was done by the juniors. There was a ward domestic who did the floors but the tops were done by the nursing staff: lockers, bed ends, backs of the beds. Every ward had a little pedestal basin in it and a treatment room. And the food, that was all cooked on the premises, downstairs in the kitchens so it all had to be carried upstairs.

In the early days, the laundry used to go to Alresford, to the nursing home Matron used to have. The babies' laundry was all done on the premises. Oh, it was lovely. Mrs Rolfe did it all. Out on the line blowing away. It was all done with soap flakes, it wasn't done with harsh detergents; but then of course they realised it had to go to a laundry. It did not seem the same, it wasn't Persil whiteness, I can tell you that.

The old house had been converted into a maternity home with some ingenuity.

In the old days there was just the labour ward, but leading off it had been a bedroom and a dressing-room. The bedroom became a three-bedded first stage ward. What it meant was that in the first stage of labour we could bring them along and they could be labouring along quietly there with us in and out, and then into the labour ward. Now the labour ward only had one bed, it was very well equipped. Next to the labour room was a sterilising room with the steriliser and an autoclave for dressings. Opposite the labour ward was the nursery. So it was a very easy area.

When you went up the front stairs of the Shrubbery, as you came to the top, there were three steps going up into the suite. Then the other way was the wards. Obviously you had to get patients down from the labour ward to the wards and there were these three steps! No way could they walk. There were two rings underneath the top step, as you turned right there was a banister, and hanging from the banister was a ramp. So when a patient had to be transferred to a ward after being delivered of a baby, we used to lift the ramp off - hook it on to these rings and then the two of you would push the trolley down the ramp. The poor soul at the bottom was pulling and the one at the top pushing and gradually you would get them down, the woman on the top hanging on for grim death - but no wonder us nurses had bad backs!

There were times obviously, before we had the new suite built, when two babies were arriving at the same time. We did have a small room with a bed in and we used to cope but it was, fortunately, very rarely that we had to deliver in one of the wards. I did. I remember delivering big twins in this ward, a boy and a girl, 8lbs 9oz and 9lbs. I knew she was going to have twins but I didn't know they were going to be so big. The little nurse that was with me said, 'Sister, there can't be

another that big,' and the mum said, 'Well, there is something else in there!' They were beautiful babes, they really were.

It is difficult to say how many single mothers there were in the early days because they used to go to St Thomas's Lodge in Darlington Road up to six months before the baby was due. They would stay there until they went into labour, then they transferred to us. They came to us as an ordinary booking, had their babe, then went back to St Thomas's for another six weeks. During this six weeks they had to make up their minds whether they wanted to keep their babies, have them fostered or have them adopted. So we lost them once they left us. They were put into a normal ward with the other ladies, it did not matter to us. They were called Mrs Jones or Mrs Smith or their Christian names if they preferred. What they told the other ladies was entirely up to them. The Registrar would visit them to register the babies. They were allowed six weeks, 42 days, to register the baby's birth, that was the legal requirement. Now the only way that little girl could register that baby in her boyfriend's name or the baby's father's name was to take him with her. When the Registrar arrived, I used to go into the ward and say, 'The Registrar is here, ladies, anyone want to come and register your baby?' But I would have already said to the single girls that if they wanted the boyfriend's name on the certificate, they would have to go down to the office with them or they could register there.

The other mothers had a sympathetic ear for them because they knew what they had been through. They knew their labour had been just as difficult as theirs, if it was their first baby.

1000th baby born at The Shrubbery, Dr Radford Potter extreme left

I delivered just over a thousand babies at the Shrubbery and in total 2,000, because I have my old register before I came to Basingstoke. As a pupil midwife, you delivered a lot of babies that you could not count. Your exam was based on a book of 26. You would have had to book them, admit them and do post-natal, you followed them right through and it all went into your book, your exam book. You were questioned on that.

Looking back at how babies and nurses were dressed.

When I think of the difference with what the babies used to wear and now! They used to have little vests and binders round their tummy buttons. Little frocks and mittens, and the tiny babies used to have bonnets on. Disposable nappies were unheard of then. When I think of it now - we had the domestic, May, who did the laundry. We used to have to brush all the dirty nappies, then she used to soak them in a big trough sink and boil them, so white. Her linen was lovely. The babies used to look so nice. The babies looked cared for, it looked as if the mothers cared.

When I first went to the Shrubbery I think I wore a checked uniform with aprons and short sleeves, frills. They were material caps, not paper. Then, when I went into Sister's uniform, it was navy blue with long sleeves and cuffs. Of course, dog collars, as we called them, and the caps all went to the laundry. We didn't have to deal with them. Navy-blue belts and a buckle. Miss Bainton gave me my buckle, but it was silver and pointed, so I had to be careful wearing it in the nursery with the babies. I used to put it round the back. Then paper caps came in, which I suppose was sensible. The old ones had to be all gathered up, then we went to pointed ones which were folded over, then the paper ones came in. Now of course they don't wear caps at all, do they, or aprons?

Matron and Jessie

We wore the bib aprons with our Hospital badge, and usually a gold pin like a tie pin, and a union badge. The Junior Staff, Patsy Crownan, was a State-Enrolled-Nurse, so she wore green. The auxiliaries wore white coats in the early days but now I think they wear a sort of biscuit check. The auxiliaries were very good girls. They took up the meals and they took the babies out for feeds. They did flowers, bedpan rounds, and they did some of the ward cleaning. We also trained them up in the labour ward. They were not there to deliver but to help us. So, when the baby was born, we would wrap it up and give it to the nurse, who would show it to the mother. Then she

would put the baby into the cot. Then off she would pop and make us all a cup of tea. A lot of the mums were smokers and would be dying for a cigarette. I used to have to tell them, 'I can't let you smoke in here because of the cylinders, the gas and oxygen.' In the middle of the night I used to push them onto the landing so they could have a cigarette there before they went into the ward. Creeping into a ward in the middle of the night. The other mums used to rouse but sometimes they used to say, 'When did she come in?' It was about 3 am.

In the early labour, for pain-killing they had syrup of chloral, which was a draught, but when the pains began to be well established we gave them pethadine, then the inhalation of gas and air.

Where the RSPCA animal charity shop is used to be Brooks, the florists, before it became Thoroughgoods, and we used to have all our fresh vegetables from them. We had them from the gardens first of all but when the National Health took over, the gardener was made redundant. It seemed daft to me, because all those fresh garden vegetables - well, time marches on and you have to go with the crowd.

We had single rooms. Upstairs, there were three bedrooms. When I first went there, there was a cook and her two children in one room. There was a single girl in the middle room, she came from Hook/Fleet way, then in the other room were two domestics. Matron was on the same floor as myself. Downstairs, there was Fairfields wing with three rooms; the bottom room was Matron's, next door was mine and next door there were two staff nurses.

Christmas was a time to remember.

Mrs Burberry used to come, to go into the garden to see old Mr Cooper. He was a great man. At Christmas-time he used to come with his wife and help decorate. They used to do the hall and the dining-room, but we used to do all the wards and the clinic, we used to have a great time. It was a lovely house to decorate because it had wooden panels and there was a lovely wrought-iron fireplace in the hall with a copper hood. It was beautiful. In the dining-room that eventually became a ward there was another one.

We all used to arrive on Christmas morning to have breakfast together. No-one used to have the day off. The only ones that used to go off eventually were the night staff. We used to give Matron her present and she used to give us all little individual ones. All the mothers and the babies had presents. All day long we were entertaining the patients, really. If we were busy with deliveries of babies, well then we did what we could.

Early in the morning, ten-ish, the doctors used to come. Not particularly to do rounds but to wish the patients 'Merry Christmas', and they used to bring their kids. Oh, it was great. Then the Salvation Army used to come. If it was nice and sunny and crisp, they would be out on the lawn to play carols and the patients would have a whip-round for them. If it was raining, they would come into the hall. There was a well that you used to look up, and there was a sort of balustrade where, if the patients were up and about they would stand and watch. When they had finished, we used to give them mince pies, coffee, squash, whatever they wanted.

One of the doctors used to come to carve the turkey at dinner. In the afternoon the patients could have as many visitors as they wished and we gave them tea. Oh, it was murder at times, because the children came. But Matron was very understanding. They used to sit on the beds and run around but they all had tea with Mum and Dad, whoever had come to visit. Cook always made a gorgeous cake. Matron or I, whoever was on, would cut it. Everyone used to have a piece. It must have been a massive thing - when I think of it now! I always say, 'If the boss eats well, the rest of you eat well,' - and we did.

We did not go off duty till nine at night and then we would walk home. Then on Boxing Day most of us would have a half-day. It was the fairest way to do it.

Jean Holloway

born 1938   *interviewed 2001*

I was a theatre nurse at the 'Mini' hospital when it opened in 1969. At the time, maternity work was still done at the Shrubbery, though if the patients needed caesareans they had to go to Winchester. And then Mr Payne came to the 'Mini' and he set up a little theatre in the Shrubbery, and I used to be on call, and I used to help him there with the caesars. I did three in one day. The Shrubbery was lovely. I had two nieces born there. A lovely little place.

Val Cole

born 1940   *interviewed 1995*

When I had my daughter up at the Shrubbery, they said, 'Oh, if you have any more children they'll all be born up at the new hospital,' but they never were. It took a long time to build it. The Shrubbery was very nice. It was friendly.

Ante-natal care was a lot different from what it is now. There were no scans or anything like that. I suppose we had more or less the same as they have now but obviously not so modern. We used to go to the doctor's once every so often and you saw your midwife, you had to go to the Shrubbery for check-ups about once a month.

Joan Metcalfe

When I came to have my fifth baby in 1949, I could not believe it. We were given £4 a week for six weeks. This was because of having a young family and having a home birth. So from having to pay them, suddenly they were paying us.

The Isolation Hospital

Dr Sandy Smeaton

born 1916   *interviewed 1998, 1999*

The interesting thing is that the Isolation Hospital was never really in use in my time in Basingstoke because of the success of the immunisation procedures post-war. The immunisation of children must be one of the most cost-effective health programmes ever undertaken.

The Isolation Hospital was refurbished in the 1950s to become an annexe for Hackwood Road Hospital but it was never used as such. It was used by the Health Authority's Finance Department for many years until it was sold for office development.

Hackwood Road Hospital

Mr Frank Tovey

born 1921   *interviewed 1999*

The Cottage Hospital was very much a Basingstoke hospital. People took a great interest in it. Financially they made a very big contribution to the running of the hospital.

At the beginning of the NHS the Women's Institute made cretonne curtains to go round the beds.

Dr Sandy Smeaton

born 1916   *interviewed 1998, 1999*

In 1949 there were some 30 beds, mainly in two wards, an X-ray room, an operating theatre and the Board Room which was used as the out-patient clinic most of the time. The operating theatre may have been primitive by modern standards, although it seemed perfectly adequate at the time. Accidents were dealt with in a small room off the entrance hall, when it was not being used by the anaesthetist. It was round about 1956-57 before Hackwood Road was extended and proper consulting-rooms and treatment-rooms were established. This made a very great difference.

Before the introduction of the NHS in 1948, most provincial hospitals were staffed by the local GPs. Over the years some of them had acquired expertise in a particular field and were able to give up general practice and concentrate on their chosen speciality in hospital and, hopefully, private practice. Higher qualifications, as we know them today, were not essential except in surgery. With the advent of the NHS this was to change. Those in post in 1948 were given consultant status, but all new appointments had to have the approval of the relevant College.

Ex-Service doctors were offered a 'study grant' on demobilisation, and many of them took advantage of this six months to study and take a higher qualification which would enable them to apply for one of the many new consultant posts in the NHS. It was hoped that, in time, the standard of hospital care would improve and be more evenly spread throughout the country.

It appears to have been the practice, going back many years, for consultants, at that time called 'honoraries' from the London hospitals to venture out of the Metropolis into the Home Counties and beyond to do out-patient clinics and operating sessions. So in 1949 specialists still came from

(TO THE EDITOR)

Sir, May I call the attention of the readers of the Hants and Berks Gazette to the memorandum published by the British Hospitals Association, with the concurrence of the Ministry of Health. The memorandum stresses the fact that the new services will be administered not from a centre but by local Committees of Management composed of public-spirited men and women giving voluntary service. In this way local knowledge and experience can contribute to the new service no less than in the past, and the channel is still provided through which local people generally can take a personal interest in the Hospital's affairs. In welfare of patients the Hospital will need just the same personal interest and sympathetic care as at the present time, and there will be many ways in which the patients' physical and mental well-being can best be promoted by voluntary effort. The visiting of patients - particularly those who have no friends or relatives in the immediate neighbourhood - and bringing them in touch with other contacts from the outside world suggest themselves as fields in which there is considerable room for continued service. In other ways the patients' stay in Hospital can be cheered and progress encouraged by personal help.

Although the full maintenance cost of the Hospitals will be a public charge, provision has been expressly made by the National Health Service Acts for the new Committee of Management of Hospitals to enjoy the use of 'free moneys' to be spent as they think fit for Hospital purposes. The Hospital Committee of Management will have at its disposal income from past endowments, and will be able to receive and hold future voluntary gifts. None of these gifts (including annual subscriptions and donations) will be transferable to the State, or used to meet the Hospital's cost of maintenance. On the contrary, the Committee of Management will be free to apply them (subject to any express wish of the donor) in providing additional amenities for the patients and staff, or in supplementing in other ways the resources of the service.

It will be of the greatest benefit to the Committee if the Hospital has at its disposal funds which can be used at discretion to meet the infinite variety of special circumstances and peculiar needs which are bound to arise, and which may not easily or appropriately be met through the expenditure of public funds.

The first and most obvious object is the welfare of the patients. There will be additional comforts and amenities which the Hospital for one reason or another will not be in a position to provide from its budget and which can be provided for by gifts of money.

By the use of their 'free' funds the Committee will be able to develop new welfare activities and constantly to assist in raising the standard of Hospital care. The Committee will also be able to provide for additional comforts and amenities for the members of the nursing staff.

In view of the above facts, I would most strongly appeal for a continuance of the interest and generous help the Hospital has for so many years enjoyed from the people of the town and district.

Yours faithfully,

R F NEWMAN

Chairman, Basingstoke Hospital

London for a day once or twice a month. I am sure they all enjoyed their day in the country, each having their catchment area for private practice, and not infrequently returning home with a couple of dozen eggs and a brace of pheasant - very welcome when food was still rationed. GPs undertook after-care. But within a year or so of my arrival in Basingstoke, the London consultants had gone, to be replaced by the new appointments to the Winchester Group of which Basingstoke was a part. They all had the necessary qualifications, but were very short on experience, compared with their predecessors. Our 'local' consultant was Cuthbert Roberts from Winchester, a general surgeon who had out-patient and operating sessions weekly and covered for emergencies.

Barbara Green

born 1921   interviewed 2001

After training at Lord Mayor Treloar's Hospital, Barbara was a nurse at Newbury and then in the Emergency Medical Service at Winchester during the War, before working at the Hackwood Road Hospital.

I was a theatre nurse at Hackwood Road when the National Health Service first started. Before that, the hospital relied upon help from people to run, I think it was in a trust or something. They got money from carnivals and voluntary contributions, and if we had patients in, or visitors, and they were pleased with what they'd had done, they would pop some money in the little voluntary boxes that we had in the hall and in the wards, for donations to help the hospital. Early on the first morning of the National Health Service, we were doing out-patients injections - they used to call in and have their penicillin and stuff, before they went to work - and we heard some noise going on and there was a couple of people going round picking up the boxes, and emptying them. We didn't see any of that money, and we were most distressed.

There weren't a lot of nurses in Hackwood Road, because we were only a small hospital. We all worked hard, and it was a happy place. We weren't allowed out after ten o'clock at night. I was in the nurses' home. Well, nurses lived in. Uniforms were done for you. We had clean uniforms - clean aprons, sometimes twice a day. Hats lasted a week, and your uniform dress lasted a week, providing it didn't get soiled. You had black woollen stockings, and when I've had a hole in my stocking at the heel, I've painted my heel with ink, so that the hole didn't show, because you'd get into terrible trouble if the hole showed. We had red capes, navy blue outside and red in. They were lovely and warm. On night duty we wore monkey jackets to keep us warm. It wasn't very hot on the wards in those days. They were centrally heated - I suppose these great big pipe things that used to go round - but it wasn't very warm. The patients had woollen blankets on their beds, and later a sort of cottony, honeycomb arrangement. They had hot water bottles too.

At Christmas-time, of course, all the poor little single jobs had to stay there. We used to make sure the hospital was full at Christmas. Not empty, full. So that people who were poor could have a good Christmas; and little children especially that were poor were going to have a good time. They had lovely food, and happiness, and presents. Now they try to keep wards empty. You mustn't be ill at Christmas now.

At harvest festivals, we used to have vegetables and fruit brought into Hackwood Road Hospital, our little Cottage Hospital. And there was also a Pound Day some time during the year, autumn, I think. All the children used to take a pound of rice or a pound of sugar, anything that was a pound they'd take to school and that was all brought to the hospital.

Once a year there was a Town Hall dance. We all went in evening dress, of course. Dr Bowen-Jones was a lovely man, and he always wore white gloves as well. There were doctors and nurses, physios, all of those people. I don't know whether domestic staff came or not. We had lovely times. Lovely food, little titbits and cakes and things. And drink, of course.

There was a regular routine.

Night duty was very peaceful. You sat at the table in the ward, and there was a little light, and you heard them all snore, and cough, and scream, and cry, and you just went over to them and helped them. There would be about two nurses, a junior and a senior, on a ward. But then you used to have what we called a 'runner', a junior nurse, and if you were getting a bit behind, the runner came in and helped. It was a ward of 25 beds. We used to go round to each patient about every quarter of an hour to make sure they were asleep.

We woke them up taking their temperatures, then we used to give them their early morning cup of tea, and then we did a bedpan round and they were washed. We used to give them all their breakfast. Sometimes they brought in eggs and we put their name on them and boiled them. And toast, bread and butter used to come up from the kitchen. We used to boil porridge. If we'd got any theatre patients, we used to do them about five o'clock, make them comfortable, change their nighties and wash them thoroughly, make their bed and make them nice. Night duty went from eight o'clock at night till eight in the morning. And with two people only you couldn't have a rest. You couldn't go off and have a couple of hours kip. That wasn't done.

When the patients had had their breakfast, it was cleared away, and then ward cleaning began. We had to push all the beds into the middle, then sweep along the backs. We put red polish on the floor, then we had a dumper to go backwards and forwards to rub it in, and then we had another piece of blanket on another big dumper to polish it. We used to love doing it, because it made our waists nice and slim! And we used to slide it up and down, up and down. We used to damp-dust the backs of the beds, so that they were all clean, no dirt or dust or anything; then we pushed them back and did all through the middle. The flowers would be done, and put round the wards, because they were taken out every night and put into the sluice. After that, the patients had their coffee; then we did a bedpan round, and then they were all tidied and cleaned up, and the dressings began and the doctors' rounds. When all that was finished, we prepared the patients for lunch.

Sister served the patients' meals. Towards the end of the time, it used to come up in a big trolley. Sister would do it, and the nurses would take it round. The patients were all sat up ready for it, and waiting for it, and if someone couldn't eat we used to feed them. We made sure they always ate their food.

After lunch, they were all ready then to have a nice sleep. And we did another bedpan round. And so it went on. We had to clean the bedpans. Wash them thoroughly by hand - no gloves - we weren't allowed gloves, because they were an expensive thing to buy. And you had the sputum mugs to clean, which was quite a joy, I can tell you! So we did all these dirty old jobs. Today everything's thrown away, disposable. So the girls needn't bother too much to grumble.

When you were on the wards, you gave injections. You had a quarter of morphia in a little tablet. You had a little Bunsen burner and a teaspoon and some water. You put your tablet in the spoon, you mixed in the water, and then you boiled it over the Bunsen burner. You had to be very careful you didn't burn your fingers, because you'd tip the tablet off. Then you drew it up in the syringe and gave it. The syringes were not pre-sterile, you had to boil them. And, when the needles had barbs on the end, we used to have to sharpen the barbs.

For urine testing, we used to have a Bunsen burner, and a test tube, and we used to hold the test tube with a spring peg, and according to what you were going to do with it, you'd add a little something to it, and then you boiled it. If it was orange you had a lot of sugar, if it was green you had a little, and so on. So that's how we did the sugar test. We didn't have any bits of paper for acid and alkaline, so we had to put drops in to do that.

If you wanted anything at any time, you rang the GP and he'd be there, quickly. And if there was an operation over here at Hackwood Road, you rang the surgeon who came from Winchester, and he used to come within half an hour. So that by the time you'd got the patient ready for theatre, the surgeon was there. And if you were on call for theatre, the anaesthetist or someone would come to the nurses' home, or, I believe, to your home if you were married and lived outside, and pick you up and take you back to the emergency. If you were in the cinema with your boyfriend, and there happened to be an emergency in the evening, your name would go up on the screen, that you were 'Wanted in the foyer, please. Emergency!' And you'd leave everything and just go back and do your job, till about three, four, five, any time, but you didn't get paid for it.

In theatre, when you did an operation, you got your list, you took your tray from the instrument cupboard, and you filled it up with the instruments you knew you would want to do the operation, and then you boiled them. And set your trolley. Before you set your trolley, that was all disinfected, of course, they were all very sterile. Although they do say today that boiling's no good, that they have to be autoclaved at high rates. Sometimes if we were in a very great hurry, we would pour methylene spirits all round bowls of sterile water and light them. And that sterilised them.

When we were in theatre we washed all the swabs. Packs, even if they were pus-y, we washed them, and boiled them, and cooked them, and they were used again. Nobody suffered a bit. And also we had to scrub and clean everything,

obviously, and we used a lot of disinfectant. The theatre floor was always sluiced all over with a lovely hot cocktail of phenol, which is pure carbolic, Dettol and Lysol. We used to make this up with boiling water from the sterilisers, and throw it all over the floors and the open radiators, a wooden shelf, and we all smelt of disinfectant: the whole hospital smelt of disinfectant. It doesn't today. But it's the only thing that'll get rid of the bugs, isn't it? There's plenty of germs about now. There never was that amount, never as bad. We never grew bugs at Hackwood Road.

We also had to patch the surgeons' gloves. We washed them after the theatre and patched them with another glove. We used to just pinch the bits off the other gloves, and put the stuff on and stick it on, leave it to dry. Like a tyre-kit, really. But if the surgeon's first finger had a hole in it, we didn't do that. That was put on one side, that was no good. Because, you see, they dissect a bit with their finger. Well they used to, I suppose they still do. Mackintoshes that we put on the top of the patient before we put the drapes, they were all washed and cooked, sterilised by us.

When a patient died, the routine was to cover them and leave them half an hour. And then you laid them out. That meant washing them, cutting their nails, and putting cotton wool in their mouths to fill their mouths out, and make a little smile, and cotton wool up their noses, to make them look pretty. Well, I had to put cotton wool in every hole, really, so that nothing happened. And then, if they were children, specially, we used to put their hands together, and put a little flower in their hands. I don't think they do that these days. Undertakers do it, I was told. Not a very pleasant job, but I'll tell you a very funny thing. I was laying out a man with another nurse. We turned him on his side to wash his back, which the other nurse did, then we turned him over. Well, she bent down to pick something up as we were turning him over, and his hands flopped over, hit her on the head and she fell forward and knocked herself out. So he knocked her out when he was dead! Knocked her out for a few minutes. And I was left in limbo, really, because of course, I couldn't move, I had to scream for help, for someone to come and help pick her up.

Hackwood Road Hospital's not there any more. It's all pulled down, gone. I think they should have done a little more, had it as a little Nursing Home, or as a Home For The Elderly or something, because it was a beautiful little hospital. It was beautifully built, and perfectly all right, no need to pull it down. I was very sad about it. Very sad indeed.

Jack Clarke

born 1925   *interviewed 2005*

In 1959, when Rooksdown moved to Roehampton, I opened a small laboratory at the Cottage Hospital. Before that, doctors used to send samples on the bus to Winchester to be analysed at the County Hospital.

Bobby Pearce

born 1924   *interviewed 2002*

I was paid for one dental session a week, which covered anything I might do on call for the hospital as well as the Basing Road Hospital. It was essentially an out-of-hours appointment, after all the dentists had gone home. Usually, the Out-patient Sister on duty would provide aspirin or veganin to the patient but, should she regard the situation as serious, she would telephone me at home. You seldom had a person that was a stranger to the town; most of the emergencies were bleeding from the sockets of teeth which had been extracted earlier in the day or from wounds where sutures had come adrift. It seemed to me that at that period nearly all the dentists were ex-directory.

Injuries to teeth and gums provided most of the problems on Saturday evenings, following excessive enthusiasm on either Rugby, Soccer or Hockey pitches. I think on average I probably got six calls a week, unless it was Christmas Day and Boxing Day, as well as Christmas Eve, when all dentists seem to have a day off for shopping. That was my busiest time. People that might have put up with discomfort at any other time of the year were determined not to have to do so over Christmas.

I also had the opportunity to use the operating room facilities at Hackwood Road Hospital for difficult cases: multiple extractions, cysts and the extraction of impacted teeth etc. The session, with a consultant anaesthetist, commenced at 8.30 am. When each patient had been operated upon, they would be wheeled to their respective wards, male/female, and the fittest patient would be asked to leave the bed and sit on a chair so that the unconscious patient could recover. With any luck, the dental patient would be sufficiently recovered by 10 am to enable the bed occupier to return.

George Doel

born 1918   *interviewed 2001*

Matron at the old Cottage Hospital ruled it with a rod of iron. It didn't matter if you were a patient, you had to do what she said. No sitting on the beds, either. She used to come round, everybody used to quiver.

We had such great nurses up there, with their starched bonnet, starched collar, starched belt, white apron, navy blue or light blue and striped dress, black stocking, black shoes.

Vicky Simmons

born 1920s   *interviewed 1995*

I fell off a ladder out here, looking after kiddies, and cracked my ribs. They took me by ambulance to the little hospital that was there at the back of Webbers. And my doctor had to come out on a bike to see me, because you couldn't see anyone else, you see, you went to this little hospital and waited there to be X-rayed and things like that and they dealt with it all.

Jo Kelly

born 1947   *interviewed 1999*

As well as all her time in Lord Mayor Treloar's Hospital as a child, Jo also spent time in the Hackwood Road Hospital.

I had my tonsils out in June, 1953, when I was nearly five. At that time they didn't like taking your tonsils out until you were five, but I kept catching colds, and they couldn't operate on my legs at Treloar's if I was having colds. So they actually took my tonsils out just as I was about to be five, not because they were hurting particularly but because they didn't want infection, so 'Whip the tonsils out!'

So I went into the Cottage Hospital up by the park to have my tonsils out. I did very well there because I was the youngest on the ward. They had Carnival early that year because of the Queen being crowned, and the Carnival Queen came in and I had the Carnival Queen's bouquet, so that was very good. But the bit that I really remember is that you were allowed to have jelly and ice-cream. My cousin, who was six years older than me, had been doing some jobs and earned some money. And he went to the Kiosk, the little shop which is now the flower shop by the gates of the park, and bought me a choc-ice. It was sixpence, in a silver and turquoise paper, and he handed it in to the hospital, because he was only ten, so they wouldn't allow him in to see me. When my mother and his mother visited the next day to see me, they asked whether I'd had a choc-ice, and I hadn't, so my mother asked the staff and a choc-ice had not arrived, so that was the end of my choc-ice - or so everybody thought.

Unfortunately, my aunt went back and told my cousin and he turned up at the hospital and demanded to see the Matron, and I think that they were so surprised that there was this young child that would speak to nobody except Matron,

that Matron decided that it might be something very important, so she had better see him. Well, he went in and demanded an investigation take place immediately because he had spent sixpence on a choc-ice for his cousin. And who had had his choc-ice? I never had the choc-ice. But a letter was written apologising to my cousin and that was one of his first victories. I don't know whether he got his sixpence back or whether they actually bought him an ice-cream as well, but he did get his letter. And we had forgotten all about that until his mother died a few years ago and he went through her stuff and amongst all the papers that she had kept was his letter from the hospital, apologising for the loss of the choc-ice. So I think that must have been an interesting hospital board-meeting, when that was brought up on the agenda.

Ann Broad

born 1935   *interviewed 2003*

In the early 1960s, when I was in my mid to late 20s, I spent two or three days in hospital having a D & C. Whilst I was in there, my husband Michael and a friend went and bought a new-to-us second-hand Morris Oxford Traveller and they brought it into the area outside the ward window so that I could see it.

After I had the minor operation, my stomach was painful, as was to be expected, but my back was also sore down the spine. When I mentioned it to a nurse, she looked and found the skin had been scraped off various parts of the spine. How, I never discovered!

Basing Road Hospital (Cowdery Down)

Rita Phillips

born 1942   *interviewed 2004*

Cowdery Down Hospital was known as the old Workhouse in Basing Road, and I started an evening and night shift work there. It was a very large austere building, very much like an old workhouse, although clearly they'd worked hard to try and improve the image. The front of the hospital was the brick building which mainly had the overspill or the patients recuperating from the Cottage Hospital in Hackwood Road. And then at the back there were the two 'Huts', which were 'Bramley' and 'Candover', and they each housed about 35 to 40 patients: females on 'Bramley', the gentlemen on the 'Candover' ward.

The nurses in those days were all female. There were very few male nurses around at that time. The only male nurse that I came across in Cowdery was a lovely gentleman called Albert, who was a nursing orderly and, I believe, worked for a funeral director during the day - so he had a vested interest in both ends, really!

We had a Matron in those days but she was always located at Hackwood Road Hospital. One of the senior Sisters would come out throughout the night hours to visit us and make sure that we were caring for our patients and behaving. We'd get a call from Hackwood Road to say 'Sister So and so is on her way.' We'd all make sure that everything was up and running as it should be. I wouldn't say they were dragons. I think they had a very difficult job. They worked extremely hard. We worked very hard hours, very long hours, the standards of nursing in those days were very high and very difficult to maintain and I think the Sisters and the Matrons had quite a hard job. The responsibility was for the whole hospital, for the patients' care, for the nurses, and in some respects for the consultants and the doctors as well. So they were strict but I think it was just making sure that standards were kept to. I'm sure that most junior nurses would respect them and the job they were doing. They were very much there for the nurses, very interested in our welfare, making sure that we stayed well, that we were looked after as well.

If you had, for example, an appendix removed, you would be in hospital at least 10 to 14 days. And that was the expected norm. So the operation would take place at Hackwood Road. Two or three days later, the consultant or the surgeon would come in, and say 'This patient's well enough to transfer over to Cowdery Down for convalescence,' and there you would stay for 10 to 12 days until it was right for you to go home. The nurse here would be responsible for wound care, for general hygiene, for preparing the patient for discharge, making sure she had organised a district nurse to call, that the local GP was informed that you were going home, that the social worker would be involved or the Almoner as it was then. These are all things that have faded away now and it's very different from discharging a patient from hospital these days.

But the main purpose of Cowdery Down Hospital was to house the something like 80 to 100 elderly patients who probably didn't have a family - and really, Cowdery Down was their home. Most patients, regrettably, stayed in till they died. So this tied in with the old memory of the place as the Workhouse. There was a very very strong feeling with the local people that if you go into Cowdery Down you actually never come out.

What about visitors?

Visiting was very strict in those days, literally between 2 and 4 in the afternoon. After lunch the patients had to have a rest, whether they wanted it or not. It was snuggle down, be comfortable and have an afternoon doze. At two o'clock the ward would open. And at four o'clock it was the junior nurse's responsibility to ring the bell to make sure that all the visitors left. Because by that time the patients would have had enough or be tired. Though if someone was particularly sick they would have 'open visiting', which meant that the visitors, the family, could come at any time. And that would include nights as well. It's a very different concept to now.

Today times are restricted again.

We had hospital chaplains who would travel between Hackwood Road and Cowdery Down and they would visit frequently. Church of England, Catholic, Jewish, whatever. We would have names of the appropriate vicar or priest that was needed for whatever denomination of religion the patient had. They played a very important part in patient care.

The dentist would come too. Particularly on the elderly ward because, obviously, as you get old, your teeth do tend to deteriorate. Or patients would be transported to a dentist. So we would know when the dentist was coming and who he or she was seeing. Probably the optician too. Thursday afternoon was 'Hairdressing Day' when the local barber would come and the men would all get a haircut, and a hairdresser came on the female ward and everyone looked very smart on a Friday morning. Nurses used to do toenails and fingernails - we're not allowed to do that now - and just generally make the patients look nice and feel presentable.

We had quite a lot of local volunteers from Basing, people who would come out on a voluntary basis and do the teas for us, bring the library books round, come and do the flowers. There was always a lot of local input, a lot of charity work really, because they weren't paid, this was all 'Let's go and help the people of Cowdery Down'. There was quite a steady stream of fairly regular helpers that the patients looked forward to, because they built a relationship up with them and I think nurses would probably have struggled a bit to do all those things, so they were very welcome indeed.

The changeover came very suddenly one Saturday in December. The night sister rang me to say, 'Rita, is there any chance that you could come in and help us tomorrow, being Sunday? Because we are going to have to transfer all of these patients and all of their belongings to the new hospital.' The very antiquated plumbing and heating system at Cowdery Down had given up.

Bobby Pearce

born 1924   *interviewed 2002*

As dental surgeon for Basingstoke, I was responsible for dentistry at Basing Road Hospital, which was the geriatric unit. There was always someone there that had denture problems. It was a sort of workhouse atmosphere, just several huts with about 28 beds in a hut. A lot of them were the destitute long-stay geriatric, often with what we call almost Alzheimers sort of conditions so they couldn't talk very clearly and there were long wards of them moaning from morning till night, and all of them needing medical attention. The nurses used to take all the dentures away from them every night, because otherwise they broke them. They put them all in the same bowl, but it was quite extraordinary how a person who has been wearing dentures recognizes them immediately among 20 others. I'm not going to attempt to describe how you take impressions of someone's mouth when they are lying in their bed and reluctant to have it done.

Park Prewett Hospital and Rooksdown

Chairman's address

The Chairman stated that in the first place he desired to convey a very hearty welcome to each and every member of the committee. They all realised what a very important part they would be taking in the administration of the benefits that ALL are now entitled to under the National Health Service Act, 1946. A number of them had served together as members of the Park Prewett Visiting Sub-committee and he appreciated the support given to him in the past. He felt sure that he would get the very closest co-operation and support from all members of the present Committee in their endeavours to make the service of this Hospital second to none. HMC (48) 1 and HMC (48) 2 had been circularised to every member. The special items requiring the Committee's immediate attention were on the agenda. The efficiency and success of the services rendered by the Hospital, with its many different forms of treatment, would, in some measure depend upon the work of the committee. The future policy and development of the Hospital and the services made available would again, to a great extent, depend upon the Committee's careful examination of proposals before them and their considered judgement. They all realised the powers within their hands and should all make very certain that such powers would be utilised for the benefit of the community in general. They were very fortunate in knowing that, initially, they had upon the staff of the Hospital, either in a full-time or consultative capacity, some very eminent members of the medical profession, in different spheres of treatment. During the war years the name of Park Prewett was known - and is still remembered by very many grateful patients. Competition was a very excellent way of promoting effort. If they could demonstrate, to both officers and patients of this Hospital, their determination to keep Park Prewett in the very front rank for the beneficial treatment of bodily and mental disorders, there was no doubt that they would have made a success of their work.

Extract from the Chairman's Address to the Inaugural meeting of the Park Prewett Hospital Management Committee held on 5th July 1948.

The Minutes reported that the Minister of Health had designated the Park Prewett Mental Hospital as a Mental Hospital for the purposes of the Lunacy & Mental Treatment Acts as amended by the National Health Service Act, 1946. The following groups of employees were to be designated as Mental Health Officers for the purposes of the National Health Service (Superannuation) Regulations, 1947: Secretary, Finance & Supplies Officer, Dep. Sec, Finance & Supplies Officer, Store Keeper or Clerk in Charge [Stores], Dispenser, Engineer, Asst. Engineer, Occupational Therapists, Laundry Superintendent, Laundress, Laundrymaids, Cooks, Asst. Cooks, Kitchenmaids, Housemaids, Messroom maids, Sewing Mistress, Seamstresses, Kitchen Superintendent, Wardmaids, Shoemaker, Butcher, Kitchen porter, Baker, Asst. Baker, Storemen, Coalman, Drainman/Gravedigger, Motor Driver, Sewageman, Sweep, Gen. Labourers, Laundrymen, Plantsmen, Under Gardeners, Poultry Women, Cowman, Farm Labourers, Shepherd, Farm Servant, Hall Porter, Messroom Attendants, Kitchenmen, Farm Bailiff, Gardener, Upholsterer, Asst. Upholsterer, Tailor, Pigmen, Carters, Joiners (Foreman), Painter (Foreman), Stokers, Tinsmith (Foreman), Bricklayer (Foreman), Fitter (Foreman), Plumber (Foreman).

At Rooksdown another children's ward was to be opened, due to the increasing number of cleft-palate cases and Tangier House, Wootton St Lawrence, was acquired for the nursing staff. A plan was submitted for the provision of a car park approximately 6,000 square feet, by the annexation of part of the pig field adjoining the Hospital main approach, at an estimated cost of £155. This is still a car park, by Harness House. Mortuary Refrigeration facilities had been advised by the man from the Ministry on his recent visit at a cost of £495. The Committee would consider further.

The Minutes of 6th September 1948 reported that the wards had competed for best garden and prizes were awarded. A free sweet ration was to be issued. Psychiatric clinics were now organised at Aldershot, Odstock, Park Prewett and Winchester. Twenty-four patients were to be sent on holiday in Switzerland, organised and paid for by the Swiss Red Cross.

Extracts from Park Prewett Hospital Management Committee Minute Book 1948-49

23rd June 1948
A recital of Old English Songs in Costume by Mary Bonin (soprano) and Daphne Ibbott (piano) was greatly enjoyed by 225 patients.

4th October 1948
A number of fractures of the femur were occurring during ECG treatment.

1st November 1948
Decided not to purchase a refrigerator for the Mortuary but to use solid CO_2.

This year the farm had won prizes at The Oxford Agricultural Show, the Royal County Show, The Royal Agricultural Society Show, The New Forest Show, The Romsey Show and the local Basingstoke Agricultural Show.

Cows in milk 31, dry 12; average milk production 64 gallons per day; 461 fowls, 323 pullets, 71 chicks, 109 turkeys, 330 cockerels, eggs 72 per day.

The Committee were informed that considerable extra duty had devolved on Mr E E Shorney, in the rearing of turkeys for Christmas. RESOLVED that the Secretary be authorised to allow one turkey for the personal use of Mr Shorney.

> This Minute was repeated the following year.

6th December 1948
Nursing staff: as from the 28/11/48 male staff should work a 48-hour week (2 shifts). After a deputation by representatives of the female nursing staff, it was resolved it should also be introduced for the female nursing staff.

English classes for foreign personnel have started, tutored by Miss K Phillips: three sessions weekly at 7s 6d per hour.

It is noted that Miss Pollock, Welfare Officer, holds a catering licence and with assistance it was sure she could manage to supply light refreshments to out-patients and visitors between 1.30 pm - 3.30 daily.

Dentures were to be provided for patients.

Since the 5th July to date the MoH had issued an ever increasing number of memoranda; 19 alone were laid before this committee today, including one with regard to Christmas Festivities!

2nd May 1949
A sculptor has been appointed: 2 sessions weekly, each 2 $\frac{1}{2}$ hours, £1 per session.

Owen (Don) Blissett

born 1930   *interviewed 2003*

One could literally describe Park Prewett as a self-contained village, with two rows of its own cottages situated just outside the main boundary of the hospital, in Kingsclere Road and Dunsford Crescent, together with the farm cottages within the confines of the grounds. It was a real family affair, when Dad worked the morning shift and Mum worked the afternoon/evening shift, the children were brought part-way to work with Mum and then handed back to Dad to take them home again.

The advent of the National Health Service on 5th July 1948 was good not only for the patients, but also for the staff, where improvements in terms and conditions of service were laid down. Whitley Council Handbooks listed rates of pay, terms of sick pay, holiday pay, compassionate leave etc, real 'bibles' for the Pay Office staff. One grade that I shall always remember being in the Ancillary Staffs' Handbook was that of 'needle sharpener' - no disposables in those days.

July 1948 brought into being the Health Services Superannuation Scheme, (I can't say 'It was the best thing since sliced bread', as that had not been invented then). This meant that all full-time employees aged 18 plus had to compulsorily contribute to the superannuation scheme at 6% or 5% of their salary or wage (my contribution was 1s11d per week), which gave them a pension, salary related, at age 60 or 55 in some cases and based on their years of service. In later years part-time staff had the option of joining the scheme; however, membership is no longer a condition of employment. I still have the original Superannuation Scheme booklet that I was issued with in 1948, price threepence, old ones at that.

In contrast to my early days in the Wages Office, when wages envelopes and the wages records were written in ink, (real ink where you dipped the pen in the inkwell and used blotting paper as well), this system was superseded by a Kalamazoo system, where indelible pencils were the writing medium, though eventually Biros became the 'in thing', refills for the pens, which were expensive, and could only be obtained from W H Smith on an official order; throwaway versions that we have today did not exist.

Twinlock displaced Kalamazoo, which in turn was displaced by Machine Accounting, using a Remington Rand machine. These latter three systems did away with the writing of pay envelopes, as the pay slip was produced at the same time as the wages record, and only needed to be folded and placed into a wage envelope, and finally we have the present day computer systems. Wages paid today are by electronic transfer - pie in the sky, possibly, in 1948 when only a few were paid by cheque and the rest were paid by cash in envelopes or by cash direct from a till. Pay parades were held in the Main Hall, attended by a pay clerk and the Head of Department of the staff being paid.

To sum up, I would say Park Prewett Hospital was a happy establishment where the staff were brought up to accept that 'if it was not for the patients, you would not be here.'

For myself, one lasting happy thing for me was meeting my wife on a blind date at one of the hospital dances in October 1950.

Mr Frank Tovey

born 1921   *interviewed 1996*

When I first came to Basingstoke in 1967, I would quite often do a mini-surgical round in Park Prewett Hospital. When the 'Mini' and later the main hospital were built, they and Park Prewett benefited by being side by side, with combined laundry services at first. The Park Prewett boiler house supplied heating for the 'Mini' and their parks management looked after the gardens. There was a good sports club at Park Prewett, with a golf course and tennis courts as well. The resident patients contributed to a lot of the running of the farm and they had a horticultural department with large greenhouses, beautiful flowers. The whole grounds were well planned so that there was always something flowering. There were industrial workshops where the patients made furniture and other things.

Bobby Pearce

born 1924   *interviewed 2002*

In 1951 the hospital was a 'locked unit'. Movement throughout the hospital was possible only with a male nurse, who ensured that doors were unlocked to obtain entrance and then relocked, having passed through. Most patients were suffering from senile dementia and were treated with mild sedatives. A minority were in a younger age group and were treated with a variety of therapies for schizophrenia, personality disorders and phobias. All wards, which were segregated into male and female areas, were equipped with both full- and half-padded rooms, into which violent patients were placed if they were harmful either to themselves or others. The entire hospital had been decorated with either dark brown or dark green ceramic tiles and the floors of the passages were of green and brown mosaic tiles. Most patients would spend their waking hours sitting on kitchen-style chairs against the walls of the main passages. A duty nurse could thus 'cruise' along the passages and keep an eye on 40 or 50 patients.

The dentistry one could provide was mainly for the relief of pain or infection; four or five patients in pain were priorities. If there were no emergencies, I was able to examine elderly patients for signs of dental problems, of which they were totally unaware. It was absolutely appalling there were people I saw at Park Prewett in 1951 that hadn't had a proper medical check-up, some of them, for 20 years and it was a dreadful situation. A great deal of time was spent extracting diseased teeth or roots. Theatre sessions would often involve the total clearance of all remaining teeth and roots for as many as six patients - this with the help of a consultant anaesthetist. It was possible in a few cases to provide artificial teeth. Often the provision of dentures had a dramatic effect on the demeanour of a patient, a re-establishment of self-esteem.

I continued my duties at Park Prewett Hospital for about four years; this seemed to be the average length of time for

The Pantomime 'Cinderella' at Park Prewett 1954/5

the visiting dental surgeons. There was always a sense of frustration at being unable to do more than the most simple tasks to help the patients.

Margaret O'Boyle

born 1935   *interviewed 1992*

My first sight of Basingstoke was in January 1953, by train. I was aged 18 and born in India. I saw the tower of Park Prewett and people said it was a mental asylum.

In 1958, when I was about 23, I was a secretary at Park Prewett Hospital on the administrative side for six months, while expecting my first child. There were tall, tall hedges around all the villas and iron railings inside. It was a focal point for Basingstoke socially and the big bands came, like Ken McIntosh, Cyril Stapleton, and there were evening-dress balls, decorations, lights. There would be a theme, such as 'Cinderella', with a coach slung across the ceiling.

If a patient had no family, the secretaries used to be asked to attend their funerals at the cemetery church, with numbered graves. No-one was buried alone, but it was very sad.

Kate Webb

born 1942   *interviewed 1995*

The patients at Park Prewett had quite a lot of freedom and they used to be in and around the spinney, which isn't there now. The spinney was a big square of trees which we used to play in and it really encompassed and surrounded a lot of the farming land that Park Prewett owned. We used to play there

and we used to meet many men and women who were going for walks. My parents were working on the wards. I used to go up to the wards to visit, when I was on my school holidays, and I got to know lots of the patients and nurses. We had a very happy time.

We had lovely times at Christmas, because my parents had to take their turns in working the Christmas shift. We often used to go and have Christmas lunch on the ward. We used to have great big trees and lovely lights.

There were a lot of Irish people there. Of course, the Irish are a very close community, so there were lots of people that we knew and got very friendly with.

The hospital was very big in those days, enormous. It seemed to go on forever. Even now, if you think about where the new Newbury Road is, that seemed to me to be the boundary, right over to the Aldermaston Road, and that's the whole estate - lots of wards that spurred off the main building and lots of villas. You would often hear about Villa 5, Villa 4, Villa 3, and they were units really for some specialised nursing of some kind. Some were for more severely mentally disabled people and some were for less disabled people, who could look after themselves up to a certain point.

Mental illness is something that's not very tangible. If you have a broken leg, everyone's very sympathetic, but if your mind's disordered it's sometimes very hard to see initially. Park Prewett was, and still is, the butt of many jokes, but people got used to it. I think it became quite an establishment in the town, and with the way the Health Service is going at the moment, people feel that it's been a security for many people who have been sadly disordered and a lot of people are concerned about that prop being taken away and they are just

pushed out into the community. Whereas, many years ago, Park Prewett was where you had to go if you were mentally ill, and perhaps that wasn't so good either, but they need to strike a happy medium somewhere.

Every holiday I used to come home and I actually worked at Park Prewett on the wards as an ancillary nurse. My word, that was an eye-opener! Having been around all my life, when you're actually in there working you really see what it's all about, but I thoroughly enjoyed it. I had a really good experience.

People died round me and I'd never seen a dead body. I was expected to lay these bodies out and to look after them. It was just an amazing experience.

Mrs Elsie Garnett née Evans 1911 - 1995

An appreciation by her daughter-in-law, Jane Garnett, 2005

Elsie Garnett had trained at Park Prewett in the 1930s and worked there till her marriage in 1939. When the National Health Service began in 1948, new rules allowed married nurses with families to work and nurses were encouraged to be recruited back into the service. So Elsie returned to work at Park Prewett part time. On May 9th 1952 Elsie Garnett was admitted to the General Nursing Council for nurses trained in nursing persons suffering from Mental Diseases. Full time work followed, where she progressed to become a Sister for many years, finally retiring on November 26, 1972.

Elsie's family and her work, where she cared for not only her patients but her colleagues too, meant everything to her. She was a wonderful person with strength of character and cheerful disposition, whose outlook on life was making the best of every situation. She always befriended young student nurses away from their homes, inviting them to tea with her family, as she knew only too well how lonely one could feel. Many of her fellow work-mates became lifelong friends.

She was always dedicated to making the lives of her patients as comfortable as she could, with fund raising events to raise money to purchase extras for the ward, such as different coloured eiderdowns and bedspreads to give patients individuality and brighten what was their home, as many were long term patients. She always worked at Christmas, with husband Tom and son Michael joining her for Christmas Day lunch on the ward. Taking part always in the Best Dressed Ward competitions held at the hospital, she and her staff were presented with the cup on more than one occasion. She gave heart and soul to her many rôles at the hospital, taking part in the nurses' races at the summer fêtes, dressing up in topical fancy dress at the many fancy dress

balls and taking the responsibility for patients on coach trip outings. Her love of dancing with husband Tom was much enjoyed at the notable Park Prewett New Year's Eve Balls and other dances held in the superb Park Prewett hall. On retirement, for many years she helped voluntarily in the 'Blue Room' at Park Prewett, where patients that were able could come for a coffee and a chat away from their wards.

The letter she received on her retirement from Park Prewett is testimony to the person Elsie was and that working at Park Prewett was not simply a job but a love and caring for people, especially those that were unwell and disadvantaged.

Pauline Deacon
born 1948   *interviewed 2005*

Susan Brown
born 1951   *interviewed 2005*

Our uncle, born in 1921, had been mentally affected by the First World War and was a patient at Park Prewett until 1997 when Park Prewett closed. At first they put a straitjacket on him, in a cell, he was very very disturbed, but as time went by the medication changed and he settled down. We went there every week from North Baddesley with our mother, father and Nan. It was quite a journey every week, in a car that often broke down. We left about half past three because he was worried about having his tea at four o'clock, having things on time was very important to him.

They used to give us children sweets and fruit. We used to sit in the main hall sometimes, but our uncle didn't like to stay in the building, even if it was very cold. We used to walk around and sit in the sports pavilion. Even though we were a bit frightened, as children, we used to go and look for birds' nests in the hedge or get conkers and we used to go into a small area where lots of marigolds grew. We did talk to our uncle, but he was very quiet. Sometimes we watched the archery and the cricket. He used to go to a little shop and buy cigarettes. He got some money from working in the workshop, making wicker stools, something he'd learned to do at Park Prewett. He sometimes went with other patients to Butlins for a holiday and loved that.

Visiting her brother was a big part of 60 years of our mother's life - every week until our father died and then once a month. For us, seeing Park Prewett again recently was sad but happy as well, reliving such a large part of our childhood, and now we are looking up everything we can find out about Park Prewett.

From the Rooksdown Club Magazine

Ian Riches
2005 issue

1953

There appear to have been a number of meetings in June leading up to the reunion. The Royal Naval Merchant School Band of some 30 members would play at the reunion. Lime Green Café would provide refreshments. Side shows included ring on the slide, bowling for a pig and a treasure hunt.

Rooksdown Was Child's Play

Rosemary Johnson
2001 issue

Rosemary was born with a birthmark which was later badly affected by radium treatment. She arrived at Rooksdown in 1951, aged 10.

I had many operations during the first six months and hoped they would turn me from monster to beauty. The worst period was when a pedicle from my arm was attached to my face by securing my hand to the top of my head using a plaster cast. This was extremely uncomfortable and made it impossible to scratch an itchy head. Fortunately, this lasted only two weeks when the plaster was replaced with a strap.

...The Reunions were always very good fun with all the cheerful people and lots of exciting activities. For a while I was in a wheel chair when the donor area on my leg would not heal. My friends pushed me around, getting up to much mischief by giving me high speed rides, particularly by releasing the chair at the top of the slope to the lower lawn. We were soon spotted by the staff and this exciting entertainment was then banned.

50 Years Ago: Rooksdown Reporting

2002 issue

A stranger to Rooksdown, paying a visit, perhaps, during the siesta hours in the summer, might have been rather startled to see a tall figure in the grounds viciously slicing the sleepy air with a lasso, but the habituees were undisturbed - though careful to keep well out of the range of the rope - knowing that it was only Dr Ralph Millard doing his 'daily dozen'.

The football season was rather late in starting at Rooksdown this year, as the one and only football was mislaid, but we are glad to say it is now being kicked around again. It is rumoured that it was eventually run to earth in the anaesthetic room where it was temporarily taking the place of the anaesthetic 'bag' that was being repaired.

Paul Evans
Born 1939

Apart from some initial ops for a congenital cleft palate, most of my treatment consisted of dental attention - as I outgrew my plates it became necessary to visit Rooksdown every year to obtain a new one. One of these initial ops occurred at Christmas time, having to arrange visits during school holidays. It was great at eight, spoiled to death! In fact, I believe I managed to wangle two further Christmas stays.

The years passed and I became so used to travelling back and forth to Rooksdown that in 1951 I was, at the tender age of 12, allowed to travel alone from Cardiff to Basingstoke, changing trains at Reading and hopping on the 137 to Park Prewett. I was so proud, booking myself into Rooksdown on that occasion.

Suddenly it happened - July 1952 - at 13 years old - I attended for one of my annual fortnightly dental visits, so I thought, but didn't walk out of Rooksdown till 5 1/2 months later. Sir Harold Gillies delegated my case into the hands of another Welshman from Llanelli, namely Jim Evans, who should have played centre for Wales as a safer pair of hands to be passed into could not be found. If Max Boyce from Llanelli has talent and a way with words, then Jim Evans from Llanelli was a poet with his hands where plastic surgery was concerned.

My one saviour at this time was an Aunt of mine who actually lived in Basingstoke, which is how I first learned of Sir Harold's whereabouts. She was a nursing sister at the "Main," and was my one visitor, did my washing and taught me that old truth of life - "there's stranger ones loose on the outside than those kept on the inside" - I think I met some of them at Rooksdown!

A series of ops followed and this young Rookie was befriended by a young orderly, Lil, whose sister worked as an usherette in one of the cinemas in Basingstoke. Whenever we went there we paid cheapest prices but were shown to the dearest seats. The programmes used to change mid-week and I remember three of us going five times in one week! There was a queue at one performance - oh, how they gaped as we tumbled out of the taxi - a motley lot, one cross arm flap, one on crutches, and one toothless wonder!

Eventually the big one came along and jaws were wired apart in preparation (what an easy way to diet!). Despite my previous false disdain, I didn't bounce back from this operation - it took quite ten days. Thank God for Taffy Evans, whose jaw had been blown off on D-Day and ended up with his tongue sewn to his cheek for as long as I can remember. He more than anyone saw me through the first few post-operative days.

Looking back, I'm quite positive these informal impromptu kindnesses of other patients and staff outside their normal official routine helped me over the difficult periods. I believe this constant support is what pulled most patients through their trials.

The Lord Mayor Treloar Hospital

Jo Kelly

born 1947   *interviewed 1999*

I spent a lot of time in hospital as a child in the 1950s in the Lord Mayor Treloar Hospital at Alton. I visited it within the first few weeks of my life, but I started my 'holidays', as my mother called them, at Treloar's, when I was about 18 months old. And until I was 17 I went on a regular basis to Treloar's, usually in the summer holidays because my mother had this awful idea that I shouldn't miss schooling. But there were periods when I was at Treloar's for longer - the longest that I was ever there at one go was just over a year.

I was normally at Treloar's for three months to six months at a time, because I had a lot of straightening surgery and Treloar's then was an orthopaedic hospital. It was painful and I was given a lot of morphine as a child. When I was 16, my mother was told that I could have become addicted to it. In those days, it was just surgical operations and then they just gave you injections. I loved the injections after operations because it meant that it controlled the pain, but after a couple of days they would give you these great big WB tablets, great big white tablets that had 'WB' stamped on them. I hated it because you would be strapped down, lying flat, they would be impossible to swallow because they were so big, and they did not have the immediate effect that that lovely injection had.

Treloar's was nearly a town when I was a child. I used to think of it as an upside-down type of hospital. The workings of the hospital were underneath, on the first floor, and then, of course, the wards were on the top floor and it was a verandah hospital. It faced absolutely south. The wards were open to the elements, because in the south part of the ward, the doors folded completely back and there was a glass roof over the verandah. Every day, half of you went out on to the verandah unless it was really howling a gale. And sometimes in the summer we would stay out overnight. We would be put underneath the glass, but we would be out on the verandah. Of course it meant that if you were out in the night and there was a change in the weather, the whole ward woke up because they had to move the beds that were in the ward, swing open these doors and then push you back in. And when you think that, on a ward, you would have two nurses and an auxiliary and there would be 30 beds in a ward, that was quite an endeavour. Also, they weren't the normal iron bedsteads. They were very, very heavy because most of you were already on a frame on the bed. You would also, post-operatively, be up on blocks to stop the bleeding, heavy wooden blocks. It must have been tremendously heavy for the staff to have actually moved you backwards and forwards. So you can understand why the staff didn't really like you being out at night. But a couple of the consultants thought it was very good for you, so you stayed out there.

At Treloar's I started off at the furthest end from Alton, where the baby wards were, and as I got older I moved along. The orthopaedic surgery there was mainly for children, so there were six wards - boy, girl, boy, girl - as you went up, and then adults in the last four wards. During the 50s, the time that I was there, a lot of children came in for corrective surgery because of polio.

All this treatment didn't need payment up front, it was the 50s and there was the NHS. I was told that I was very lucky because the RAF paid for me to be born, because I was born a year and a month before the NHS came in. And they started operating on me a few months after the NHS came in, so that was very nicely timed!

Down in the basement at Treloar's, you had a complete workshop that did all the artificial limbs and the different callipers. They made my callipers. And there was a leather workshop that did all the leather of our equipment. It was all done on-site in those days. And they had at one time four theatres in the main hall of the hospital.

When I was about four or five years old, the consultant I had was Mr Wilson. And he had different views from other surgeons of the time. He asked my mother if she was prepared to have faith in him, because he felt that he could correct my congenital dislocation of the hips. That also meant that my knees were knock-kneed and my feet were bowed. I know people of my age and older that have had congenital dislocation and they are still what I think of as quite disabled. So he wanted to manipulate me every three weeks. I had a particularly bad couple of years where he manipulated me under anaesthetic one week, I would then sort of recover in the second week, the third week I would be fine, and then the fourth week I went back into theatre again and was manipulated into another position. But in fact this has meant that I don't limp. He straightened my feet by 21 operations in the end and several on my knees. I think the treatment worked. Old age is creeping up on me now, but you know, I've had 50 years! One person told my mother that I wouldn't be able to walk by the time I was 25, and that didn't happen. And I think I can thank Mr Wilson for that.

In those days, the consultants there were gods and they came round on their ward day, and Matron came with them, and they swept onto the ward with all their hangers-on in their white coats - just like James Robertson Justice in the films! We would be in our beds and we couldn't move, because the nurses would tuck us in, in our clean sheets.

Because we were children and we were there for so long, we would have school in the morning and in the afternoon we would do things like art or cookery. Cookery was a laugh. I enjoyed cookery. They used to take us down to the kitchen once a week - and we would be wheeled down. Now, Treloar's was designed so that there were no stairs. So although on terraces there were steps down into the grounds, the actual hospital itself was corridors and slopes. So, if you were in a wheelchair, you had access everywhere in that hospital. And the beds could be pushed anywhere. We would be pushed down to the kitchens for cookery. And we only ever cooked one thing. There'd be about six of us in our beds. And they would take the bowl from bed to bed and we would stir it and that was our cooking. So I'm not good at cookery.

Treloar's was at the forefront of using electric trolleys. All the stores and everything were taken round the hospital on them. They weren't so bad on the actual levels in the hospital, but all the other buildings - the private wing, the nurses' home, the doctors' home, the chapel, everything, and the boiler house - were up a slope, quite a steep slope behind the hospital. And these electric trolleys in the 50s were forever breaking down. I think their battery only lasted for about five minutes, especially if they'd got a load up. And on a Sunday, if you went to church they would dress you and put you in the back of one of these trolleys. And many a time the trolley broke down with about eight of us kids lying in the back of it. And we looked upon it as great fun! I would hate anybody to think that I was that anxious to go to church every Sunday. But there were two good things about it. It was always an exciting occasion, because the trolley might break down. And they always gave you cocoa when you came back, because you'd been out in the elements and so you needed a hot drink. I quickly locked on to the idea that it was a good idea to volunteer to go to church on Sunday.

Treloar's children

I've got a very biased view about the food in Treloar's. I don't like milk. And because of these trips to theatre every three weeks, I was on the building-up diet, which meant a lot of milk, and they also gave you mince and mashed potato. And so I had a lot of milk, mince and mashed potato. But the best thing about hospital food was at weekends. Saturday you always had fish and chips, and it was really good fish and chips. And that was from my first Saturdays there, right the way through to when I was 17: every Saturday you had fish and chips. And on a Sunday it was always roast dinner, and ice-cream for pudding. It was canister ice-cream, it wasn't the little bricky things, it was scooped-out ice cream. So that was really good.

I got into a lot of trouble when I was about seven or eight. I'd gone into hospital, it was a new Sister and everything, and they'd come round and they'd said to me that they hadn't got what religion I was. So I said that I was Roman Catholic because I had spotted that I could get away with it because of my name and Roman Catholics had fish and chips on Friday as well as Saturday. This large clergyman, or priest as of course

he was, came and spoke to me and started giving me instruction. And he was a very nice man and I didn't mind talking to him. That was fine for about three weeks. And then my mother found out! Something was mentioned to my mother about it and my mother went ape! And I had to apologise to the priest and my fish and chips were cut off. I didn't know why my mother was so upset. My grandfather thought that it showed initiative, he was quite proud of me.

If you were naughty, you were taken off the ward. There was the main ward and then there was the little cloister part that went on to the back of the hospital. And there were two bays where you usually were when you came from theatre. You'd be there so that they could watch you. But you would be put out there if you were naughty. Unfortunately, one day a week you had mashed potato and poached egg, and they would break the egg over your mashed potato. And I wouldn't eat it, so it was served up for the next meal. Cold. And I wouldn't eat it. And I was then put outside overnight, and the next breakfast I wouldn't eat it, and the next lunch-time I wouldn't eat it, and the next dinner I wouldn't eat it. On the third day I still hadn't eaten it and I had got a very high temperature. So the medical staff were called. And my surgeon came to see me, because he was operating on me that week and he had known me since I was this big, so he sat on the bed and I in self-righteous sniffs told him why I was outside and why I was naughty. And he himself pushed me back into the ward and told the Sister to give me whatever I would like to eat. And that was not good. That was not good!

Once a year a full-staged fair would actually come in to the grounds of Treloar's, so you would have a helter skelter, and you would have the roundabouts, and on the grass in front of the hospital would be a fairground. I assume it was a local fair, most likely from the Stokes's from Basingstoke, I don't know. It was always in August and I was always a little upset if I wasn't in hospital over that period of time. That was another thing I held against my mother. She was always trying to get me home for Easter and Christmas. And they would allow me to go home. And of course that was always a very good time to be in because you got freebies. And also the local Hunt used to come to see us children once a year. Well, the nurses hated that. Because we would be out on the verandah, the dogs would come out on the verandah and they would just put their paws up onto our nice clean beds. Great muddy paws. And we kids loved it. And the nurses had to change our beds because Sister would say the beds had to be changed again.

Treloar's was a home from home, really, for a lot of us children. Some of the children were there for years, some in their spinal frames. There were also children that came there from the Channel Islands and I know particularly one friend whose parents came over once a year and would stay for a week and visit her. They were not allowed to visit more than three times a week, even though they had come over from Guernsey. There was visiting for an hour on a Wednesday afternoon, and then you were visited on a Saturday afternoon and a Sunday afternoon. So us children got quite used to being our own little organisation, really.

One reason for restricting visiting hours was that you couldn't have parents there when it was one of the consultants' theatre list because of the disruption of children going on and off the ward. But of course that wouldn't have really caused a problem. And obviously it doesn't cause a problem now. I think now they have suddenly realised that the parents can actually help with the nursing of the child. But in those days they just thought that it upset the children, having the parents, because you sometimes got very homesick when they went home for a bit. In fact I suppose for about half an hour after visiting-hour on a Sunday especially - Saturday wasn't as bad, because you knew somebody would come and see you on the Sunday - but Sunday evening for about half an hour we'd all snivel in our corners.

But I've always said to parents, when they've said that they hated leaving their children because their children were so upset, 'You're upset, but usually half an hour after you've gone, the children resurface and they're fine,' and definitely, that's how it was with me. I think it was harder for the parents than it was for the children, really. But we did become very institutionalised.

At Treloar's there were specialist Sisters, some of them ex-army. Sister Brian was the plaster Sister. She always had the one joke. Whenever you went to have your plaster cast off, she always told you not to worry, because of course once the blade reached bone it would automatically stop. One of the reasons I learned not to trust anybody was what happened once when I had sticky bandages on both legs. I was taken to the plaster room. They cut through both bandages and the Staff Nurse held one lot of sticky bandage and the Sister held the other, and the Sister said, 'Oh, Josephine, look at that aeroplane,' and I, like a twit, looked out the window. And of course there wasn't any aeroplane and they did the almighty rrrrrp on both legs - which of course was the best way to do it, but it just didn't feel like it at the time! I must have been about six and I thought, 'Right. I'm never going to look at an aeroplane again! You won't catch me again!' She actually ran physio, she was the Sister for all of the treatment, the out-patient treatment as well the plaster rooms, the dental surgery, the physiotherapy department. And she was a force to be reckoned with. A large-ish lady, very nice lady, but everybody quaked, including the consultants.

She was one of the ex-army Sisters. In the 50s there were several, of course, as you would expect. Sister Gardner and Sister Gurney were two totally different people. One a softer sort of woman, and we all adored her. And the other one, we always did whatever she said because we were all quite petrified of her. And I think maybe the other Sisters were as well. As I got older, I realised that everybody sort of tiptoed around her. But she was very good.

I can't say that there were any practices that were really medieval. Except certain practices that had to be done. These days I don't know whether they would be done 'just because it has always been done'. Every Sunday you had your hair looked at for nits, so the nit comb went through your hair. And as they washed your hair every three weeks, by the third week it was like marcel waves, it had set. You had a throat swab taken once a week to make sure that you hadn't got anything nasty lurking. And that was the thing I hated, because I hated the wooden thing holding your tongue down. And I am ashamed to say they used to strip my bedding off the bed, so

I couldn't get down under the bedclothes as they came towards me. And then, even though I was young, I would have two nurses lying on me to hold me down while it was done - it was not a nice experience, I was very naughty. I quite often got sent out of the ward for that. And also we used to have cod-liver oil and malt. Every week it came round on the trolley. And the syrup of figs. We all had it - you had the three spoonfuls every Sunday night. So you'd had your nice ice-cream at lunch-time, so I suppose it couldn't all be good on a Sunday. And the malt was okay, it was a bit sweet for me, but cod-liver oil I hated. I seem to think that the malt was on a wooden spoon, so I am sure that couldn't have been all that hygienic.

Jean Holloway

born 1938   *interviewed 2001*

Before the 'Mini' was opened, Jean Holloway was a theatre nurse at Treloar's.

I enjoyed Lord Mayor Treloar's very much, it was great fun. It was an orthopaedic hospital, with surgery as well. I did most of the surgical work in the theatre. I did some of the orthopaedic as well, and I found it very enjoyable. While I was there the new hospital was built in Basingstoke, which was called the Mini-hospital. And then the doctors started coming to Lord Mayor Treloar's, the ones that were going to move across, like Mr Payne, Mr Tovey and Dr Evans-Prosser. And then of course when the 'Mini' was opened, we all got transferred over. That was 1969. There were probably about a hundred beds.

The 'Mini'

Dr Sandy Smeaton

born 1916   *interviewed 1998, 1999*

In the 1960s the Basingstoke and Alton hospitals were included in the Winchester Group; the Royal Hants County Hospital in Winchester being the flagship, Alton next with three hospitals, and Basingstoke a poor third. The County Hospital was over a hundred years old and there was mounting pressure from the local consultants to build a new hospital, and a reluctance on the part of the Wessex Regional Board to admit that Basingstoke would require a new District Hospital to cope with the great increase in the population of the town arising from the 'London overspill'. It was most unlikely that the government would allow two District Hospitals 20 miles apart. Seemingly endless meetings, some quite heated and acrimonious, resulted in much delay, with Basingstoke 'making do' by opening two medical wards at Basing Road Hospital, taking over orthopaedic wards at Treloar's for medical and surgical patients from Basingstoke and having to borrow Villa 5 and Villa 6 from the psychiatrists at Park Prewett for medical and geriatric patients. These arrangements caused much inconvenience to patients, their relatives and the consultants. The population continued to grow steadily but by the mid-1960s the decision about a new District Hospital in Basingstoke had still not been resolved.

To build a new town requires a Town Plan and town planners. Basingstoke was allocated a group of young professionals who were particularly concerned about traffic flow and their answer was to build ring roads and roundabouts - so much so that Basingstoke has been labelled 'Doughnut city'. One part of the ring road on their plan involved demolishing the Shrubbery Maternity Home, which set alarm bells ringing locally and also at Regional Board level. The Board responded by agreeing to build a new maternity unit in the grounds of Park Prewett and the planners agreed, as a temporary measure, to construct a single instead of a dual carriageway.

The new maternity unit was completed in 1970, by which time the pressure on beds was such that the powers-that-be decided that the new building would have to be used as a 'Mini' general hospital, housing all departments, including casualty. The Shrubbery continued to function but with our new consultant obstetrician, Peter Payne, on site. The Regional Board had committed themselves to go on and build a District Hospital but it was another four years before the main hospital was completed and we were able to give the orthopods back their wards in Treloar's and return Villa 5 and Villa 6 to the psychiatrists at Park Prewett.

When the Basingstoke District Hospital opened in 1974, the 'Mini' became what it was originally intended to be - a maternity unit, with 25 GP beds on Level 1 and 25 consultant beds on Level 2 and SCBU (the Special Care Baby Unit) on the ground floor. What had been the casualty department became ante-natal clinics.

Dr Peter Arblaster
from THE MAKING OF A HOSPITAL, 1996

Two doctors in the mid 1960s merit special mention - Sandy Smeaton and Don Burrell. Both were GPs; they were fearless in committee, a constant support to Hospital consultants, dedicated to the Basingstoke project and gave up much leisure time attending frequent meetings in Winchester.

When commissioning the 'Mini', new staff were urgently needed - in particular, doctors and nurses. For the latter, we argued and gained acceptance that a State-Enrolled and State-Registered Nurse School be started in Basingstoke. We needed doctors headquartered in Basingstoke to develop Medicine, Surgery, Orthopaedics, A & E, Pathology and Radiology Departments. We were extremely lucky with certain Departments, of which Obstetrics, Anaesthesia, Pathology and Radiology were supreme. Medicine was established in Villa 5, Park Prewett and the RHA generously sent the, then, only consultant to America to observe the first and rather primitive Coronary Care Units. Back in Basingstoke we were able to

Jack Clarke, who had been appointed by Sir Alexander Fleming to the Rooksdown pathology laboratory in 1947 and had set up a small laboratory at the Cottage Hospital, now opened a larger one in the 'Mini'.

experiment with early cardiac resuscitation methods and even bend the nursing conventional wisdom so that senior nurses actually gave emergency life-saving electro-cardioversion.

After much debate and guidance from Lord Rosenheim, then President of the Royal College of Physicians, it was established that for the first time in a District General Hospital there would be GP beds for Maternity and General Medicine; he also kindly agreed to support medical appointments to Basingstoke by offering Consultant sessions at University College Teaching Hospital in London. We believe that these arrangements, the first of their kind in the country, added to the attractions of Basingstoke Hospital as a great place in which to work.

Dr John Williams
born 1939   *interviewed 2002*

What became 'The Mini' was built in 1969 as a maternity hospital only, with no support facilities. I remember saying, 'How can we have a maternity hospital in Basingstoke, if the paediatric unit is in Winchester? And where's the pathology going to be? Because that's in Winchester at the moment.' There wasn't anything in Basingstoke. It was all done at arm's length. Then the penny dropped with the powers that be, and so they turned the 'Mini' from being a maternity hospital, as it was planned to be, into being a mini-general hospital (it was the late sixties, mini-skirts and that sort of thing). It had twelve surgical beds, twelve medical beds, six ENT beds, six eye beds , and so many paediatric beds, and a small special care unit, and obstetric beds. The Shrubbery went on being the maternity unit, with the appointment of a gynaecologist, Peter Payne, to Basingstoke.

A big change was happening. From having all our consultants coming up to Basingstoke from Winchester, we suddenly started having Basingstoke consultants. Peter Arblaster, then Frank Tovey, and then Peter Payne. And then gradually over the next five years a whole series of Basingstoke consultants were appointed, culminating in people like Bill Heald and Brian Elvin, and all these people who are retiring now. The GPs had always had a good relationship with the Winchester specialists, because we had shared coffee with them, and when they opened the new hospital we sort of moved into the new hospital with them.

Mr Frank Tovey
born 1921   *interviewed 1996*

I came here as a locum consultant surgeon, after running a hospital in Mysore, South India, because Basingstoke at that time was growing. We had outstanding general practitioners and it was amazing what they covered, but the town was rather thinly served from the surgical point of view. There were visiting surgeons from Winchester and they had to fit it in with their daily work. They wanted a locum consultant surgeon until they actually started the plans and commissioning for the new hospital. For a time I had a single room at Park Prewett Hospital, so I got to know the ambiance. Then eventually in 1968 I was appointed to the substantive post of consultant surgeon.

Dr Peter Arblaster had been appointed as the dedicated consultant physician to Basingstoke, and the two of us were to work together with the commissioning team for the opening up of the new hospital. The small Cottage Hospital was very friendly and run by the GPs. We would have lunch with the GPs every day. They would often come to Out-patients, sitting with us and actually help us in the operating theatre. We had no Junior Doctors in the hospital, so the GPs also shared the care of the patients on the ward, and this really was a very good basis for developing relationships in the future.

In September of 1968, they were just digging the foundations of the first part of the hospital, which is now the Maternity Hospital. We called it in those days the Mini-Hospital. This took two years to build and during that time some of the surgery was being done in the Cottage Hospital at Hackwood Road, but the bulk of it took place in Lord Mayor Treloar Hospital, the orthopaedic hospital down in Alton, where we had borrowed medical and surgical beds. Much of the day was spent there with the major operations, but also we had to spend time in the Cottage Hospital and we had convalescent beds in the Basing Road Hospital, which also for a time had a geriatric unit with physiotherapy. So every day we were travelling from place to place. Often at night we had to go down to Alton for emergencies. I think people were extremely patient about this, because if they had a relative down in Alton it meant an uncomfortable bus journey - and the bus services were not very great - or getting a friend to take them down by car. I think they put up with a lot of inconvenience.

The amount of time I spent on administration or actual surgery varied from day to day. There was a lot of planning to do. We had to decide on ward furniture, I had to decide on all the instruments and equipment for the theatre and so on. Most of the planning was being done from Highcroft, the Regional Health Authority building in Winchester. They used to come up from day to day and we would meet with them. There was also the Area Health Authority in Winchester, but the responsibility for building the hospital was with the Regional Health Authority, which employed me. It was not very long before the Area Health Authority was disbanded.

The plans had been drawn up early in the 1950s but they had lain on the shelves for over ten years before permission and finance was available for starting to build the hospital. They were based on the concept of Progressive Nursing Care, with patients around four sides of a square. One side would be high intensity nursing and as you went round it would change to medium intensity nursing, ending up in low intensity where the dayroom was, where patients could sit and be ready to go home. This Mini-Hospital opened in 1970, with surgical, obstetrics, gynaecological and ENT beds. The medical beds were over in a borrowed ward at Park Prewett. We had to set this progressive nursing care concept into action but it just did not work. Patients didn't like being moved, nurses didn't like moving their patients and I rather likened it to 'Chinese Whispers', because instructions you gave in one department were passed on in a different form as the patient was moved on, and on, until the initial instructions were almost unrecognisable. Within a few months we had to

split up the squares into four corners. This introduced staffing problems, because our staffing levels had been worked out on the old Nightingale pattern, so many nurses to a 20-bedded ward and so on. That was all right when you could sit at one end of the ward and see all your patients, but when they were at an angle of the square and you had to walk along, looking into the wards one by one, it just did not work with those staffing levels. One of our early problems was getting adequate nursing staff

Basingstoke District Hospital

For some the move to the new hospital came sooner than anyone expected and it took a lot of organisation.

Rita Phillips

born 1942   *interviewed 2004*

We were planning anyway to be closing Cowdery Down Hospital down in the Spring. The new hospital had just opened and the wards were almost ready. I can remember us ringing everyone up and saying 'Can you come and help?' And on the Sunday we'd got volunteers and people with cars and vans to help us to move the patients up to North Hampshire Hospital. Some of them hadn't been out of Cowdery Down for 25 to 30 years, so under their beds were their lifetime belongings, and it was a nightmare trying to sort everybody out with all their belongings. And to take them to a brand new hospital on almost the top floor - it never failed to amaze me, why they put the elderly patients on F floor, which was nearly the top floor in the hospital. Nearer to God maybe, but certainly not nearer to fresh air and where we could wheel patients out. They'd been used to that at Cowdery Down. They'd been able to go out in the gardens, and even if patients couldn't get out of bed we were able to push the beds out onto the verandah and let them have sunshine.

> Recent research suggests that patients recover more quickly from illness and operations if they can see sky and trees.

A lot of the patients were extremely upset and very confused. They didn't quite understand what was happening and why. We spent a lot of time telling them that this was the new beginning and that they would be going into a nice new home and the staff would be going in there with them. It took us probably about four days in total to move the patients, lock stock and barrel, up to F floor and also to tell the staff that they were no longer working at Cowdery Down, that we would now be working at the Basingstoke District Hospital.

It was just two or three months too early. But maybe in a way we didn't have time to worry, we just had to get on with it. However it was going to be, it was going to be upsetting. Very sadly, a lot of the patients died within that first year, just didn't settle.

I didn't like working on F floor. It was very different from what we had been used to. I stayed about three months and then decided that I didn't particularly want to work in that environment, so then changed my tack completely and went to work in the Accident and Emergency Department. But I still used to go up and see 'my old gentlemen' as I called them.

There were good things about the move. It had been getting increasingly difficult nursing patients at Cowdery Down with antiquated systems. The heating would always pack up in the middle of the night, it was very cold. Although it was only in Basing, it was still quite difficult for some relatives to visit, whereas with the new hospital there were bus services. And a patient needing an X-ray had to go to the Hackwood Road hospital, whereas in the new hospital everything was on-site.

Mr Frank Tovey OBE

born 1921   *interviewed 1996, 2004*

From the 'Mini' we moved to the new main hospital, which was opened in 1974 (formally in 1975). By then we had established our nursing levels. I would never say that we could not have done with more nurses, but we had worked out the principle by then. Once the surgery was brought to Basingstoke, we were able to surrender the wards at Treloar's, and a little later we surrendered the wards at Park Prewett and brought the medical patients over to the main hospital. C Floor was for surgery, with ear, nose and throat, D floor was orthopaedics and gynaecological beds, E Floor was medical, F Floor was geriatric and G Floor was paediatric. The old 'Mini' now became Maternity.

'…that enormous car park!'

I remember when the main hospital was being built, we saw that enormous car park and said, 'This is ridiculous, we will never need that size of car park,' because in those days not many people had cars. People came by bus, they cycled, they walked, only the minority of the hospital staff had cars. Now, of course, virtually everyone has a car, and so staff, patients and visitors have to have parking spaces.

Bit by bit we built up our own staff, starting off with anaesthetics, the appointment of an obstetrician and a gynaecologist and then building up the laboratory staff and the surgical and medical staff. Early on, also, a paediatrician was appointed and we had our own radiologist and our own laboratory staff, instead of making use of the visiting staff from Winchester. They were all recruited by the Regional Health Authority. One of us was allowed to sit on the appointments board but the rest of the board were appointed - there were statutory appointments, the colleges, the board and the health authority were all on. There would be just one interview but a lot of behind the scenes work was done beforehand, phoning around about candidates, taking up references. I think we've been extraordinarily fortunate in Basingstoke. It started off working on an extremely friendly basis and it is still known, really, as being a friendly hospital. There have been good relationships right through.

To begin with, of course, we had an accommodation problem and the local Council made council housing available

to staff. Some was in Oakridge, some in Popley, some in Winklebury and of course there was Wellington Terrace, where most of the Park Prewett houses were.

We needed nursing staff, laboratory staff, domestic staff and kitchen staff, Even in the days of the Mini-Hospital, from 1970 to 74, we went through very difficult periods with regards to industrial relationships and trades unions. I think it was because we were getting established as a unit and we had to define boundaries. In fact, this industrial unrest continued until about 1976, the first two years that we were in the main hospital. It was really with the domestic and the service personnel from the staff where the trades unions were involved, and we had very militant trades unions at that time. To give you an illustration. Supposing something was spilt in the ward and it splashed onto the wall and the floor. The doctor and the nurses had no authority to ask domestic staff to clean it up. They had to get the domestic supervisor to ask the domestic to do it. The domestic would be willing to do the floor, but the wall would be another person's responsibility and they also had to be found to do it. We had to establish the principle which eventually was called 'sapiential authority', whereby a senior medical person or a nurse could actually ask a domestic to do a task. There was a two-day strike when the doctors just took over and did the cleaning and they served the meals and so on. Some of the doctors took home the laundry, such as theatre suits, put them through washing machines at home and brought them in again the next morning. That did not go on for long and we made sure these problems didn't affect the care of patients. By 1976 we had got through our troubles and since then everything really ran very smoothly. My rôle in this was just being with the Medical Staff and negotiating with Administration.

Later we had a lot of trouble with flat roofs, and with leakages, but by then we had a good administrative staff and that was their problem, not ours.

We had a Post-graduate Society for medical staff and nurses, and we did a lot of social activity with our junior staff so that they felt cared for and one of the family. We had a Benevolent Fund, which my wife started off. It had an Annual Dinner, a friendly get-together, and she introduced Indian Curries, which carried on for quite a long time. The Christmas Pantomime was great fun but I am afraid for the first three years I was the butt of much of it.

We had our own Anglican hospital chaplain and the chaplaincy, and other denominations appointed ministers to act as chaplains for their patients in hospital. The Chapel was there, right from the beginning of the opening of the main hospital and it is centrally placed and, particularly on Sundays, members of the staff can come to morning chapel service and bring patients who want to attend the service.

To begin with, when I was the only dedicated surgeon in Basingstoke, I was happy to cover most fields, apart from orthopaedics, but as we got other consultants appointed we each took up our special interests. My greatest relief actually was when I had to give up urology. Later I concentrated mostly on gastro-enterology. I retired in 1998 but for six years I was asked to carry on with the Neuropathic and Diabetic Foot Care.

There was the question of private care.

When I was first appointed, I accepted that there was a need from the point of view of surgery to cover the private patients. I was never very happy, because they were nursed in the same wards in the hospital, except that they had single rooms, and I very much disliked the two-tier system within the hospital itself. There was considerable resentment among nursing and domestic staff that some people should be more privileged than the others.

As other colleagues came along, I decided that I would give up private work so that I could give all my time to the development of the hospital. So from about 1976 onwards, I stopped doing private work. In those early days there were no outside private beds in Basingstoke; first of all they were just in Winchester, later on there were beds in Crondall, but it meant adding long journeys to your day's work to look after private patients and if consultants chose to do private work they had to be part-time. There were so many sessions for the National Health, which would leave them the sessions for their private care, but they still continued the daily visits in addition to the hospital work. It wasn't until the Hampshire Clinic moved here that it became much easier for people to do private work. There are still private beds at the Basingstoke hospital, because there are certain facilities which the Hampshire Clinic cannot provide.

Professor Bill Heald

born 1936   *interviewed 2005*

On 1st January 1973 I was appointed as a Consultant General Surgeon to the Basingstoke District Hospital which was to open the following year. Basingstoke has represented one of the great adventures of my life, and I have seldom been made to feel so welcome at any phase of my life, first of all by the Chairman of the Medical Staff Committee, Dr Caryl Evans-Prosser who hijacked me and took me home to celebrate with champagne in his house, with his lovely wife, Joan.

Peter Arblaster had been the architect of a clinical team which had started out as the 'poor cousin' of Winchester - that entirely desirable ancestral home to the peers of British Medicine. Peter had taken on a task which he discharged with the most amazing unselfishness - always seeking out and finding the best people he could and then persuading them of the huge potential that really existed in Basingstoke. His choice for example, of John Fowler as a running mate in the Department of Medicine was a remarkably statesmanlike choice of an outstanding physician who might well have out-shone the existing team. In the event he was a true Basingstoke team player with his own unique commitment to a dream that was increasingly shared by all the new consultants who arrived during the seventies. On the same day as I started my work, for instance, Dr Peter Baxter became a Consultant Anaesthetist (I believe, the youngest consultant in the Country at the time) and the rather new concept of a

Consultant to run the Accident and Emergency Department in the form of Dr Brian Elvin who also made major contributions over the following years. Basingstoke has made so many contributions in so many different areas and most of this must be put down to the far-sightedness of Peter Arblaster, Frank Tovey and the nucleus of more senior people who welcomed into their midst a new team of youngsters like myself in their early thirties.

Any newly appointment consultants in the new 21st Century who are still reading this, will be intrigued by the next sign of welcome that I received. The Regional Medical Officer, Dr Revans, rang me and asked me whether he could take me out to lunch. He made me feel that I was about to take on a massive responsibility with limited resources but had the absolute backing of the only manager, Mr Harry Barrow, and of the backup team of Region, largely led by Dr Revans himself. He had a special fund for new consultants which he would make available to me for any specialist requirements that I might have. At the time, gastric surgery was a particular fascination to both Frank Tovey and to me and my special treat from Dr Revans was a gastroscope.

During the course of the next twenty years, I migrated distally in the gastrointestinal tract and eventually based my surgical career on refinements in the surgery of rectal cancer. I would never have been able to do this if it had not been for the support and guidance of Frank Tovey. I well remember him asking me to take over a young patient of his with rectal cancer. He stood behind me and watched me try painfully to show him my ideas about peri-mesorectal excision, and his thoughtful comments thereafter formed the basis of the whole of my surgical life. He said to me, 'I think you have got some very interesting ideas there and I think that I should stop doing rectal cancers myself and give you the opportunities that come from dealing with all of them in this District.' This decision by Frank was a typically unselfish one, since he had a personal interest in rectal cancer which would have made most surgeons hostile to a youngster who sought to intrude on his hallowed territory. This was absolutely typical of the man who, many years later, so surprised the applicant for a new consultant job to replace him (Mr Merv Rees, now so well known), as the potential new consultant found the retiring one difficult to get to speak to because he was away applying for new research monies for his new research project. Frank is still publishing well into retirement and his contributions to gastric surgery remain something of which everyone in Basingstoke should be extremely proud.

Another astonishing aspect of a consultant appointment in the 1970s was the manner in which one was taken to the heart of each of the general practices. There were few of the local general practitioners who did not invite myself and my wife, Bounce to dinner and few with whom we did not become personal friends. It is impossible to measure the benefit that patients received from such a relationship existing within a medical community. One immediate example is that my amazing and dedicated secretaries, of whom I shall mention only three - Jill Stevens, Rosemary Sexton, Pat Caballero - would never allow me to keep a woman patient with a lump in the breast waiting more than a week or two to be seen. It mattered not whether the lump was thought to be benign - the secretary knew that the woman would be worried and that therefore Bill or Frank, or Tony Richards who soon joined us, would see that patient at the earliest possibility. Furthermore, each of our secretaries had clear instructions never to keep waiting any patient about whom one of our GPs took the trouble to ring.

Of course, what we did was not always perfect, but we did try to be a medical community and almost all of us tried to keep our enthusiasm for private practice within the limit set by proper ethical behaviour in relation to waiting times. There was no private hospital in Basingstoke and our operating lists were besieged by the need for surgery to NHS patients. For many years, I had no less than six NHS operating lists, whereas today the surgeon often has to make do with two or three. However, I and most of my colleagues would not allow a private patient with a more trivial complaint to queue-jump over an NHS patient with a more serious complaint. Thus it was that for fifteen years or more I trekked on at least half my working days to Winchester to the Winchester Clinic and later Sarum Road Private Hospital to do any such patients out of NHS working hours. Looking back, I do not think that many of us were guilty of abusing our right to private practice or short-changing our NHS patients. Indeed, our respected GP colleagues would, I suspect, have rapidly grasped what we were up to and would have sent their private patients to other surgeons or indeed to London, which had been commonplace in the past. There was no doubt in those days that private practice acted as an incentive bonus scheme and rewarded one with private referrals for good service provided to NHS patients.

Thus it was, with the support of my colleagues, that I was able to develop a special interest in cancer of the rectum. I think that I can now claim that the town of Basingstoke, though often not known in foreign places, is a word to conjure with in every place in the world where rectal cancer is discussed. We now have a team with such outstanding colleagues as Merv Rees and Brendan Moran but it would be improper to mention simply my own colleagues because so many of the other departments have made outstanding contributions and so many of our colleagues in every discipline have been exceptional. As far as I know, no other district hospital has been awarded a personal Chair for one of the ordinary consultant staff and certainly no other district hospital has a specialist contract with the Department of Health to handle a certain rare form of cancer - in this case, the NSCAG contract for Pseudomyxoma Peritonei which is run in such a dedicated manner by Brendan Moran.

It would be possible to go on and on about how much better the NHS seems to me to have been in the 1970s than it has become all these years later. Professional standards were guarded by the communal conscience of the profession itself, which I believe was very well developed indeed. Mutual respect and understanding between General Practitioner and Consultant was constantly renewed at the Wednesday lunch-time meetings - which I note, sadly, have now gone into history because of poor attendance. When one reflects on how everything seems to have got worse, it would be less than fair to leave out one group that has maintained its selfless set of standards entirely from personal motivation -

these are the medical secretaries - where the government bureaucracy has not yet spread its claws. Indeed there are many others - our operating theatres are a joy to work in and the selfless toil of so many still makes our hospital unique despite the background of widespread National gloom.

Perhaps, the politicians who reflect on why these good things from the past have been sacrificed might just ask themselves whether it is not the burgeoning bureaucracy that makes the doctor look nervously over his shoulder instead of into his own conscience that has been the root of this sad decline. Perhaps the professions in this town can grasp again the sense of pride and shared achievement that can come from a medical community that sets and shares its own standards of care for its patients.

Dr John Williams

born 1939   *interviewed 2002*

GPs continued to visit their patients in the new hospital.

When the new hospital, the main hospital, finally opened in 1974 (the official opening was in 1975), we had a GP medical ward. That was a very unusual thing, it took a lot of negotiating; a lot of the young specialists in the hospital were very dubious about this concept. It subsequently went, due to pressures of General Practice changing and hospital medicine changing.

The GPs looked after their own patients. One GP was appointed to be the medical officer for the ward and he liaised with the Sister and kept a watching brief that all the other GPs were behaving in accordance with the rules that had been laid down when it was agreed we could have our own beds in the hospital. So patients were not to be kept in for three months or so. They were supposed to be out within a fortnight. If they weren't, the doctor in charge would be saying, 'What's going on here? Why isn't this patient out?' But sometimes there were good reasons, and that was fine. Sometimes it was because the doctor was being lazy. At one stage, I was medical manager for that ward for about five years, which was quite an interesting job to do.

You would use it for things like respite care. I can remember a young man in his forties with quite severe Parkinson's disease, whose wife would periodically have respite from having to care for him 24 hours a day, seven days a week. Or perhaps he'd become unwell, and we would get him in. Or you would have patients in who had advanced cancer, and you would look after them during the dying part of their illness.

Every Wednesday for many, many years most of the GPs in the area would go to the hospital, have their lunch and have a post-graduate meeting. One of the specialists said to his junior, 'When a GP rings you up to admit a patient, you just ask what the patient's name and age are, and what the problem is, and then you find where you are going to send them. You don't cross-examine them as to whether or not the patient needs to be in hospital.' Cross-examining the GP was the pattern, particularly in the 1960s. A lot of GPs would dump patients in hospital, particularly in big cities ('I don't know what to do with this patient. Send them to hospital' and it was called 'the Friday Afternoon Syndrome'. A lot more patients were admitted on Friday afternoon than other days of the week because the doctors didn't want to be bothered with them over the weekend.) The hospital doctors in big city areas became very suspicious of GPs, but in Basingstoke it was accepted that if the GP says, 'I want the patient in,' the hospital would take them in, see what the problem was, perhaps send them out the next day if it all resolved itself, but they would accept that the patient needed admitting. The standard of General Practice has always been very high in the area.

One of the jobs of a GP is to be what I used to call a progress chaser, which is to see that the correct things have happened to your patients, and the good GPs would be in the hospital knowing the consultants' secretaries and chasing things up, finding the consultants over lunch and talking to them and saying, 'You saw Mrs So and So last week. The family are very unhappy about what happened,' or 'You didn't see them, your junior saw them.'

But by the mid-1980s the concept of actually having GP beds in the hospital had become impractical and GPs found it more and more difficult to get into the hospitals because they were so busy in their surgeries, so they stopped going. In the last ten years the relationship between the GPs and the consultants has changed, because the young consultants who are appointed now don't expect to meet the GPs and the young GPs who are appointed now don't expect to meet the consultant.

Jeanette Patterson

born 1938   interviewed 2001

If you want to know anything in a hospital, ask the domestics!

In 1988 they had a recruitment campaign going on at the hospital, so I went up there one night. To start off with, they didn't have any vacancies for nursing auxiliaries, which was what I was looking for. I was desperate for the money, so I took a job as a domestic, which again stood me in very good stead, because if you want to know anything in a hospital, ask the domestics! Especially when I started up there, the staff actually relied a great deal on the domestics. Apart from the cleaning of the wards, you had to give out coffee at mid-morning, you helped give out the lunches, and you also did afternoon teas. On F floor, which was elderly care, very often the nurse said, 'If you've got a minute, could you help us feed Mrs So-and-so?' When I first went there, the nurses did rely a lot on the domestic staff because they were busy, and when you're going round cleaning and dusting, if somebody's falling out of their chair, or somebody's pillows need adjusting, you were allowed to do all that. Unfortunately things have changed now, I think for the worse. I think there's a few more restrictions now, since we've gone into Europe, because everything's ruled by Brussels and everybody's got to be accountable for their actions. There are lots of things you were allowed to do, like being a volunteer in hospital, that you can't do now.

I remember one sad incident one morning. At half-past seven in the morning, you've got to be quite bright and cheery for the patients, and I bowled in and I said, 'Oh good morning Mr So-and-so, here's your cup of tea,' and then I realised that the gentleman wasn't quite with us, in fact he definitely wasn't with us because I think he'd just died! And so that was quite a shock. But I just went and said, 'I think the gentleman in such-and-such a bay is actually, you know, not with us any more.' And they were full of remorse because they knew, but they hadn't put a sign on the door.

I used to say, 'Oh, Mrs So-and-so wants the loo,' or 'Can somebody come and help this gentleman? He's slipped down in his chair.' They didn't mind, because we worked on the ward regularly, so they got to know us, and they knew who they could trust. When I first went there, the standards were much higher, and there was a different rapport with the staff, it wasn't so much 'Us and Them'.

Jean Holloway

The new hospital saw many developments in surgery.

The main hospital was officially opened on the 5th November 1975, by Her Royal Highness the Princess Alexandra, and I had a special invitation. We all had the day off. It was a very nice day, as I remember - didn't rain. It was very pleasant, and she's a lovely lady.

At the new hospital, first of all we opened two theatres. I think the first operation was a gynae case. The other one was a surgical, and I took over running the surgical theatre. With Mr Heald, now Professor Heald, we started the general surgery. And then he started his gun surgery. That is a stapling gun where, in a bowel operation he staples the two pieces of bowel together so the patients don't need a colostomy. First of all we had the American gun and eventually we had the Ethicon gun, which was much better, and I think he still uses it now. It was a fairly big operation, taking probably about two to three hours in the beginning, but it's certainly much quicker now. I can remember when Mr Heald first came, and he was the new surgeon. He did a big operation and I was very impressed with his operating. I thought, 'My goodness, we've got a good surgeon here!'

I did shift work, and I did calls. I enjoyed the hours I did. It wasn't so nice doing the calls, but in fact there were junior staff on at night and if they couldn't cope they had to call somebody in. It could be about three o'clock in the morning, you'd be fast asleep and the phone would go, and they'd say, 'We've got this large operation going on, can you come and help?' and you just got in your car and you went. Simple as that. You were paid extra money for that.

Over the next few months, as we got more staff, we opened up more theatres. And more orthopaedic cases came over from Treloar's, and we opened up an orthopaedic theatre. And then they opened up another orthopaedic theatre, and gradually we opened up an ENT theatre, and an eye theatre, and eventually we had several theatres open.

Then Mr Rees came as general surgeon, with a leaning towards liver surgery, and we were then introduced to this big machine called the CUSA machine, which Mr Rees managed. It removed parts of liver, without any bleeding. And it was excellent, and it made life so much better for the patient, and the operation was so much easier. Mr Rees did most of it. And then eventually Mr Ward came to do our vascular surgery.

Jeanette Patterson

born 1938   *interviewed 2001*

A vacancy became available in the operating theatre. That was basically just helping the nurses keep the cupboards stocked and all sorts of jobs there, anything from getting sandwiches for the doctors in between operating, making lots of teas and coffees, just generally making sure they had their uniforms to put on: a bit of everything, really. And I enjoyed that. As soon as the post became available for a nursing auxiliary, because of my past experience of working as a volunteer, they gave me a job in the operating theatre.

Then I trained as a nursing auxiliary in theatres. That involved actually going into the theatre and assisting the trained staff, so you might do anything. You might be a runner, the one who passes the instruments to the scrub nurse. The scrub nurse is scrubbed up the same as the surgeon, so she's sterile. All the staff help to get the equipment ready, but once you take the outer wrappers off, the scrub nurse is the only one that touches the instruments, and she actually passes them to the surgeon. The runner's job is to help get the trays ready, before they take the sterile wraps off. And you could do anything from laying up the trolleys before the operation, getting all the equipment plugged in, meeting the patient, taking them into the anaesthetic room, helping the anaesthetist just by attaching equipment and things like that. And then, once the operation is underway, if they require instruments that aren't on the tray. you run for them. You also count the swabs, you count the needles, you measure amounts, you take the specimens and you write them in the book, and then you check all the equipment when the operation's finished, with the scrub nurse. Each patient has their own set of instruments. If it has been somewhere infected, then the instrument will be put to one side and it won't be used in that area again but if it's all the same patient, then that set of instruments is for that patient and the surgeon probably will use it again.

At the end of each list, you're responsible for washing all the furniture down, and, if you're not using the theatre that afternoon, then all the equipment has to be tipped outside and the theatre's scrubbed. All the trays go to the sterilising department and the runner is responsible, with the staff nurses, for making sure that all the instruments that were on the tray to start with are there at the end. So you count them before the operation starts and you count them at the end, as you do with the swabs and the needles, and it's all written up on the wall. You have to keep the place tidy, keep the gloves stacked up, make sure that all the drawers are full up with all the equipment so that you're not running here there and everywhere, and you just generally assist. When I first went there, you were actually allowed to scrub up and help, if it was a minor case, and it wasn't invasive, going inside. Things like dentistry, some of the ears, nose and throat, and some gynaecological things like a D & C, you'd be actually allowed to scrub for that, and pass up. But that has been stopped now with the new laws.

The only time I've ever felt queasy is during an eye operation, which I'm not that keen on. I've never fainted. But it's probably to do with my background, because I was brought up with a family of nurses, and my mum was always going out to other people's houses to bring babies into the world, or lay people out. So we grew up with all that sort of thing.

We wear greens (well, they're called greens, though sometimes they're blue). In some theatres they have special colours. The doctors have one colour, the trained nurses have others, the auxiliaries have others. But because there's always a problem with the laundry, you often just wear whatever's available.

If you're working with surgeons and doctors long enough, they know who you are. You meet before the operation starts. Most of their instructions would be to the scrub nurse, and she would say, 'Jan, go and get so-and-so.' But when you get to know the doctors, if it's not convenient for the scrub nurse to do something, he'll say, 'Oh Jan, can you do this?', or, 'can you adjust my mask, can you wipe my forehead, can you move that, can you plug this in?'

I'm not in main theatres any more. When I was up there, we were doing all sorts of things like bowel resections, liver resections, hip replacements. You name it, we did it. When we first did a liver resection it could take, six, seven hours. The team would obviously have to take a break, and they would have somebody stay with the patient - the anaesthetist, and one other. Some of the big bowel operations still can take four or five hours. The department I work in now, I would think the longest operation, a hernia, was probably three-quarters of an hour to an hour, and varicose veins about the same.

There are so many people involved, it's such a huge team, and nobody can work without the other. Nobody can work without the sterilising department, because very often, when there are lots of operations going on, (there are seven theatres upstairs, we've got two theatres, that's nine) they've got to clean and sterilise all those instruments; it's a mammoth thing. Sometimes they run short of trays, so they're under great pressure there. Then there's the cleaning staff as well. Then you've got the porters: they rely very much on them. So you have to work very much as a team. That's why I enioy working in the theatres.

Changes in the funding of medicine

Mr Frank Tovey

born 1921   *interviewed 1996*

About 1980 we founded what was called then the Medical Trust - it's called the Medical Fund now. The National Health Service never had enough money to buy all the sophisticated equipment, particularly to keep up with developments, and the Medical Trust was established to raise money for buying the more expensive equipment to supplement what the National Health Service was able to supply. The Medical Trust has always been helped by local firms. I can think particularly of De La Rue, Wiggins-Teape and Eli Lilly. A good many others have taken part. Vickers Medical helped with items of equipment.

I think there have been many mistakes in hospitals in the last ten to twenty years, partly because of shortage of funds and ward closures and perhaps poor nursing pay, lack of adequate career structure and there are so many factors which I am not really qualified to comment on.

From about 1978 to 1982 we coped with these problems because there were efficiency drives and, being more efficient, we could cope, but every year there was a cut in the money that the hospital received. From 1982 onwards it literally meant hospitals were closing wards and cutting down beds or, when staff left, not replacing them and it was a continual struggle to meet with the economy drives that were inflicted on us by the Government.

I think the biggest problem from my own personal experience was when they introduced the 'Internal Market'. For instance, it meant that if one hospital offered a cheaper service than the other, patients would actually be taken off the individual waiting list and moved onto the waiting list of the other hospital. That didn't actually happen in Basingstoke, but it happened to other colleagues around the country. But within Basingstoke the problems were, for instance, if the budget for hip replacements ran out by October-November it meant no more hip replacements were done until the new financial year which began in April. The same thing happened with cataract lens implants. Every department had to work to its own budget. And when you ordered investigations, the pathology department, the X-ray department, whatever you will, would then charge your department for their investigations and you had to keep within your budget, so you did not order investigations that were expensive or not strictly necessary. If I wanted to do an extra out-patients, for instance, I could go down previously to the Out-patients Sister and ask would there be a room free on such and such a morning, could I do a clinic? When you'd got the internal market, the first question was, 'Have you got the money in your budget to pay for it? This altogether hampered the Health Service. I am glad to say that that is finished now, but this is an illustration of the type of economy they were trying to make, that really interfered with the work of the hospital.

I think there have always been waiting lists, even in the days of the voluntary hospitals. And, of course, what can be done and is available now is so much more than the earlier days. But there's no doubt about it that, even now, in 1996, there are beds closed partly for lack of funding but also largely because of a lack of nurses. One of the big changes in recent years has been the big increase in day-case care. So much more from a surgical point of view is being done on a day-case basis. The patients just come in for a day and go home and then the general practitioner takes over, with the community nursing care. This has introduced problems in that, with fewer beds being available in the hospital, and a much greater turnover, patients who are admitted to the wards go home much earlier than before, with a nursing package. But the community care resources are such that there are not always people to meet them, and I think because of this patients have suffered.

Innovations

Jack Clarke

born 1925   *interviewed 2005*

When I started work in pathology, 'in mediaeval times', most examinations like blood tests were done manually. For instance, blood counts were done by diluting the blood and putting it into special counting chambers marked out in squares. You counted out about 500 cells and did various calculations. When I retired in 1984 we were getting patients' details on computer and there might have been one automated machine in the department. Now a computer analyses 30 to 40 samples at once.

Mr Frank Tovey

born 1921   *interviewed 1996*

I am trying to think of various landmarks. Early on, for instance, I was very concerned for our service for patients with breast cancer and the aftercare of them. In those days the operation for breast cancer used to be removal of the breast, with its psychological effects, and we managed to establish a breast care service, as we called it, with a nurse who was dedicated to looking after patients who had had mastectomies and helped them with appropriate prostheses to get back to normal life and gave general support and advice.

There was a big problem too at that time for people who had stomas - those are artificial openings of the bowel onto the wall of the stomach. When I first came to Basingstoke, stoma appliances were extremely crude and, with the help of Leslie Kingston (a Basingstoke man who founded the Ileostomy Association) we developed a stoma care service. In the early days the only way we could examine the inside of the stomach (apart from X-rays) was with a rigid telescope and a light. It was in about 1970 that they introduced fibre optic instruments which were flexible and we had some of the very earliest instruments in Basingstoke. I was able to start an endoscopy service, and this has built up through the years. Now there is a first-class endoscopy service in Basingstoke.

While I was working abroad in India, I became very involved with the reconstructive surgery for leprosy, because surgery on leprosy patients had become possible during that time because of new drugs which cured leprosy. One of the things I was involved in was the care of feet which had lost their sensation - what we called neuropathic feet, which needed very special care and special footwear for protection. We pioneered and developed appropriate footwear in India. When I came to England I realised that there was no suitable footwear for patients with neuropathic feet in this country. Diabetic patients often get the same sensory loss as leprosy patients used to get. With the help of Lord Mayor Treloar College, who had a vocational workshop - in fact, several vocational workshops in those days to train the boys, and one was for surgical footwear - we developed a prototype of suitable footwear for diabetic patients. About 1976 we were able to get this taken up by the shoemaking industry. So early on with this we had established in Basingstoke a diabetic foot service and we were able to pioneer the making of suitable footwear for these patients. All these really are firsts for Basingstoke, which we were able to pioneer.

I think we have been very blessed with the type of consultant we have had. I speak really from the surgical point of view but it does apply to other appointments. When Mr Heald was appointed, he had a particular interest in colo-rectal surgery, that's surgery of the large bowel. I said to him early on, 'If this is your interest, we will send you all the cases.' He specialised in that way and developed his own surgery for carcinoma of the rectum, the lower part of the large bowel. He achieved the best results literally in the whole world, and the international surgical field was taken by surprise. As a result he has travelled widely throughout the world, telling people about his results and teaching them his procedures - to the States, West Germany, Europe, so many many countries. In fact, the Scandinavian countries have adopted his technique and he has been to each of the major centres to instruct them in his surgery. So Basingstoke has come onto the international map from that point of view. As a result of it, people are anxious to work in Basingstoke and we have a very high quality staff. My successor, Myrddin Rees, has extended this surgery in his field in cancer in the liver and his results too are outstanding.

I helped with the organisation of the 21st Anniversary of the hospital and then with the 50th anniversary of the Health Service. My main contact has been with the Medical Fund, which organised public appeals for things like the CT scanner and other equipment. The Fund is still needed, even though now the public finance initiative helps to get some essential hardware.

Dr Sandy Smeaton

born 1916   *interviewed 1998, 1999*

There have been several advances in obstetrics in Basingstoke. Aroo Moolgaoker designed a pair of obstetric forceps which were an advance on anything we've had in the past and are now widely used (he had been a pilot in the Indian Air Force before studying medicine and listed among his leisure pursuits tiger shooting in Bengal and rifle shooting at Bisley).

The obstetric department at BDH got an ultrasound scanner in 1979 for scanning pregnant women and I was asked to operate it as I had been a clinical assistant in the obstetric department at the ante-natal clinic for some years. The scanner was a post-war discovery, really, when Professor Donald in Glasgow found a machine used in the ship-building industry for looking for flaws in metal and so on and thought we could use this for looking for abnormalities in pregnancies. I went up to Northampton for a one-day course with lectures in the morning, and in the afternoon we had actual patients and machines there so we could practise on them. The images on screen reminded me of John Logie Baird's early efforts with television. One can produce much the same effect by watching TV with the aerial cable taken out! As I drove home that evening I began to realise the enormity of the task ahead of me.

Fortunately, Margaret Holt, a radiographer, had used an ultrasound machine, but not for obstetrics, and together we set up the obstetric department. At the time there were few textbooks on the subject, so we had to build up our own mental picture library of the images we were seeing and as the months passed there were fewer and fewer 'don't knows' in our reports to the obstetricians. Then Margaret Holt went on a course at King's College Hospital, run by Professor Stuart Campbell, the kingpin in the UK of obstetric ultrasound.

I was there in all for about seven years and we got a new machine after about four or five years with much better definition. I enjoyed this enormously. The first picture was just a little flicker - the baby's heart. You could see the baby's head and the outline of things and it enabled one to forecast the expected date of confinement, because we could assess the rate of growth.

Dr Smeaton and scanner

Dr Gill Williams

born 1939   *interviewed 2002*

I did a clinical assistanceship in gynaecology for Mr Aroo Moolgaoker. It was an honour to work for him, he was quite outstanding. And then in 1987 Dr Sandy Smeaton retired and he asked me if I'd like to try the ultrasound, so I did. It was, as he says, like looking on at the first television, it was like a snowstorm, you could hardly pick anything out. And I went on a week's course to King's College Hospital, which was *the* place, and it was incredible. It was where all the pioneering work on obstetric ultrasound was done. I worked twice a week, two sessions a week in the maternity department with Margaret Holt, the radiographer in charge of the ultrasound department. She was a delightful person and became an excellent ultrasonographer. And then they got a new ultrasound machine, and then another one. Once you had the more sophisticated machine it was just amazing. And sometimes tragic, because people would come in so excited about seeing their baby on the screen and you found it was an anacephalic; you had to break the news. It was one of the etiquette things that doctors were allowed to talk to patients and tell them things but radiographers weren't. They had to have cover from a doctor or refer the patient to a consultant.

Once it came in, scans were done at 20 weeks routinely, unless people objected on religious grounds. We also did them for threatened miscarriages, which were very upsetting for patients, and for us sometimes. Because you could see a little flicker of a baby's heart at four weeks, it was just amazing.

Some people had repeated miscarriages and you'd get to know them and they'd come in and you'd hope so much that this time it would be all right, and it wasn't.

It was fascinating to be at the start of something. But now it's technically very very sophisticated.

North Hampshire Hospital

Mary Edwards

born 1959   interviewed 2005

Mary Edwards trained as a nurse in London (Middlesex Hospital and London University) and joined the North Hampshire Hospital NHS Trust in 1995 as Director of Nursing and Patient Services. She became Acting Chief Executive in January 2003 (on secondment of Mark Davies) and was appointed Chief Executive in November 2003 when Mark took the CEO post at RUH Bath.

The North Hampshire Hospital celebrates its 30th anniversary in November 2005, having been opened as Basingstoke District Hospital in 1975 by HRH Princess Alexandra. The hospital changed its name in 1994 following yet another reorganisation in the NHS that resulted in the introduction of NHS Trusts, which were meant to be free-standing organisations with quite a level of autonomy - sounds mildly similar to the principles being discussed with the introduction of Foundation Trusts in 2005!

I joined the North Hampshire Hospital NHS Trust (to give it its full title) in 1995 as Director of Nursing and Patient Services. This rôle is the closest the NHS now has to the traditional rôle of hospital matron many years ago. Over the last 10 years I have witnessed a period of enormous growth; for example we employed 48 medical consultants in 1995, we now have 103; we saw 128,896 out-patients then compared to 130,315 now and did 30,021 in-patient/day-case treatments/operations then compared to 41,332 now. This growth has resulted from a number of things. In my early days the NHS had an internal market whereby we were paid for the number of patients we treated and GPs could choose where their patients were sent. As a reflection of our good quality, and particularly some of our specialist services, we were able to attract ever-increasing numbers of patients and therefore could grow our services. More latterly there has been a significant growth in funding and staff numbers across the whole of the NHS and we have benefited from that.

I have many memories from the last 10 years; however, a few stand out as memorable milestones in the development of the hospital. In 1997 Princess Alexandra returned to open our refurbished and expanded X-ray and pathology departments. In that same year we signed the first NHS private finance initiative (PFI) deal in the southern region with Scottish Power. This provided us with a new heating and power system to replace the boiler that was part of the old Park Prewett Hospital. This was closely followed by another PFI deal with Lodestone to build and run our MRI scanning

The MRI Centre

centre. The MRI centre saw the arrival of a new radiologist, Dr Delia Peppercorn, who leads this service.

1997 also saw the start of our now annual pantomime which was the brainchild of Dr John Ramage; it was called Sinderella and the Ugly Blisters and was a high quality production with lots of irreverence and leg-pulling against hospital staff, including myself!

1999 heralded lots of change in the A&E department. The Prime Minister, Tony Blair, visited to announce that the Trust had been given £650,000 to modernise the A&E department. This work was led by our newly appointed A&E Consultant, Dr John Kitching, with a long-standing consultant, Dr Brian Elvin, who has since retired. HantsDoc, the GP out of hours service also moved into the hospital, right next door to the A&E department at the same time, which meant the services could collaborate and complement each other.

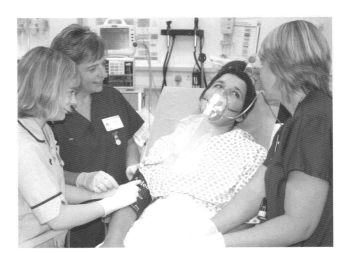

2002 was another red-letter year for the hospital. It saw the opening of the ARK, our state-of-the-art education centre that had been built with the generosity of the local community and other major charitable donations. Fundraising for the ARK was led tirelessly by Mr Myrddin Rees, who is one of our renowned liver surgeons, with the support of many other staff across the Trust. It was more than 10 years in the planning but definitely well worth waiting for. It now houses Southampton University's study centre, our own postgraduate education team as well as education and research teams for our colorectal, liver, cardiology and rheumatology services. This includes the PELICAN charity that focuses on improving surgical treatment of pelvic and liver cancer.

Another opening in 2002 was the Rotherwick cardiology unit, led by Dr Andrew Bishop, another charitably funded benefit for the hospital. The unit includes a specialist laboratory to enable angiography scanning of the heart to be undertaken. In 2004 the Cardiology Team set another 'first' in undertaking primary angioplasty - a procedure used for patients following a heart attack and more usually done in specialist heart centres. National leaders including the Cardiac Czar, Dr Roger Boyle, who opened the unit in 2002, are watching the development with interest.

2005 has heralded another major milestone for the hospital; it is our 30th anniversary and we are opening our thoroughly modernised Maternity Unit which has been the result of nearly £2m of funding from the Dept of Health - and, boy, did we need that! The Maternity Unit was part of the original 'Mini' hospital which was opened in 1969 as a forerunner to the main hospital. It has had very little improvement since that time, other than superficial decoration. The new unit has resulted from the hard work of the midwives and doctors working with parents to identify what a modern service needs - it is barely recognisable from the original building.

Our 30th anniversary also saw HRH Princess Alexandra visiting again, this time to open our state-of-the-art Diagnosis and Treatment Centre (DTC) built on the old out-patients' car park site. This centre is the result of a successful bid for £7.5m from the Dept of Health. The DTC provides care for the majority of patients requiring planned short-stay surgery, as well as housing our endsocopy unit and breast diagnostic unit. The DTC has been led from start to finish by Miss Anne Stebbing, Consultant Surgeon, working with Alan Thompson and Rod Pope as project managers.

Having identified some of the commemorative highlights of the last 10 years, I reflected on how different the hospital feels now compared to when I joined in 1995. For a start it is palpably much busier. We see ever more patients every year, they stay in hospital for much shorter times, and they have many more procedures on a day-case basis. Some of the other things that have changed include the emphasis, quite rightly, on preventing hospital-acquired infection, and the need to involve patients more directly in deciding on their treatment options.

Over the last 10 years it has also become plain to me that we employ many superb staff and that they attract other good staff to join us. Unusually for the NHS, we do not normally experience difficulty in recruiting medical staff and some of the therapy staff such as physiotherapists. We do have the same problem as many hospitals in finding enough nurses and have had, over the last few years, successful recruitment drives in the Philippines and Dubai. These nurses have been welcome additions to our staff and have adapted well to their new culture.

We have continued to develop our specialist services, including the national Pseudomyxoma Centre led by Mr Brendan Moran, the liver cancer surgery service run by Mr Merv Rees and Mr Tim John, the Haemophilia service run by Dr Jason Mainwaring and the cardiology service mentioned earlier. Each of these services raises the profile of North Hampshire Hospital and gives us our unique position as a district general hospital with a difference!

The DTC

Jeanette Patterson

born 1938   *interviewed 2001*

The hospital has a major incident policy for emergencies, which is already worked out in advance. Each department has a copy; certain people are responsible for certain things, so we know that, if there's a major incident, one area becomes purely responsible for receiving the walking wounded, another area will be up and ready for the people that are on stretchers, various people will be drafted into various areas. But you have to stay in your own department until told to do otherwise because they don't want you running around like headless chickens. Everybody that's a key worker will know what their job is. And the rest of you just stay where you are until you're asked to do so-and-so. And you're not allowed to go home till they've got stand-down.

They would stop all things that weren't emergencies, so the run-of-the-mill operations would be stopped, so that staff were available to deal with the emergencies. If you had no power in the middle of an operation, you'd have to stop and make the patient as safe as possible. In a major operation, you might have to carry on with battery-operated lights.

When I first went there, the hospital had a social club but now there isn't any organised relaxation for hospital staff as a whole; we organise things in our own units. We play skittles, or we go out for a meal, or to the theatre or something, but it's very much up to individual units to organise. Other hospitals do have social clubs, they even have swimming pools. We've got student nurses living there, a lot of them have come from abroad and haven't got anyone here, and if you haven't got transport it's not the easiest place to get to town from. So that is a failing, I think.

I think most people do belong to a union, you need to, really. Especially today, where everybody's responsible for their own actions. And everybody's very aware of that now, especially the doctors. If there's a problem with the pay structures and things like that, that's when the unions come into their own.

People spend less time in hospital now.

Eventually, more and more people will come in as day patients. People aren't staying long in hospital at all now. Most people used to come in the night before and have all their tests done, and very often it was found they weren't suitable for one reason or other to have the operation. So now people are pre-assessed. They go to see the consultant, then they come round to us for an assessment, and we weigh them and we make sure they haven't got anything which would make the operation a risk and we give them a date for coming in. They've got to be pretty healthy to be done as a day patient

Even if you go for a triple by-pass, you're lucky if you're in for seven days. When I had a hysterectomy you were in for a fortnight; and now it's five days, if that. You can go home next day from a gall-bladder operation now, or the same day if you have it done with a laparoscope. They found that people are better getting up and moving around. They need a mixture of bed rest and movement. But they need to have somebody at home to look after them.

Dr Richard Turner

born 1946   *interviewed 2005*

There is a general practice training scheme at the North Hampshire Hospital. Church Grange has a long history as a training practice and regularly has registrars for either six or 12 month periods. Cedric Cochrane and Richard Trueman are currently the trainers. and Judith Pagdin is an examiner for video assessment for the MRCGP examination. We also teach 3rd and final year medical students from Southampton and from the London medical schools: the teaching is co-ordinated by myself and Richard Trueman. We are honorary Clinical Teachers at Southampton University Medical School.

The partners at Church Grange have a wide range of medical interests; this is encouraged and adds to the level of expertise in the practice. I started the paediatric allergy clinic at the North Hampshire Hospital in 1984, which has developed into a successful clinic taking referrals from South Berkshire, North Hampshire and West Surrey and I was appointed allergy specialist to the PCT in 2002 and provide adult NHS services within Church Grange. Previously I had helped Hugh Platt and Professor Alberti set up the Diabetic Clinic in 1976 at the then, Basingstoke Hospital. Judith Pagdin worked as a clinical assistant in the Breast Clinic, Gemma Adamson was previously a clinical assistant in dermatology and ophthalmology. David Knight was previously a clinical assistant in a diabetic clinic and now, with Dr Steve Colley of Tadley, provides a sigmoidoscopy for the North Hampshire area in conjunction with consultant surgeon Brendan Moran; he also provides a sigmoidoscopy service within the practice. Andrew Cole performs vasectomies within the practice and Cedric Cochrane has developed an interest in travel medicine and recently obtained an MSc in this subject.

The League of Friends of The Basingstoke Hospitals

David Anderson

born 1919   *interviewed 2005*

In 1958 the Rotary Club of Basingstoke decided to form the League of Friends for the Basingstoke Hospitals, with an annual subscription of half a crown. Letters were sent to all the service clubs, all the Women's Institutes etc and a meeting of representatives of the clubs was held at the Town Hall. At the meeting a formal decision was made to form the League and a committee was elected.

I became a member of the committee in 1967, and in 1969 I was elected Chairman of the League, a position I have held ever since. The main purpose of the League is to provide amenities for hospital patients and staff and to provide equipment for the hospital. The League initially ran a tea bar at the Cottage Hospital in Hackwood Road. This was followed by a trolley service at the 'Mini' Hospital when the Cottage Hospital closed, and subsequently a tea bar at the Out-patients' Department in the present main hospital. This went on for about 17 years until, about 1992, the hospital authorities decided in their wisdom to put the facility out to

The League of Friends – Hazel Minter and Mary Melton

tender. We were not successful in our bid and a private firm took over. We then decided to set up a Welcomers' Service in the main corridor of the hospital, to give patients and visitors a friendly welcome and a helping hand where necessary. That carries on today. The desk is manned by two volunteers on all weekdays.

Amounts spent on provision of equipment for the hospital have varied over the years according to the money available. During the three years ending in February 2003, for example, the total was in excess of a quarter of a million pounds. Unfortunately at the present time we do not have as much money as that to spend. Income comes from a variety of sources, such as legacies and donations from grateful patients and their relatives. League members pay subscriptions and a lot of effort is put into money-raising activities such as a twice-yearly raffle, and sale of books and diaries at the desk. We never have enough money to provide all the facilities we would like and are always looking for alternative sources of income. Just one recent example, in 2004 we ran a stall at the Overton Sheep Fair.

Hazel Minter   *Interviewed 2005*

There are some thirty of us on the rota for the Welcomers' Service, some doing a weekly morning or afternoon stint, others preferring every other week. We work in pairs, so that the desk is always covered if there are flowers to be taken to the wards, prescriptions to the pharmacy or people to Patients Support. We help people having difficulty with the telephone, wanting a reviving cuppa or a proper meal, or just wanting to talk to someone before they go home.

The ARK

Myrddin (Merv) Rees
born 1950   *Interviewed 2005*

I qualified from Westminster Medical School in 1973, spent three months in Canada, then worked all over the South of England and in St James's and St George's Teaching Hospitals in London. I spent two years in the Ochsner Clinic in America, and that was quite an important time for me because whatever pre-conceived ideas I had about American medicine were blown out of the water. Alton Ochsner had founded his clinic on the basis that he wanted to treat the patient and the family as one, so we were encouraged to keep everybody informed. At that time in the earlier 1980s in England we often were not prepared to explain too much to the patient. I still had bosses that would tell the truth to the relative and a version of it to the patient, which wasn't my style at all. I think we only guarantee that we'll do our best and that we'll be honest with people, no matter how hard that is sometimes. I've always tried to include the family where we can - we will routinely phone the relatives after major surgery, for example, which is the least we can do. I'd like to have a huge room where they could all come and stay and we could come and see them immediately afterwards. That's one innovation I still haven't achieved, but there's time.

Alton Ochsner taught younger surgeons that, no matter how much technology they had, they'd always got to listen to what the patient had to say, because sometimes technology gets you off on a tangent. So I came back from America with renewed vigour and determination to improve things in this country and then in 1986 Professor Bill Heald phoned me to invite me down here to have a good look around. Basingstoke chose me but I also chose Basingstoke because it was a relatively young town. To me it had a feel of America - the skyscrapers, the fact that we had roundabouts and not traffic lights (though they have come back since), the fact that things were happening and that if you were going to achieve anything you'd do it from ability and not because we had a cathedral in the town and because other people had built up a reputation.

Professor Heald encouraged me to see what Professor Scheele was doing in liver surgery in Germany, so I introduced his techniques and then evolved them here.

To start with, nobody believed that you could do liver surgery without major blood loss. Nineteen years later, everybody is interested in what we are doing, how we are achieving it. We've just been involved in writing National Guidelines for Managing Liver Cancer and that's really quite a plus for Basingstoke and our unit. Amongst the surgeons here are all these young guys - Tim John, Brendan Moran, Tom Cecil, Chris Eden and Anne Stebbing -, who have carried on this tradition of just doing that bit more, looking for ways of improving outcomes for patients, but above all working in a team.

If we had one frustration it was the fact that, despite the advances we were making, we did not have an education forum where we could share that knowledge I went to the Mayo clinic in Rochester, America, for a workshop and I realised that most of the fantastic new buildings had been paid for by charitable donation. Now their tax laws encourage that, as people get the tax returned, but it sowed the seeds that well, maybe we could do something similar in England. I also visited a nice little education centre in Chichester and went to see one of the Trustees for a Trust Fund for building and encouraging education in Postgraduate Doctors. After a lot of negotiating they put a million pounds on the table if we could match it. I then asked all the local doctors and got a hundred thousand off them from their private income - it was actually the individuals who pledged a hundred thousand and started the ball rolling! Our mission statement was 'A centre of excellence for the sharing of medical knowledge', the emphasis was on sharing. At that stage sharing with nurses, the public, other health workers was a pretty avant garde idea and drew a lot of criticism. We needed to raise initially £3.5 million to get the building contract done and it was a massive effort by the team of volunteers led by Lieutenant Colonel Stuart Rowsell , with a generous donation by Lord Portsmouth. So we then had the building and we had a year to find the money to kit it out and we found another two million - the local Borough Council were very supportive and we opened the building two years ago last September.

It's achieved so much and yet we still have work to do. I think that perhaps what pleases me the most is that on any one day there's somebody in there. Already we're getting over 70,000 people every year and that will go up to 100,000 in no time. When people walk in and they've never seen it before, they say the one thing I wanted to happen, they go, 'WOW, this feels good, I like being here,' and that's the environment we wanted to create. We wanted to make it different from the normal hospital environment where you walk in and you think, 'God! - low ceiling, no light, grubby,' whatever. If each of those 70,000 people through the door learns just one thing, it's worth it and is a ripple in the water to spread that knowledge.

The building itself is fantastic, the environment is fantastic, the food is fantastic, the library is great, the partnerships with Nursing Learning in there from Southampton University, the Pelican Cancer Foundation, it's all come together. If you talk to our junior staff who come here from elsewhere, they rave about this place - the amount of consultant involvement, the amount of personal involvement, the amount of pastoral care the patients and the junior doctors get is far superior to anywhere else. I'm not satisfied with that. I want it to be even better.

We have a community education programme for health related matters. The first people to grab the opportunity were the Breast Cancer group and they have helped us in return by raising funds. That was a fundamental ARK principle: ARK meaning 'Noah's Ark', everyone gets on board, but everybody helps each other too. In the fullness of time we want more businesses to come on board so that they can bring some more money into the equation that we can then use to help fund more health initiatives. My view is until it is full one hundred percent every day of the week, we haven't finished our task. Already we are looking at expanding it because we need to make it more user-friendly for bigger groups. We want Basingstoke to be known as the place for medical education.

I'd like to continue to develop the ARK, to the point where it becomes a Golden Goose that lays golden eggs, and year in, year out generates huge income to be dished out to improve health care in North Hampshire, to send nurses to learn new techniques, the community worker to learn something from Newcastle or wherever. And that model could be repeated throughout the country so I'd like to see in twenty years that everybody has an ARK and it all comes under one umbrella and that educating on health matters includes the public as well as health workers and there's an openness and honesty to it as a process.

I'd like people to look back and think how ridiculous it was that they had waiting lists. I'd like everybody to have access to reasonable care where the people that can afford it pay for it, and the people that can't afford it have it for free. I truly believe we will be a grown up society when that's happened and that I could investigate people thoroughly and quickly, I could then operate on them at their convenience, depending on the urgency. I'd like the public to help in that process by accepting responsibility for health care, because I don't see it as a one way ticket, I see it as a partnership - the ARK emblem of the two giraffes hugging is to indicate partnerships. We have perhaps pampered people for too long and we waste a lot of time because people fundamentally misused the concept of health care free at the point of delivery. Health care just might require some kind of nominal charge that's means-related, because it's very difficult for an individual to appreciate something when we haven't put any value on it. For example, for our catchment area we could have a forum and ask people to buy into Health care, just donate £1 or perhaps, if you're wealthy, £100.

Rita Phillips

born 1942   *interviewed 2004*

The ARK is going to make so much difference to so many people. It's a wonderful facility. The Hampshire Clinic supports the ARK whole-heartedly and we will use it, we use the library facilities, we use the rooms - I believe the lunch up there is rather nice! I think it's an excellent opportunity for nurses, for doctors, for surgeons, for every walk of life to actually use. It has put Basingstoke on the map.

Hampshire Clinic

Rita Phillips

born 1942   *interviewed 2004*

In 1984, when I heard that they were building the Hampshire Clinic, a new private hospital on the site where Cowdery Down was, I went down and saw it when the bulldozers had been in and everything was flattened. I was living in Basing then so I felt I was just coming home when I started here as the nurse on night duty.

The Hampshire Clinic

But it was a very different concept from Cowdery Down. Brand new hospital. State-of-the-art. Everything was modern. When we first opened, we were about 30 beds, we had X-ray, we had physio, we had out-patients, we had operating theatres, but not to the extent that they had at the main hospital. We were here to complement the main hospital, to offer the people of Basingstoke choice as to whether you stayed with the NHS or whether you opted for private health insurance.

Most of our patients in the early 80s were insured. Eli Lilly, Lansing Bagnall, the big companies in Basingstoke at the time were offering private health insurance to their employees. Now 20 years later, that has significantly changed. Although we still have a very high insure-penetration of Basingstoke, there's an awful lot of self-paying patients as well. And we also do a lot of NHS-initiative work, doing operations and surgery here for some areas of the NHS, to assist them in getting their waiting lists down.

Providence associations, for example, BUPA, or PPP, will look at what a patient is coming in for, and they will negotiate with us how long that patient should be in hospital. They will say, 'This gentleman is coming in for hip replacement. We will allow up to 10 days.' So it's in our interest and the patient's interest within 10 days to get that patient well enough to go home. Now in the unlikely event that that patient is not well enough, then there's no way that patient will leave this hospital. We can't just say 'Your 10 days are up. Out you go.' Then it would be my responsibility to negotiate with the insurance company and say, 'Look, Mr Bloggs isn't well. This has happened, that has happened. He's probably going to be in another two or three days.' And that will be agreed. We would have the same aftercare as in the NHS, when the GP would be informed. If they needed a District Nurse to go out,

then we would ring that District Nurse and say 'This lady is leaving tomorrow. Could you go?' That would be on the National Health because the patient is still paying for National Health. Or we would say, 'You need your stitches out in three days' time. Come back up to us and we will do it.' So it's a little bit of both. We have physiotherapy here and a hydrotherapy pool, so the patients would have that here. And then they would come back for their out-patients' physio and hydrotherapy if they needed it. That's all arranged before they go home.

We do elective surgery at the Hampshire Clinic. What we don't do is trauma, so we wouldn't have road traffic accidents, people who'd had heart attacks, people who required neurosurgery. But we do care for terminally ill patients and we do now have a critical care unit, which is new to us. So over the 20 years we've expanded quite a bit and from 30 beds to 66 beds and from two theatres to four theatres.

Surgeons come from other hospitals, but some nurses come from even farther afield.

Surgeons come from other hospitals. Mostly North Hampshire Hospital but we do get visiting surgeons from Frimley Park and from Windsor. The majority of our nurses are local. But we, like the NHS, have had quite a difficulty in actually obtaining nurses, because there is a shortage of nurses within the United Kingdom. Our group runs 47 hospitals in the UK and for the last three or four years we have recruited nurses from the Philippines for all of our hospitals. That's quite interesting, because you get a different type of nurse, different culture. It's been quite an experience for us to learn about them as well as them learning about us, and how we can look after them and make them feel very much part of the team. They are highly trained nurses in their own right already when they come, using the American system. We put them through a period of adaptation, anything from three to six months so that they can then be registered on the NMC Register, so we are all working from the same standard. They work under a mentor who will oversee and be accountable for their actions until we deem that they are sufficiently confident and competent to work alone in our hospital.

We have a fair mixture of male and female. Sometimes the nurse will come over here to send money back for a younger brother's education or for a child's education or for a cousin's education - it's very much into family, and they all support one another.

We used to have a Nurses' Home at Basing Road, but now we rent accommodation for them and they all live in and around Basing, maybe a three-bedroomed house for three nurses. We have one couple who have married and have had a little girl since they've been here so they've got a house. They clearly have to be within walking distance of the Hampshire Clinic because they don't have cars and there's no buses that come down here, so they do walk or get lifts in with other nurses. I'm not particularly happy for nurses to be walking early mornings and late at nights, so we do have a driver who takes them home at night.

There have been lots of changes, in the 20 years since the Hampshire Clinic opened.

The main change has to be how surgery is performed these days. A patient having an appendectomy used to be in for 10-14 days; now that will be a day, maybe two days. Major surgery patients will come in and go home in a day, too, which is quite phenomenal. We have consultant surgeons who are specialists in their field - and Basingstoke has quite a lot to be proud of with the likes of Professor Heald, Mr Rees, Mr Eden, all the consultants who do amazing, amazing work.

Patients' expectations have changed. Patients won't settle for second-best. Twenty, thirty years ago, it would have been unheard of for patients to complain. If Sister said, 'Stand on your head in the corner,' a patient would do it! I think television and the internet have opened up all sorts of information for people. Patients don't just take it that the doctor's word is gospel or what Nurse says is right. They'll question and ask. They'll read about it. They'll research it. They'll want to know who the best person is to do the job. And that has to be right. We have to be safe. We have to offer patients what they want, which is the right to ask, to inquire, to choose.

What the Matron does.

I'm the hospital Matron, nobody stands to attention when I go round now, but it's all very nice, very informal. I want to know why the patients are here, who they are and if they're comfortable and happy with us. And I find that by visiting them every day, just spending five minutes talking to them, I can pick up what they are happy about, what maybe they're not happy about and we can do something about it while they're here. It also supports the nurses, because, I'm not just Matron shut in an office below stairs. I'm actually out there. I'm in a uniform. I hope I look like a nurse, I'm trying to act like a nurse. Nurses are encouraged to come down and talk to me. It has to be teamwork in a hospital. I can't do without the housekeepers, I don't want to do without the gardener. I need my nurses.

It's like no other job. The people that you meet, the opportunities you have, the privileges that you are allowed, it's just amazing, there can't be anything else like it. I don't know what other people can do that's so fulfilling. And I go home every night and I think 'Have I made any difference to any one person today?' and if I have I'm happy. Just one little difference. And you can, because you can be an agent for change. Yes, It's good. I wouldn't want to do anything else.

St Michael's Hospice

Dr John Williams

born 1939 *interviewed 2002*

Throughout the time when GPs could admit patients to their own beds in the 'Mini' hospital or later the main hospital, one was conscious of the varying standards of palliative care, the terminal care being given to patients who were dying, perhaps of cancer. There were lots of young doctors who were discovering the same things all over the country, like the way you should use morphine. The pattern in those days was to give morphine only when the patient was in pain, then wait till the pain had come back and give them some more. But morphine should be given every four hours, because it is gone within four hours. Around this time Cicely Saunders was

The Hospice

starting the concept of palliative care and opening St Christopher's Hospice in London.

I got more interested in this in the late 1980s and started doing courses on it, and realised that we really needed a hospice in Basingstoke. Margaret Weston, when she was mayor, made having a hospice her mayoral project. We put a huge amount of work into it and the hospice opened in 1992, with Hugh Freeman as the hospice medical doctor and our practice providing all the out-of-hours cover. A couple of years later I did a diploma in palliative medicine - as a distance-learning course over a year, through the University of Wales.

St Michael's Hospice has been a huge success.

St Michael's Hospice (North Hampshire) is a voluntary sector provider, with negotiated partial funding from the NHS. In 1989 Mayor Margaret Weston launched an appeal for funds to renovate Park Prewett House and to erect a purpose-built Hospice. Although it was to be built in the grounds of the North Hampshire Hospital, for medical support, it was deliberately placed on the perimeter of the site, to provide a non-hospitalised atmosphere. It was to have accommodation for 15 in-patients, a treatment room, a consulting area, a conservatory and a chapel. It was to act as a centre of excellence, staffed by volunteers and professionals. HRH the Duchess of Kent agreed to become the Patron.

'Everyone is helping, doing work free of charge or at drastically reduced rates.'

F James, Chair, Building Committee 1991

'Left or right, rich or poor, support has been universally generous.'

Alan Turner, 1991

A sizeable proportion of the building funds came from the Basil de Ferranti appeal. The District Health Authority leased the Hospice the building site and Park Prewett House, which became the day-care centre. A new building accommodating the in-patient unit was constructed adjacent to the original house. The Hospice opened on 3rd April 1992, and soon provided care for 15 in-patients and 30 day-care places per week. In 2001 20 Marie Curie nurses were transferred to the Hospice for care in the community and became the St Michael's Hospice Community Nursing Service under a joint-funding arrangement between St Michael's Hospice and the North Hampshire Primary Care Trust.

A day-care patient [1997]

A day at St Michael's is like a breath of fresh air. It's like one big, happy family. There's not many places you can go and get fed, waited on, plied with alcohol, shouted at, insulted, pampered with complementary therapies, hand and foot care, and your hair coiffured all in one day. Also, the friendly physio stretches and bends us, all for our good. Then we go home, thanks to the volunteer drivers. Well done to Aileen and the team for making us feel special, and having something to look forward to.

Les Picket

born 1940   *interviewed 2003*

I contracted cancer two years ago, had an operation, I did get the all-clear in June 2002; in October it all came back. I've since had radiotherapy, chemotherapy and the Macmillan nurses suggested that, as a way of bettering my life, I attended a day-care centre which I came to on a Tuesday and then it was suggested I come on a Friday as well. I can honestly say I really look forward to coming, because the people are first-rate, the care is all done by voluntary people and they cannot do enough for you

At the moment we are making bird tables and bird boxes as a means of raising revenue for the day-care centre. After dinner, Tuesday and Friday, we do the *Daily Mail* crossword and the word game and it's very interesting because everybody has a chance, though I get frowned upon because I shout the answers out because I do so many crosswords sometimes you can see the answer before the clue comes up.

Kate Kersley (Matron)

interviewed 2005

St Michael's Hospice provides specialized supportive and palliative care for people with advanced progressive life-limiting illness. We recognize the devastating impact of an incurable illness for a person and their family, which may leave them feeling out of control and isolated. Our purpose is to provide a quality service that addresses the total needs of a patient, providing holistic care through a multi-disciplinary team aimed at providing the best possible quality of life for them and their families. We have an in-patient unit, a day-care unit, a community nursing service and offer a range of supportive services including family support, complementary therapies, bereavement support and carer support.

The ethic is that the Hospice was built by the community and is largely maintained by the community.

The Hospice is constantly looking to enlarge its enthusiastic body of volunteers who help in day-care, the in-patients unit, fund-raising, in clerical and administration rôles and as receptionists and drivers. Volunteers also help in hospice shops which provide good quality donated clothes, books and household items at attractive prices. All profits go to support the work of St Michael's Hospice (registered Charity Number 1002856; www.stmichaelshospice.org.uk)

Conclusion: compare & contrast

How can Basingstoke's experiences be matched in other Hampshire towns?

Like Basingstoke, its Hampshire neighbours felt the economic and social effects of two World Wars, depression, inflation, prosperity, technological advances, the landmark event of the National Health Service Act and all the subsequent changes in health provision imposed by central and local government. They could no doubt gather similar memories from health workers and patients of all kinds, but it would be interesting to see what local variations might emerge, reflecting the different ways their demographic and economic profiles developed over the years. The changing hospital provision in, say, Andover, Winchester and Alton is partly the result of political manipulation and partly the result of varying needs and resources.

Andover is perhaps the Hampshire town that has most in common with Basingstoke as a market town with a strong agricultural basis that was dramatically expanded in the 1960s. An article in 'Lookback at Andover, 1999' describes Mrs Newman (perhaps a fore-runner of our own Jessie Jack), who 'helped so many of the town's babies into the world at the beginning of the 20th century' and 'Lookback at Andover, 1991' tells of '150 years of pharmacy in Andover' and the effects of the 1911 National Health Insurance Act.

Two books give us an overview: 'Andover: an Historical Portrait' by John Spaul (Andover Local Archives Committee, 1977) and 'Andover Past' by Anthony C Raper (Historical Publications, 2001). Andover had a Workhouse, just as Basingstoke did, but the Andover one became notorious when 'The Andover Scandal' of 1846 revealed atrocious conditions there. Eventually it became St John's Hospital for the aged and handicapped. A Hospital dedicated to St Mary Magdalene as early as 1249 was apparently originally a leper house. When the bubonic plague reached the town in 1605 nine separate pest-houses were set up in the fields and in 1757 a Corporation Pest-house was erected, eventually becoming the Infectious Hospital until it was replaced by a joint Isolation Hospital for Andover and Weyhill in 1910. The Cottage Hospital, built in 1877, was replaced in 1926 by the War Memorial Hospital - which, like Basingstoke, gained much of its funding from an annual Carnival. Like Basingstoke, Andover was greatly expanded to allow for "London overspill" in the 1960s, but this did not result in a new hospital. On the contrary, in 1966 the Wessex Regional Hospital proposed the closure of Andover Hospital, everything except a geriatric department to be transferred to Winchester and Basingstoke. A deputation of councillors, doctors and clergy lobbied Parliament and succeeded in keeping the hospital open. The Andover NHS Trust was created in 1993 and was dissolved in 2000 when it became part of the Winchester & Eastleigh NHS Trust. At the time of writing Andover's hospital is under threat again!

Odiham, which now counts itself as a large village rather than a town, had a vigorous and successful campaign from 1996 to 1999 to keep open its Cottage Hospital. This had been opened in 1910, funded by a charity set up by Dr John McIntyre and by annual Hospital Sundays, whist drives, dances and concerts. See Daphnie Reggler's book, 'The story of Odiham Cottage Hospital' (Odiham Society, 1999).

In Alton a hospital was built by public subscription with the help of the **Daily Mail** in 1901 for the sick and wounded soldiers returning from the Boer War (which ended before the Hospital was commissioned). It became an Army hospital for the RAMC until 1905 and taken over, in a dilapidated state, by Sir William Purdie Treloar (Lord Mayor of London). He founded the Lord Mayor Treloar Cripple's Hospital and College and the first 18 patients were received at the Hospital in 1909. See 'The Lord Mayor Treloar Hospital and College' by G C E Moynihan (Paul Cave Pubications, 1988). The hospital treated children with TB, and then became a regional orthopaedic hospital. Orthopaedic work is now done at Basingstoke and the old Lord Mayor Treloar Hospital has been demolished, but the Community Hospital continues to serve the local community. Interestingly, Alton still has GP beds, unlike Basingstoke. And most of the consultants who visit the Out-patient department come from Basingstoke. The website says 'The community hospital is now well placed to face the uncertainties of the 21st century.'

As might be expected, Winchester, with its castle and royal palace, monastic establishments and eventually its cathedral, had even more mediaeval hospital provision. Some of my information here comes from 'A History of the Royal Hampshire County Hospital' by Barbara Carpenter Turner (Phillimore, 1986). I am most grateful to Barbara Selby, Hon. Archivist of the Royal Hampshire County Hospital, for giving more detail of the early years and for the panel of later developments below.

The three great monastic establishments of the Priory of St Swithun (Winchester Cathedral), St Mary's Abbey (Nunnaminster) and Hyde Abbey (St Grimbald's Abbey) also had infirmaries and took in the poor and the needy and Winchester College produced many distinguished men of medicine. In the eighteenth century several of the Lyford family were surgeons in both Basingstoke and Winchester (see pages 5-6).

Like Andover, Winchester had a leper hospital dedicated to St Mary Magdalene, on Morn Hill. St John's Hospital for men and women, attracted donations from the wealthy and the St John's Winchester Charity has now become an important independent housing organisation for elderly people, with a combined residential and nursing home in Devenish House. The famous hospital of St Cross was founded by Bishop Henry de Blois about 1136. 'for old men who were so feeble that they could not stand without help' but eventually it became an almshouse rather than a nursing institution. Christ's Hospital was founded in 1607 by Peter Symonds 'for the perpetual maintenance of six poor, old, unmarried men and four poor young children' and the present Peter Symonds Sixth Form College is the most recent development of his Charity.

Winchester's Workhouse of 1796 was replaced by a new one in 1837. That was used during both world wars for service men convalescing after surgery and in 1948 became a Geriatric Hospital. As in Basingstoke, there was a name change (St Paul's Hospital) .

The City Isolation Hospital of 1887 became the Victoria Hospital, with tuberculosis patients transferring in 1955 to the Mount Chest Hospital at Bishopstoke. It became merged with the Royal Hampshire County Hospital (RHCH) in 1957, closing in 1987 after the opening of the Nightingale Wing at RHCH, eventually becoming an Adolescent Psychiatric Unit. An isolation building in Crab Woods had treated patients with smallpox, with Weyhill Hospital near Andover 'kept in readiness for smallpox patients'.

The first County Hospital was in Colebrook Street, moving in 1759 to Parchment Street. Like Basingstoke, Winchester had problems with drainage and sewerage, leading to 'the Battle of Winchester' of 1844 when ratepayers described as 'muckabites' opposed drainage improvements. In 1861 a civil engineer's report on 'The Sanitary Condition of the Hants County Hospital' was damning and recommended the complete removal of the hospital from its polluted site in Parchment Street. But even in the new site on Romsey Road (approved by Florence Nightingale as being 'away from the miasmas of the lower town', there were problems with drainage and it was eventually put onto main drainage in 1896.

Winchester's Pound Day to support the Hospital began in 1906, when donations from all over the county included 230 lbs of tea, 10 lbs of soap, 1 lb of prunes, 844 lbs of rice, 10 lbs of table salt, 2 lbs of starch. .

At the beginning of World War 1, beds in the hospital were made available for the sick and wounded, with four wooden huts in the grounds for service men and in World War 2 patients who were fit enough were moved to other hospitals to make room for evacuees and people on essential 'war work'. Five hutted wards and an operating theatre were put up on land which had been used for growing fruit and vegetables. Like Basingstoke, Winchester became a Transit Hospital for wounded servicemen from mainland Europe, especially after D-Day.

The Hospital became part of the NHS in 1948, in spite of the strongest opposition of the Management. A new development was the Physical Medicine Department, with a Daily Living Occupational Therapy Unit and a residential Agricultural/Horticultural Rehabilitation Department, which was used quite widely by patients from Basingstoke. A small bungalow was built in the Hospital grounds to accommodate the relatives of critically ill patients, - a very progressive move for the time. In 1964 the first Post-Graduate Medical Centre and Library was opened, replaced by another in 1982, generously equipped with computers, and having a lecture theatre, seminar rooms, an Education Centre and its own restaurant.

The major new wing, the Nightingale Wing, opened by HM The Queen on 27 November 1986, has operating theatres, an Intensive Care Unit, Accident and Emergency Department adjacent to the Fracture Clinic and the X-Ray Department (now called the Medical Imaging Dept.). There is a Rehabilitation Department. with a hydrotherapy pool as well as conventional physiotherapy. The secure Children's Department is quite independent with its own out-patients' facilities. On the ground floor is a modern chapel designed for either denominational or non-denominational use - very different from the magnificent chapel in the original Butterfield building, which was closed in the 1960s because of fears of infection, as it was very close to the Main Theatre.

1989/90 saw the start of the Breast Screening Service, with a mobile unit for the more rural areas and a well-qualified Breast Care Nurse / Counsellor. (Recently a proposal to move Basingstoke's breast-screening service to Winchester has been strongly opposed.) The Brinton wing, opened in 1992, houses the medical wards and their diagnostic units, the Rheumatology Department, Electro-Cardiogram and Endoscopy Units. A third phase of new building houses the Microbiology and Pathology Departments. In 2000 the long awaited MRI Scanner was installed.

In 1994 the Winchester Health Authority became the Winchester and Eastleigh NHS Trust.

continued over

One of the problems of the Hospital site is the steep gradient from north to south. However, this has been turned to advantage in the development of a six-storey car park with a rising number of spaces on each level, which opened in 1994. Melbury Lodge, a very progressive Mental Health Care Unit, opened in 1996. Yet to come, currently under construction, is a building for a comprehensive Cancer Centre, a Day-Care Treatment Centre and a much needed Out-patient Department.

Barbara Selby, Honorary Archivist, Royal Hampshire County Hospital

Basingstoke's relationship with neighbouring hospitals has changed over the years. As we have seen, for many years Basingstoke relied on the visits of Winchester consultants, while some difficult maternity cases and even what would now be routine fractures were sent to Winchester and orthopaedic cases were sent to the Lord Mayor Treloar Hospital in Alton. Today Basingstoke is not only independent but has become a pioneering centre, sending out experts to explain their techniques around the globe, and welcoming health workers of all kinds to The ARK.

It has been a fascinating job, putting together this collection of Basingstoke memories, a real learning experience.

I can see several strands emerging, closely interwoven.

There is the impact central and local government have had on health care and the quality of people's lives, from Lloyd George (and his folders!) to the great watershed of the National Health Act, followed nowadays by so many new initiatives: Care in the Community, Primary Care Trusts, Foundation status etc. But how much should these be affected by the pendulum swings of politics? Is there a danger that ambition - personal or party - might give too much emphasis to one particular idea or need at the expense of others?

There is the heartening generosity of so many people: from Walter de Merton setting up his mediaeval hospital to the wide range of local people who supported the Cottage Hospital with donations large and small, Carnivals and Pound Days. Now there are contributors to The ARK and the Hospice, with donations, imaginative fund-raising events and 'street collections'. Above all there is the professionalism, care and integrity of the health workers in hospital, surgery or the community, both NHS and private. And the patience of the patients!

It has been a privilege to gather all this together and to preserve these memories not just for today but for the future.

Bibliography

Andover Past Anthony C Raper (Historical Publications, 2001) ISBN 0-948667-76-5

Andover: An Historical Portrait John Spaul (Andover Local Archives Committee 1977)

A History of the Ancient Town and Manor of Basingstoke Francis Joseph Baigent & James Elwin Millard (Basingstoke, 1889)

A History of Park Prewett Hospital Dilys Smith (Basinstoke & North Hants Health Authority, 1986) X100948995

A History of the Royal Hampshire County Hospital Barbara Carpenter Turner (Phillimore 1986) ISBN 0-85033-606-6

Jane Austen's Letters collected and edited by Deirdre Le Faye (OUP1995 3rd ed) 0-10-283297-2

Lookback at Andover 1991 and 1999 (Andover History and Archaeology Society ISSN 0960-5738

The Lord Mayor Treloar Hospital and College G S E Moynihan (Paul Cave Publications Ltd 1988) ISBN 0-86146-072-3

Sherborne St John and The Vyne in the time of Jane Austen Rupert Willoughby (2002) 09534428-3-7

The Making of a Hospital: A Digest of Personal Recollections of the Early Years of the North Hampshire Hospital, Basingstoke
    (Basingstoke, 1996)

The Story of Odiham Cottage Hospital Daphne Reggier (Odiham Society 1999)

Then and Now: A Pictorial Account of Lilly, Basingstoke: 50 Years 1939-1989

Unpublished manuscripts:
History of Basingstoke Hospital Dilys Eaton

History of Infectious Diseases Hospital Dilys Eaton

History of Eli Lilly (author and date not given)

Leaflet
Equivalent Contemporary Values of the Pound: A Historical Series 1270 to 2004 (Bank of England, 2005)

BASINGSTOKE ARCHAEOLOGICAL & HISTORICAL SOCIETY

The Society aims to investigate the history and pre-history of the Borough of Basingstoke & Deane, and to stimulate interest in archaeological and historical studies generally. There are lectures on the second Thursday of the month, from September to May, at 7.30 pm in Church Cottage, Basingstoke. As well as the Basingstoke Talking History project, the Society organises visits to places of archaeological and historical interest as well as fieldwork, training excavations and finds processing.

PUBLICATIONS

Voices of Basingstoke 1400-1600 Anne Hawker £3.00
Taken from Basingstoke records, identifying where and how people lived, describing the contents of property and the misdemeanours that led to fines

The Story of Basingstoke Anne Hawker (Revised edition) £6.95
A clear and readable account of the history of this town up to the present day.

Going Down Church Street to the Felgate Bookshop Mary Felgate and Barbara Applin £7.50
Mary Felgate's memories of her Grandmother's bible bookshop in the 1920s, with research into the history of properties in Church Street

Past Pieces Selections from the Society's Newsletter £3.00
Articles ranging from "The Royal Arms in St Michael's Church" to "The Hazards and Rewards of Culture and Entertainment in 19th century Basingstoke"

Roundabout Basingstoke Barbara Applin £1.50
Stories of Basingstoke's many roundabouts: the highway-man, the Daneshill stones, the "Chineham Wave" etc.

Beneath Basingstoke VIDEO £12.50
Archaeological discoveries made beneath and around Basingstoke from the Stone Age to the Saxons.

A Day in Tudor Basingstoke VIDEO £10.00
A historical entertainment performed in Church Cottage, based on Basingstoke's archives, showing goings-on in the Market Place, people "had up" at court and the cost of the townspeople's petition to Mary Tudor.

Quarterly Newsletter

charity no. 1000263

Secretary: Mrs Margaret Porter 01256 356012

www.bahsoc.org.uk

Index

The names of 'speakers' and the pages on which they speak are given in bold italics. Doctors, chemists, dentists etc are listed under individual names.